TREATING ADULT SUBSTANCE ABUSE USING FAMILY BEHAVIOR THERAPY

A STEP-BY-STEP APPROACH

BRAD DONOHUE
DANIEL N. ALLEN

WILEY

John Wiley & Sons, Inc.

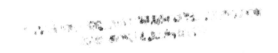

Library of Congress Cataloging-in-Publication Data:
Donohue, Brad.
  Treating adult substance abuse using family behavior therapy: a step-by-step approach / Brad Donohue, Daniel N. Allen.
    p. ; cm.
  Includes bibliographical references and index.
  ISBN 978-0-470-62193-6 (pbk. : alk. paper); 978-1-118-01320-5 (ePDF); 978-1-118-01321-2 (eMobi); 978-1-118-01322-9 (ePub)
    1. Substance abuse—Treatment.   2. Family psychotherapy.   3. Behavior therapy.   I. Allen, Daniel N.   II. Title.
    [DNLM: 1. Substance-Related Disorders—therapy.   2. Adult.   3. Behavior Therapy—methods.   4. Family Therapy—methods. WM 270]
  RC564.D66   2011
  616.89'156—dc22
                                                                                                    2010039797

Printed in the United States of America
10 9 8 7 6 5 4 3 2 1

Contents

Foreword

The authors have written a treatment guide for adult drug users that is a "must-read" for all who deal with this problem. The book is a veritable model of an effective and practical guidebook. Simultaneously, it provides an integrated approach encompassing virtually every aspect of treatment while also providing details of the specific aspects of treatment that are readable and complete as separate aspects.

No important components of treatment are left out, as topics covered separately include the initial recruitment of clients, session attendance, family member participation, treatment planning, treatment integrity measures, counselor style, treatment content, and so on. Each section is valuable in its own right whether utilized in the present program or as a component of any other program. Thus, this book is of value and utility to any other program approach.

Notably, almost all guidelines are accompanied by tables or outline charts that provide the specific steps and often sample verbatim statements. No vague generalizations or platitudes here. At the same time, the client participates actively in the choice and order of treatment procedures used. The book, as the title implies, incorporates behavior therapy, as well as the central features of family therapy, group therapy, behavior analysis, motivational therapy, and cognitive therapy. The authors have not allowed conceptual purity to obstruct the principal objective of therapeutic success. Some of the recommendations are so practical and conceptually valid that I found myself repeatedly thinking: "What a wonderful program for treating adult addiction."

NATE AZRIN

Preface

We decided to write this book while on an airplane after a wonderful experience training a treatment agency in Meadville, Pennsylvania to use Family Behavior Therapy (FBT). Although Dan and I had worked as colleagues in a number of research studies, this was our first experience conducting training together. The agency was located in a small, working-class town similar to the ones in which Dan and I were raised, and we appreciated how warmly they treated us and how passionate they were to learn FBT. We were both so excited after the training that as soon as we sat down in the plane, Dan started brainstorming methods of teaching FBT more effectively, which included the writing of this book. His generation of ideas brought back great memories for me of Nathan Azrin, who used to do a lot of problem solving in our research meetings developing FBT. Nate would start our brainstorms by asking what could be done to ameliorate some aspect of the therapy that appeared to be problematic. We'd generate dozens of solutions, with each solution building from the previous one. When we'd all agree on a group of viable solutions, we'd change the respective intervention protocol, and all therapists would attempt the revised therapy with our clients. We'd then regroup in a subsequent meeting and repeat the process until the problem was solved empirically. Nate's philosophy was that no single idea could be sufficient, although every single idea was important. He insisted that if just one client experienced a problem with a protocol, it needed to be revised to accommodate others who would inevitably have similar concerns. Having extremely high standards in the quality of service delivery, he was a model in positive reinforcement, which is embedded throughout FBT. Now, some 20 years after our initial trials, each of the intervention components reviewed in this book has undergone dozens of revisions based on the input of a diverse group of research assistants, community treatment providers, and consumers. These efforts have resulted in a robust, comprehensive, and theoretically sound behavioral intervention capable of treating a wide array of problem behaviors in addition to substance abuse, such as family dysfunction, employment, and mood disorders.

Although there are a number of innovative features making up FBT, community mental health providers consistently indicate that its comprehensive, flexible, step-by-step method of implementation most differentiates it from other intervention approaches. As will be reviewed in Chapter 1, each of the FBT intervention components is organized into a series of therapeutic instructions. Each step is part of an intervention sequence that builds upon the previous step. The format is refreshingly straightforward, as therapists are free to exercise their own positive style when implementing each step. Moreover, therapists often integrate information between steps to assist in clarification, engagement, and so on. Other innovative features of FBT include its tight integration of (1) standardized and time-efficient goal-setting procedures that are tied to specific drug use triggers and competing rewards, treatment planning, and treatment termination; (2) pragmatic utilization of therapists in assessing their own estimates of treatment integrity; (3) ongoing standardized assessment of the extent to which consumers participate and are satisfied in therapy; (4) standardized client record-keeping procedures and accompanying quality assurance system; and (5) strong evidence base in treating drug abuse and other associated problem behaviors. Each of these factors is very important to treatment delivery, although very few programs do so reliably.

This book, therefore, provides an overview of FBT as applied to the treatment of adult substance abuse, including its strong research base and step-by-step application. Although FBT has been indicated as an established evidence-based practice in both adults and adolescents, we decided to focus on adults in this book, and follow with *Treating Adolescent Substance Abuse Using Family Behavior Therapy* to appropriately address the many developmental issues that define these very distinct populations. FBT involves the administration of psychometrically validated assessment measures and well-established behavioral intervention components (i.e., goal setting, contingency management, environmental/stimulus control, self-control, communication skills training, relationship enhancement, and job-getting and financial management skills training). Each intervention component is systematically described, including an overview of the intervention approach, rationale for its use, requisite materials, and detailed description of the intervention procedures (including implementation dialogue between therapist and client). Protocol checklists that summarize each of the major intervention modules are provided to assist therapists as prompts during therapy sessions (i.e., "cheat sheets"). Within each chapter, case examples and completed worksheets assist in bringing the interventions to life. This systematic organization permits readers to quickly identify and skim through parts of each chapter that may be particularly relevant. For instance, if a therapist experiences a problem implementing a particular intervention, this therapist may quickly review the detailed descriptions of this intervention, including the appropriate dialogue, to assist in determining how to prevent or manage this problem in the future.

This book is primarily intended for mental health treatment providers who are interested in learning FBT. However, professors who teach substance abuse treatment (or other clinical intervention courses) are particularly encouraged to use this book in their courses. Indeed, there is ample information available to suggest that students who will go on to become mental health professionals need training in evidence-based therapies, such as FBT, and that these interventions should be integrated within their class curriculums. Along these lines, this book will likely be quite useful, as each chapter represents a particular intervention that may be taught in a typical academic week. Qualified community mental health treatment providers may gradually learn each of the interventions at their own pace, as each treatment component may be implemented independent of the other. Indeed, some interventions may be employed to address multiple problem behaviors, or they can be adjusted to focus on particular concerns. To assist in dissemination, this book includes all necessary materials that will be required to implement FBT in the back of each chapter, including the prompting checklists, handouts, and worksheets. Of course, the method of implementation for each of these materials is extensively reviewed in the narrative section of each chapter. We hope you find the book rewarding and the interventions exciting to implement.

Brad Donohue
Daniel N. Allen

Acknowledgments

We would like to acknowledge our families, particularly our wives, Denise and Ann, for their encouragement in writing this book and continued love and support. We are particularly thankful to Nathan Azrin for his role in leading the initial development of FBT and his continued mentorship. Of course, we would like to thank our colleagues and students who have significantly enhanced FBT throughout the years. Finally, we are grateful to the National Institute on Drug Abuse and National Institute of Mental Health for their support of FBT in randomized controlled trials.

CHAPTER 1

Introduction to Family Behavior Therapy

Overview

This chapter provides an overview of the application of Family Behavior Therapy (FBT) in adults. First, the historical, theoretical, and empirical under-pinnings of FBT are reviewed to assist in understanding its conceptualization and development during the past 20 years. The chapter then delineates indi-viduals who are most likely to benefit from FBT, and recommendations are offered in determining an assessment method that may be utilized to develop effective treatment plans. Although content of each of the FBT intervention components is extensively reviewed in Chapters 5 through 12, a summary of each component is provided in this chapter to show how they are integrated in treatment administration. The method of using checklists to guide mental health service providers in treatment implementation is reviewed, and proce-dures involved in the assessment of treatment integrity are underscored.

Chapter at a Glance

➣ Historical, theoretical, and empirical background of FBT

➣ Which clinical populations are appropriate for FBT, and in which therapeu-tic contexts

➣ General structure of FBT

➣ Maintenance and assessment of FBT intervention integrity

Historical and Theoretical Background

Family Behavior Therapy (FBT) was initially developed by Nathan Azrin, Brad Donohue, and their colleagues with the support of the National Institute on Drug Abuse and National Institute of Mental Health. In 1989, Nathan Azrin was awarded a grant from the National Institute on Drug Abuse to conduct one of the first controlled trials of behavior therapy in drug-abusing adolescents. Adults were later included in this trial, resulting in a robust intervention capable of ameliorating drug abuse and its associated problems across the life span (Azrin, McMahon et al., 1994). When Dr. Azrin initiated this seminal study, very few evidence-supported interventions were available to treat drug abuse, and those few treatments that were available were rarely developed to explicitly and systematically address complicating factors, such as effectively managing nonattendance to sessions, multiple psychiatric diagnoses, treatment integrity, and so on. In developing an intervention to address these issues, the theoretical tenets of existing behavior therapies that were found to be efficacious in treating problems that were related to illicit drug abuse, such as the Community Reinforcement Approach to alcohol abuse (Azrin, Sisson, Meyers, & Godley, 1982; Hunt & Azrin, 1973; Sisson & Azrin, 1989), were used to model FBT.

Similar to the Community Reinforcement Approach, FBT was designed to integrate significant others and community support systems into treatment planning, utilize multicomponent behavioral interventions, and encourage significant others of clients to permit negative consequences of undesired behaviors to occur. Substance use was conceptualized to be a strong inherent reinforcer (e.g., pleasurable physiological sensations, peer support, elimination of aversive physical sensations and emotions). Of course, negative consequences also occur as a result of substance use (e.g., job loss, interpersonal conflict). However, the severity of these consequences is often minimized or suppressed, or their full impact is not realized until well after the habitual processes of drug use have begun. Therefore, in originating FBT, these concepts were adopted to form a base in which to conceptualize intervention planning. FBT therapists were taught to eliminate drug abuse and other problem behaviors by (1) facilitating the development of skills that are incompatible with drug use (e.g., recognizing antecedents to drug use, controlling drug cravings, utilizing communication skills to decrease arguments and other antecedents to drug use), (2) modifying the environment to facilitate time with drug-incompatible activities (e.g., enrollment in school or work, changing driving routes to avoid drug use triggers, creating a social network of nonaddicted friends), and (3) rewarding behaviors that are incompatible with drug use (e.g., spending time with friends who do not use drugs).

Environmental/stimulus control strategies were formalized and involved teaching clients to identify antecedents ("triggers") to drug use and non–drug use, and to use skills designed to assist in managing these antecedents (see Chapter 9). A Self-Control intervention (see Chapter 10) was developed based on Joseph Cautela's Covert Sensitization therapy for alcohol abuse to assist participants in eliminating drug cravings and urges. In Covert Sensitization, clients are instructed to think of aversive stimuli just as alcohol use is about to occur during imagery trials. After repeated pairings of aversive and alcohol-related thoughts, desire for alcohol use is theorized to diminish. However, the relatively strong addictive properties of some illicit drugs (e.g., "crack" cocaine) were found to be too strong to countercondition in our earlier trials involving FBT. Moreover, Covert Sensitization did not teach skills relevant to managing substance use. Therefore, we developed the Self-Control intervention to focus on teaching clients to identify the earliest thought of drug use and consequently imagine aversive stimuli when the urge was relatively low. This change permitted cravings and desires for drug use to be easily over-shadowed by aversive thoughts and images. Once the urge is terminated, clients are taught to engage in a series of skill sets culminating in a brief problem-solving exercise to identify drug-incompatible behaviors, and imagining escape from the drug use situation. The latter skill-based modifications were unique to the previous Covert Sensitization procedure and, as reviewed later in this chapter, appeared to be quite effective.

Recognizing the pioneering work of Stephen Higgins and his colleagues in contingency management, a contingency contract was also developed for adult clients to enhance their motivation to achieve therapeutic goals (see Chapter 5). These contracts included standardized methods of determining target responses, rewards from the clients' social ecology, and contingencies. Other interventions were adopted from the Community Reinforcement Approach with few modifications, such as communication skills training (see Chapters 7 and 8) to prevent interpersonal conflicts that often lead to drug use and other problem behavior, and Job Club (see Chapter 11) to assist clients in remaining "busy" doing drug-incompatible work-related activities. Thus, FBT owes much of its theoretical underpinnings to the Community Reinforcement Approach and other behavioral therapies, but does differ in meaningful ways.

FBT has undergone continued enhancement since the initial trial now more than 2 decades ago. For instance, quality assurance programs specific to FBT have been originated to assist in managing infrastructural and administrative needs (see Donohue et al., 2009), and the method of assessing treatment integrity that is described in this volume has been favorably evaluated in a community setting (Sheidow, Donohue, Hill, Henggeler, & Ford, 2008). Easy-to-follow prompting checklists that are described at the end of this chapter have been developed to guide mental health professionals in efficient and effective administration of therapies during sessions (prompting checklists are included at the end of each of Chapters 5 through 12), and standardized telephone therapies aimed at improving session attendance have been favorably examined in controlled trials to complement FBT (Donohue et al., 1998). Standardized methods have also been developed to assist treatment providers in transitioning between treatment sessions (see Chapter 4), effectively managing treatment planning (see Chapter 6), and appropriately ending treatment (see Chapter 13). Relevant to dissemination, other standardized procedures have been developed to assist in determining readiness for FBT adoption in community agencies, and prompting checklists have been developed to guide trainers when implementing FBT workshops and ongoing training sessions (checklists are freely available from the first author). Many of the aforementioned strategies are extensively reviewed in this volume.

Empirical Background

Relevant to outcome support, FBT is one of the very few evidence-based treatments to consistently demonstrate efficacy in clinical trials involving both adults and adolescents who have been identified to abuse illicit drugs, and these results have been maintained up to 9 months' follow-up (see reviews, for example, by Carroll & Onken, 2005; Dutra et al., 2008). In the first randomized controlled trial of FBT (Azrin, McMahon et al., 1994), adults and youth were randomly assigned to receive FBT (referred to as Behavior Therapy at that time) or a nondirective control group after completion of baseline data. Results indicated that, as compared with control group participants, the participants assigned to FBT demonstrated significantly greater improvements throughout the year following baseline in various areas that were assessed (e.g., drug and alcohol use frequency, conduct problems, family functioning/ satisfaction, work/school attendance, depression, parental satisfaction with the youth). These results were maintained at 9 months' follow-up (Azrin et al., 1996). Similar positive effects were found in randomized controlled trials involving substance-abusing youth and their parents (Azrin, Donohue, Besalel, Kogan, & Acierno, 1994; Azrin et al., 2001). Based on a meta-analysis of outcome studies, Bender, Springer, and Kim (2006) concluded that FBT was one of only two treatments that produced large treatment effect sizes for dually diagnosed adolescents across substance use and internalizing and externalizing behavior problems.

Since these earlier controlled trials, FBT has evolved for use in severe behavioral disturbances that coexist with adult substance abuse and dependence. For instance, in uncontrolled case trials involving referrals from child welfare agencies, FBT has demonstrated benefits in substance-abusing mothers evidencing psychiatric disorders (i.e., bipolar disorder, posttraumatic stress disorder) and domestic violence and other problem behaviors (Donohue et al., 2010; Romero, Donohue, & Allen, 2010; Romero et al., 2010). In an uncontrolled trial involving parents at risk or suspected of abusing illicit drugs and founded for child abuse and neglect, significant improvements were found in child maltreatment potential, family dysfunction, parental dissatisfaction, and child behavior problems (Donohue & Van Hasselt, 1999).

Thus, FBT has been used to treat effectively a wide array of problem behaviors in adults (and adolescents), and these positive results have been recognized by independent scientists specializing in the addictions. FBT has also been recognized by nationally governed organizations. For instance, it is listed in national clearinghouses as a well-supported therapy (e.g., Substance Abuse and Mental Health Service Administration's National Registry of Evidence-Based Practices, California Evidence-Based Clearinghouse for Child Welfare). It was one of the first behavior therapy programs reviewed in the National Institute on Drug Abuse's Principles of Drug Addiction Treatment (National Institute on Drug Abuse, 1998), and in Module 10, published by the National Institutes of Alcoholism and Alcohol Abuse (2005), this therapy was said to be an "emerging developmentally sensitive approach" for drug use problems.

Appropriate Referrals and Intervention Settings

During the past decade, FBT has become increasingly popular in community agencies, leading administrators to query about what specific populations and intervention settings are appropriate for FBT. In answering this question empirically, FBT has demonstrated success in controlled trials involving youth and adults who have evidenced drug addiction and various comorbid problem behaviors. Adult clients are referred through multiple sources, most often including criminal justice and child welfare systems. Thus far, in controlled trials clients have received FBT in their homes and in outpatient clinics. Administrators of community-based inpatient facilities have utilized FBT as one of their treatment options, and this approach appears to have several advantages. For instance, inpatient facilities ensure easy access to FBT, restrict drug use opportunities, and provide opportunities to implement FBT intensively. In considering FBT within inpatient facilities, it is important to ensure that (1) significant others will be able to visit the facility to participate in FBT sessions, (2) patients will have sufficient time in the facility to learn the interventions (or therapists will be able to engage participants in outpatient care subsequent to discharge), and (3) patients will be provided opportunities to practice skills during brief excursions from the facility. Therefore, it would appear that the emphasis of FBT on skill-building exercises to assist in the prevention of future drug use would make FBT a viable contribution to inpatient care. However, it should be emphasized that outcomes resulting from the implementation of FBT have yet to be formally examined within the context of inpatient therapeutic milieus.

Study exclusionary criteria in outcome studies of FBT have been relatively relaxed to better approximate "real-world" referrals. Thus, there is some published data to suggest that FBT can be successful in treating adult substance abuse and coexisting psychiatric and behavioral problems, such as depression, dysfunction in family systems, stress, incarceration, and unemployment (see preceding section). Other problems (e.g., victims of rape, sexual promiscuity and prostitution, poor academic functioning) have been treated with FBT in controlled trials of adults who abuse illicit drugs. However, FBT outcomes pertaining to these problems have yet to be formally assessed. Persons who have been formally diagnosed with mental retardation, severe cognitive impairments, and psychosis have generally been excluded from controlled trials of FBT. Indeed, when persons with these disabilities have been treated with FBT, the outcomes appear to be relatively poor (see Burgard, Donohue, Azrin, & Teichner, 2000).

General Approach to Treatment and Structure

Outcome Assessment

It is generally recommended that evaluation of FBT include the administration of assessment measures before, during, and after treatment. Assessing treatment outcomes is important because the derived data may be used to guide treatment, assist in determining the adequacy of fit between FBT and the treatment agency, demonstrate program improvements, and justify costs to funding agencies.

Of course, in determining which measures to administer, several factors should be considered. First, the person administering, interpreting, and recording the respective measures and analyzing this data should be legally, professionally, and ethically qualified to do so, and the measures should be relevant to the presenting concerns. To assist in the evaluation of FBT, it is generally recommended to implement broad-screen urinalysis testing procedures to assess recent illicit drug use, hair follicle tests to assess illicit drug use that may have occurred during the past several months, and Breathalyzer tests to assess alcohol use that may have occurred during the previous day. Retrospective reports from clients and significant others regarding clients' number of days using illicit drugs and alcohol, as well as other problem behaviors (e.g., work and school attendance, incidents of domestic violence) appear to be valid and reliable up to 6 months when assessed utilizing formal assessment methods, such as the Timeline Followback method developed by Mark and Linda Sobell. In addition, depending on various characteristics of the population receiving FBT, other assessment measures may be warranted, including measures of psychiatric symptoms and mental health diagnoses, family functioning, satisfaction with family relationships, satisfaction with treatment, service utilization, and risk of contracting HIV. Additionally, when the client is a parent, other assessment methods to consider include those that assess factors that interfere with effective parenting, parental stress, and home safety. More information regarding specific assessment procedures used to evaluate the effects of FBT and other evidence-based treatments can be found in Allen, Donohue, Sutton, Haderlie, and LaPota (2009). Assessment procedures should be standardized; evidence good psychometric properties; and be quick and easy to administer, score, and interpret. Depending on the specific setting in which FBT is implemented, assessment measures vary to accommodate the unique aspects of program referral sources, funding agencies, and state laws.

Of course, immediately after the initial assessment battery is scored and interpreted, an orientation to FBT should be provided to clients that includes opportunities for clients to receive and provide feedback relevant to the assessment findings, solicitation of commitments from clients and participating family members to follow established program guidelines (e.g., attend sessions, participate in session exercises and therapy assignments, engage in appropriate communication such as speaking calmly and briefly), and a general description of treatment (see Treatment section below).

Treatment

Number of Sessions   FBT treatment usually includes 16 to 20 treatment sessions ranging from 1 to 2 hours, and is generally scheduled to occur between 4 and 12 months, depending on the setting, presenting problems, available funding, and response of clients to treatment. Sessions fade in frequency and duration as FBT progresses and therapeutic goals are accomplished.

Family Structure   The person referred for treatment of substance abuse is considered to be the identified client in the FBT model. FBT is therefore focused on assisting this individual in maintaining long-term abstinence from illicit drugs, and encouraging this individual to accomplish goals that are consistent with a drug-free, healthy, and prosperous lifestyle. Significant others, usually family members and sometimes close friends, are recruited from the clients' social network to assist clients in attending their therapy sessions, completing their homework assignments, and providing encouragement and rewards to clients when treatment goals are accomplished. During sessions, significant others can be used to model exemplary skills during role-playing exercises, encourage clients to participate in role-plays or discuss difficult situations, provide insights that are relevant to the recovery of clients, and provide clients with empathy and support. To some extent, adolescent family members may be involved in therapy as significant others. However, treatment providers need to be careful not to involve adolescents in age-inappropriate content. The role of small children is limited to reviewing the scheduled family activity during the Environmental Control intervention (see Chapter 9), and providing and receiving positive statements during the Positive Request and I've Got a Great Family interventions (see Chapters 7 and 8) and Treatment Termination and Program Generalization intervention (see Chapter 13).

Significant others should ideally be sober (or evidence a desire to remain sober), have an interest in the client's well-being, live with the client, and be relatively well adjusted. Recruiting more than one of these individuals is of course helpful, although this is often difficult to achieve because clients have often "burned their bridges" with their significant others, and for this and other reasons "ideal" significant others are often unavailable. When available friends and family are less than ideal, it may still be valuable to incorporate them within the FBT model. Indeed, the inclusion of these individuals permits treatment providers to closely monitor their behavior and encourage and assist them in accomplishing behaviors that are consistent with treatment goals. However, these persons must be carefully screened and monitored to ensure that including them in therapy is likely to put clients at relatively less risk of harm; when this is not the case they should be excluded from therapy. Of course, clients must want significant others to participate in their therapy, and significant others who are recruited to participate must be committed to ameliorating problem behaviors that have the potential to negatively influence clients. When significant others are deemed to be appropriate, it is important to tell them that although they may indirectly benefit from FBT, their role in therapy is to aid the clients in accomplishing their goals. In each of the remaining chapters, recommendations are provided for therapists to consider in regard to how and when to involve significant others in therapy.

Of course, ethical, legal, and programmatic issues will need to be considered when including significant others. These issues are customarily reviewed in state laws, and state licensing boards may be queried when relevant laws are unclear. However, legal consultation is highly recommended in the initial development of family-based treatment programming to assist in originating consent procedures and guidelines to review and implement with clients and their participating significant others, such as how various issues that are influenced by relationships will be managed (i.e., establishing firm guidelines in the prevention of "secrets" [e.g., infidelity], reviewing how significant others will be included in record-keeping procedures, consent for treatment, limits of confidentiality).

Content of Therapy   Although there are currently more than a dozen intervention components that have been utilized in FBT, this book will emphasize those treatments that have been formally examined in controlled trials involving adults. These intervention components include:

1. *Behavioral Goals and Rewards (Chapter 5):* Involves clients and potentially adult significant others reviewing a list of commonly experienced antecedents (i.e., triggers) to drug use and other problem behaviors that, when

endorsed by clients, may be quickly developed into behavioral goals for the clients to accomplish that are contingently rewarded by family members.

2. *Treatment Planning (Chapter 6):* Involves the client and adult family members choosing the order and extent to which specific FBT intervention components should be prioritized in therapy.

3. *Self-Control (Chapter 7):* Involves clients and adult family members learning to identify and manage antecedents (triggers) to negative thoughts, images, feelings, and behaviors that have become associated with drug use and other problem behaviors.

4. *Environmental Control (Chapter 9):* Involves clients and family members learning to restructure their environment to eliminate or manage negative emotions, people, and activities in the environment that increase risk of engaging in drug use and other problem behaviors.

5. *Communication Skills Training (Chapters 7 and 8):* Includes exercises in which clients and family members share what they love, admire, and respect about one another; demonstrate their appreciation for one another; learn to make positive requests; and develop conflict resolution skills.

6. *Job-Getting Skills Training (Chapter 11):* Involves teaching clients and family members how to solicit and do well in job interviews.

7. *Financial Management (Chapter 12):* Involves teaching clients and family members to use a standardized worksheet to assist in assessing current income and expenditures, and reviewing methods of generating extra income and decreasing expenditures.

Determining Which Interventions to Implement   The order and extent to which the interventions are implemented in therapy is fully described in Chapter 4 ("Establishing Effective Agendas for Treatment Sessions"). However, in short, Behavioral Goals and Rewards is the first intervention that is implemented in therapy, followed by Treatment Planning. The order in which the remaining intervention components are implemented for the first time is primarily determined by the client and adult significant others during Treatment Planning (see Chapter 6). The extent to which treatments are subsequently implemented, with the exception of Treatment Planning because it is implemented only once, will depend on their effectiveness as determined mutually between the client and mental health professional (MHP) during agendas (see next paragraph) utilizing the results of Consumer Satisfaction and Compliance ratings (see this section below), as well as objective data (e.g., urinalysis testing, session attendance).

Method of Transitioning Between Treatment Sessions An agenda is administered by the MHP at the start of each session. In doing so, therapists initiate agendas by pointing out positive efforts that may have occurred during the past session, and briefly mentioning the interventions that are intended for review in the current session (including estimated times to complete each intervention). Clients and family members are invited by MHPs to modify agendas based on unanticipated circumstances that may have arisen since the last treatment session, such as being evicted from their homes, substance relapse, and so on (see Chapter 4).

Structure in Presenting How to Implement Each Intervention Details regarding how to implement each of the interventions are described in Chapters 4 through 12. Each of these chapters includes (1) an overview and rationale of the intervention approach; (2) goals for the intervention; (3) materials needed to implement the intervention; (4) a treatment manual that includes implementation dialogues between clients, therapists, and family members; (5) worksheets and handouts to assist in treatment delivery; and (6) initial and future prompting checklists to guide MHPs during treatment delivery.

Prompting Checklists Guide Therapists During Sessions With the exception of Treatment Planning, each of the interventions includes two prompting checklists. One prompting checklist is specific to the first session that the respective intervention component is implemented (e.g., Initial Session Prompting Checklist for Self-Control). The other prompting checklist is used when implementing the intervention in subsequent treatment sessions (e.g., Future Session Prompting Checklist for Self-Control). Prompting checklists are included at the end of each of the chapters. Prompting checklists are basically summaries (checklists) of the specific steps required to implement the treatments. Because prompting checklists are designed to be used by the MHP in session, each checklist item is a succinct instructional prompt written in shorthand so MHPs can quickly glance at the instruction during treatment and consequently implement what is being prompted. The instructions are listed in the order in which MHPs should implement them.

During implementation, MHPs put the respective checklist on their lap or nearby desk. They briefly glance at the checklist, look up, and proceed to implement what is being prompted. MHPs then respond to clients as they normally would, implement the next instruction, and so on until all intervention steps in the prompting checklist are complete. Of course, comfort, confidence, and skill in utilizing the prompting checklists is enhanced with continued practice. Most MHPs will experience some anxiety in utilizing the checklists initially. However, any initial anxieties will eventually be overshadowed with successful implementation. It should be mentioned that each of these checklists has undergone hundreds of revisions based on the input of MHPs and clients in community-based treatment centers and controlled trials, in order to encourage therapeutic freedom in responding to client concerns. Using these prompting checklists is the best way to ensure that MHPs implement all critical components of each intervention and, in this way, ensure treatment integrity.

The general content or "meat" of each *initial* intervention session prompting checklist pertains to: (1) provision of a rationale for the treatment (i.e., problem behavior that is expected to be addressed, brief description of intervention, why intervention is likely to work); (2) developing the skill set through participation in simulated role-play scenarios and structured exercises; and (3) assigning homework so clients practice skill sets between sessions. The general format of each *future* intervention session includes: (1) discussing the homework assignment from the last therapy session, (2) practicing or behaviorally enacting skill sets that were assigned during the last therapy session, and (3) assigning homework to continue practicing the skill set (if necessary). Use of these prompting checklists assists in maintaining the integrity of the intervention so that all needed components are implemented, thereby increasing the effectiveness in treatment. For these reasons, MHPs are encouraged to closely follow the protocols, but in doing so are also encouraged to use nonprescribed procedures when indicated between the prescribed steps.

It is important to emphasize that treatment sessions may include the implementation of several interventions, and that intervention components may be temporarily suspended or abandoned to permit timely implementation of other intervention components based on the needs of the individual client and family. For instance, if the Environmental Control intervention were being implemented during a treatment session, and a client spontaneously indicated that she wanted to learn to be assertive when talking with her husband, the MHP could put down her prompting checklist for Environmental Control, and take out a prompting checklist for the Positive Request procedure (as well as the other requisite handouts for Positive Request) to teach her to be assertive. After the Positive Request procedure was implemented, the MHP could return to the Environmental Control intervention if time permitted, or end the session after the Positive Request procedure was reviewed. This approach to therapy encourages treatment integrity while allowing flexibility to address contemporaneous concerns of clients. In the latter example, the MHP's integrity for Environmental Control would be based on the steps she did or did not complete up to the point at which she stopped administering this treatment.

Treatment Integrity   Although there are a number of ways to define *treatment integrity* or *protocol adherence,* these terms generally concern the extent to which MHPs implement a given intervention in a manner that is consistent with the way it was determined to be efficacious. Importantly, programs that utilize standardized manuals and evaluate treatment integrity are consistently rated better than those programs that do not (Moyer, Finney, & Swearingen, 2002). As emphasized by Power et al. (2005), it is imperative that treatment programs conduct comprehensive assessment of intervention integrity or protocol adherence. They go on to suggest that protocol adherence is often assessed in a limited and questionable manner, perhaps because these procedures are often time consuming, costly, and lack psychometric support. The methods of measuring treatment integrity vary, although there is some evidence to suggest that examining audiotapes or videotapes of therapy sessions appears to be the most accurate way to assess MHPs' adherence to therapeutic protocols (Del Boca & Darkes, 2007).

FBT utilizes two approaches to ensure treatment integrity, with the first focusing on overall MHP adherence in completing the steps necessary to implement any given FBT intervention, and the second addressing the skill of the MHP when implementing the intervention. Research demonstrates that these methods of assessing protocol adherence in FBT are both valid and reliable for therapists participating in controlled treatment outcome studies (e.g., Azrin et al., 2001) and for community-based treatment providers (Sheidow et al., 2008). FBT is especially amenable to the assessment of treatment integrity because all FBT intervention components are specified in the initial and future session Therapist Prompting Checklists. These steps are unambiguous, easy-to-understand instructions that are listed sequentially, permitting MHPs to use them as prompts during treatment implementation, and permitting trainers to easily and objectively monitor them during their audio-taped reviews of MHP's sessions. The prompting checklist method of treatment administration also has practical utility. That is, it encourages MHPs to achieve a high degree of treatment integrity (implementation of one step prompts the next step, and so on), while permitting them to compute their own assessment of protocol adherence.

The Treatment Integrity Review Form (Exhibit 1.1, also located on the CD that accompanies this book) is used to record the results of protocol adherence assessments. In assessing protocol adherence for FBT, MHPs examine their completed prompting checklist after the therapy session, and divide the number of steps completed by the number of steps that were possible in the sections that were implemented. They then multiply the resulting dividend by 100. The resulting percentage score represents the percentage of steps completed for the respective intervention. Scores above 80% are generally considered to indicate good treatment adherence. Trainers or other persons examining treatment adherence may also independently complete their own prompting checklists while listening to the session audiotapes, and compute their assessment of protocol adherence in the same way as the MHP. Thus, protocol adherence scores may be derived for the MHP, trainer, or other persons or raters examining treatment adherence. Reliability is determined by recording the number of agreements between the MHP and trainer (number of items or steps both the MHP and trainer agreed were completed or not completed) by the number of disagreements between the MHP and trainer (number of items or steps the MHP and trainer disagreed were completed or not completed) *and* agreements between them. The resulting number is multiplied by 100 to yield the percentage agreement score. Eighty percent or higher means reliability between the MHP and trainer in assessing treatment integrity is good.

For example, in the Self-Control Intervention Prompting Checklist for Future Sessions, there are 24 items or steps. If the MHP indicated that 24 items were completed, the MHP's estimate of treatment integrity would be 100%. If the trainer indicated that 22 of the 24 steps were completed, the trainer's estimate of treatment integrity would be 92%. In computing their reliability, if the MHP and trainer agreed that the first 21 items and the last item were performed, there would be 22 agreements. If the trainer stated that the 22nd and 23rd items were not performed, and the MHP stated that the 22nd and 23rd items were performed, they would have two disagreements. Thus, reliability of the MHP and trainer's ratings would be computed as agreements (22) divided by agreements (22) + disagreements (2) multiplied by 100, or in this case, $22/24 \times 100 = 91.7\%$. Thus, the percentage agreement score would be 91.7 percent, indicating excellent reliability.

In both community and research settings, it is recommended that all therapy session audiotapes be submitted to an appropriate administrator, and that approximately 10% of these session audiotapes be randomly selected for review by the trainer (or other rater) to enhance feasibility. To assist in the provision of feedback from the trainer to the MHP, and enhance treatment integrity, the Treatment Integrity Review Form includes a section where the MHP's overall "skill level" can be recorded by the trainer utilizing a 1 to 7 Likert-scale: 7 = extremely skilled, 6 = very skilled, 5 = somewhat skilled, 4 = neutral, 3 = somewhat unskilled, 2 = very unskilled, 1 = extremely unskilled. The top of each prompting checklist includes a spot where the name of the trainer may be recorded, as well as the date of the review. Finally, there is a location at the bottom of each prompting checklist to write notes about the intervention to facilitate qualitative comments about the delivery of therapy.

This highly reliable and valid method of measuring treatment integrity has a number of unique advantages. Indeed, it is psychometrically reliable and valid, it is administratively feasible, and it facilitates learning as MHPs use the checklists both as instructional prompts during therapy and to score their own adherence to therapy, and as trainers use them to provide feedback to the MHPs.

Consumer Satisfaction and Compliance Ratings

After each intervention is implemented, the client is asked to rate the extent to which the intervention was perceived to be helpful, and the MHP rates the extent to which the client was compliant. These ratings are recorded at the end of each of the prompting checklists. As exemplified in Exhibit 1.2, MHPs are prompted to assess these ratings, and to facilitate discussion about how these ratings were derived, and how the intervention can be improved in the future.

Consumer satisfaction ratings are important to obtain because high scores are indicative of future interest in the respective therapy, whereas low scores may demonstrate a lack of enthusiasm or confidence in the intervention. Of course, assessing consumer satisfaction is also likely to show clients that the therapists are interested in their opinions about the treatment plan, and this procedure provides opportunities to modify treatment planning to be commensurate with clients' interests and needs. Certainly, low scores may suggest that a treatment is not working or that a treatment is not desired in its current method of implementation and may need to be adjusted. The compliance ratings include three process measures that have consistently been predictive of treatment outcome (i.e., attendance, participation, and homework completion). MHPs are also encouraged to consider significant others when compliance ratings are assessed. Providing clients positive feedback lets them know these process measures are valued. Indeed, with permission from clients, the compliance ratings are provided to referral agents (see Monthly Progress Report in Chapter 2), thus enhancing the meaningfulness of these ratings and potentially motivating clients to do well.

Concluding Remarks

This chapter provides a general background of FBT, including its historical, theoretical, and empirical underpinnings; outcome support to assist in determining appropriate referrals; and strategies to maintain and assess treatment integrity and customer satisfaction. As indicated, FBT is clearly a robust, empirically supported intervention capable of managing a wide range of problem behaviors that occur in clients with substance use disorders. In addition to being relatively easy to learn and monitor, it is exciting to implement. Whereas most of this chapter was focused on the general structure of FBT, the remaining chapters will focus on therapeutic strategies and specific content involved in the effective implementation of this approach.

Supporting Materials for Chapter 1: Introduction to Family Behavior Therapy

Exhibit 1.1. Treatment Integrity Review Form.

TREATMENT INTEGRITY REVIEW FORM

Name of Trainer (or rater): _____   Name of Therapist(s) Reviewed: _____

Date of Session Reviewed: _____   Intervention Reviewed: _____

Therapist Protocol Adherence

Adherence according to therapist: # of steps reportedly completed by therapist divided by # of steps possible $\times$ 100 = _____.

Adherence according to rater: # of steps reportedly completed by therapist divided by # of steps possible $\times$ 100 = _____.

Reliability: # of steps agreed upon by therapist and trainer $\div$ (# steps agreed upon by therapist and trainer + # of steps disagreed upon by therapist and trainer) $\times$ 100 = _____.

Therapist Skill Rating

Trainer: Indicate the extent of therapist skill demonstrated when implementing the intervention using the following 7-point scale:

7 = extremely skilled, **6** = very skilled, **5** = somewhat skilled, **4** = neutral,
3 = somewhat unskilled, **2** = very unskilled, **1** = extremely unskilled

Record Trainer Rating of Therapist Skill Here: _____

Notes (optional):

_____

_____

_____

_____

_____

_____

Exhibit 1.2. Ratings of Intervention Helpfulness and Client Compliance.

Client's Assessment of Helpfulness of the Intervention

___a.   After stating client should not feel obligated to provide high scores, as an honest assessment helps better address client needs, solicit how helpful client thought intervention was using a 7-point scale:

> **7** = extremely helpful, **6** = very helpful, **5** = somewhat helpful, **4** = not sure,
> **3** = somewhat unhelpful, **2** = very unhelpful, **1** = extremely unhelpful

- **Record Client's Rating Here:_____**

___b.   Solicit how rating was derived, and methods of improving intervention in future.

Therapist's Rating of Client's Compliance With Intervention

___a.   Disclose therapist's rating of client's compliance using a 7-point scale:

> **7** = extremely compliant, **6** = very compliant, **5** = somewhat compliant, **4** = neutral,
> **3** = somewhat noncompliant, **2** = very noncompliant, **1** = extremely noncompliant

- Factors that contribute to compliance ratings are:
    - Attendance
    - Participation and conduct in session
    - Homework completion
- **Record Therapist's Rating of Client's Compliance Here:_____**

___b.   Disclose client's compliance rating.

___c.   Explain how rating was derived, and methods of improving performance in future.

Infrastructure

Overview

This chapter reviews clinic infrastructure and quality assurance procedures, such as standardized methods of training and record keeping. It also reviews standardized forms that were developed to assist in the implementation and management of FBT in community agencies. These forms are included as Exhibits 2.1 through 2.10. The forms are also included in the attached CD to permit them to be modified to accommodate cultural, legal, and reporting requirements that may differ across treatment agencies. Updated versions are available through correspondence with the primary author.

Infrastructure and Quality Assurance

There are a number of infrastructural concerns that must be considered when implementing evidence-based treatments, such as FBT. First, treatment mental health professionals (MHPs) need to be qualified to learn and administer FBT, and agency administrators need to be sufficiently prepared to support FBT training and sustainability. Therefore, this section identifies methods of determining, securing, and sustaining appropriate resources, training, and quality assurance programming.

Mental Health Professionals and Supervisors

One MHP is required to implement FBT in outpatient or inpatient contexts, while two MHPs may be necessary if FBT is implemented in clients' homes, particularly when there are safety concerns or multiple children are involved in therapy. To make home visits with two MHPs feasible, session agendas and progress notes may be completed during travel to and from client homes, and whenever possible one provider should engage children in therapy while the other separately treats the client and adult significant others. If MHPs are not state licensed, at least one state-licensed mental health professional with an interest in FBT will need to conduct supervision. Supervisors should ideally have experience in conducting evidence-based therapies, particularly cognitive-behavioral therapies, and must have professional therapeutic experience serving the population that is being treated. Providers should be state-licensed mental health professionals (MHPs), or legally able to provide therapeutic services under the supervision of a qualified state-licensed mental health professional. MHPs should ideally have experience serving the population that is being targeted for treatment, and must have an interest in conducting therapy utilizing FBT.

Ensuring a Sufficient Number of Clients

It is certainly possible for agencies or individual practitioners to secure resources to learn and implement FBT, and subsequently experience difficulties soliciting a sufficient number of client referrals. This is usually not a fatal blow since it is important for MHPs to assume a small caseload when first learning to implement evidence-based treatments. However, within 6 to 8 months of initiating training in FBT, it is important that treatment MHPs maintain full caseloads to assist in program sustainability. A number of strategies may be helpful in soliciting referrals. First, administrators of potential referral and funding agencies should be approached, and the plan to implement FBT should be discussed to determine the extent of their interest. There are FBT presentation materials that may be obtained free of charge from the authors or prepared based on the information in this book. Of course, it may be helpful to query which specific populations the funding or referral agency is most interested in treating, and determine if plans can be made to accommodate those needs.

Another approach to securing referrals is to conduct professional presentations at referral agencies, such as child protective service agencies, correctional institutions, court, large corporations, and other treatment agencies. To assist in this endeavor, the FBT Presentation to Assist in Obtaining Referrals is included as Exhibit 2.1. This checklist includes sequential instructions and prompts designed to assist in developing the FBT presentation and in guiding the presenter when the presentation is delivered. This form is expected to be modified to accommodate the unique needs of each referral agency. In the first section of this form (i.e., "Establish contact with referral agency"), prompts are provided to encourage staff in the referral agency to participate in 30- to 60-minute presentations that are designed to enhance staff cohesion within the referral agency. These meetings are designed to be fun and demonstrate an experiential appreciation of FBT. For instance, "I've Got Great Coworkers" might be developed from the "I've Got a Great Family" FBT intervention (see Chapter 7). In the latter example, coworkers would be substituted for family members (i.e., the referral agency staff would be prompted to exchange things they loved, admired, or respected about each other). Of course, these presentations permit the referral agency staff to experience the relative strengths of FBT firsthand while enabling the treatment provider to establish rapport with the referral agents. Similar activities can be performed to solicit referrals from school administrators (i.e., "I've Got a Great Classroom). The experiential activity is followed by a 15-minute presentation about FBT services. To assist in follow-up after the presentation is completed, a sample brochure to distribute at these meetings is provided as Exhibit 2.2. The template indicates where idiosyncratic information about the agency may be recorded, such as contact information, directions, inclusionary criteria, and so on.

Methods of Learning FBT

There are a number of training options available for learning FBT. The most inexpensive method of training involves studying this book. Someone who is familiar with the treatment of substance abuse and evidence-based treatment implementation, particularly behavior therapies, may find this method adequate. Along these lines, videos are freely available from the authors that depict the implementation of FBT with actors. However, when more intensive training is desired or needed, interactive distance education and continuing education programs are available that are focused on FBT. The authors may be contacted for a list of independent mental health providers who have received extensive training in FBT and have expressed an interest in the provision of intensive on-site training. These trainers generally utilize the following consultative approach, although instruction may vary.

Overview of Consultative Approach   Of course, clinical expertise and adherence to evidence-based protocols like FBT are enhanced by intensive ongoing training (Bartholomew, Joe, Rowan-Szal, & Simpson, 2007). Intensive training in FBT initially involves a series of conference calls from a reputable trainer, and the completion of structured questionnaires by participating treatment

MHPs and their administrators to assist in customizing the FBT training experience to fit the agency's culture. There are currently four training packages available that are thematically organized as follows:

1. *Family Relationship/Communication Skills Training Module*—includes I've Got a Great Family and Positive Request (Chapters 7 and 8);

2. *Drug– and Other Problem Behavior-Specific Training Module*—includes Behavioral Goals and Rewards (Chapter 5), Environmental Control (Chapter 9), and Self-Control (Chapter 10).

3. *Job-Getting and Financial Management Skills Training Module*—includes Job-Getting and Financial Management interventions (Chapters 11 and 12).

4. *Comprehensive FBT Training Module*—includes all FBT interventions listed above.

The drug- and other problem behavior-specific training module requires an initial 2-day workshop, whereas both the Family Relationship/Communication Skills and Job-Getting and Financial Management training modules may be implemented in 1-day workshops. The Comprehensive FBT module requires a 4-day initial workshop. All workshops are followed by ongoing teleconference training calls that last between 1 and 2 hours. These teleconference calls initially occur once per week and fade in frequency over the course of 3 months to a year. MHPs who receive the comprehensive training package are additionally encouraged to participate in a 2-day booster workshop that is usually scheduled to occur 6 months after the initial workshop. Of course, the comprehensive FBT training module is recommended, but requires greater time and resources.

Initial Workshop   During the initial workshops, FBT interventions are usually taught in a conceptually driven sequence. For instance, in the full training package, the Session Agenda is taught first, then Behavioral Goals and Rewards, Treatment Planning, and finally the remaining skill-based interventions. After introductions, trainers usually present a slide show demonstrating the theoretical and empirical background of FBT, as well as a general overview of its treatment components and agenda for the workshop. Each intervention is first modeled by the trainer utilizing the initial session prompting checklist while participating MHPs sequentially take turns portraying the role of a client, each for about 5 minutes. Rather than asking questions during these role-plays, MHPs are instructed to "act out" their problems during the role-plays, which helps maintain flow and contextual appreciation of issues that are relevant to clinical management (Rowan-Szal, Greener, Joe, & Simpson, 2007). The roles are then reversed, with the trainer portraying the role of a relatively compliant client, and the trainees assuming therapist roles, each for about 5 minutes. MHPs are instructed to "work out" their mistakes as if they are in a real session. Positive feedback is offered by the trainer and other MHPs after each role-play has finished. The trainer points out clinical skills that were effectively demonstrated, and suggests ways to improve them further, whenever necessary. After initial session protocols are modeled, the trainer and MHPs role-play future sessions in a similar manner. Trainees are also sometimes encouraged to "break out" into pairs to role-play the interventions while the trainer walks about the room providing encouragement, guidance, and instruction.

Ongoing Training and Case Monitoring   After the initial workshop is conducted, the MHPs and their supervisor participate in 1- to 2-hour teleconference meetings with the FBT trainer. The meetings usually occur once per week initially and fade in occurrence as MHPs master FBT. These ongoing training sessions are feasible because supervisors usually manage their legal and ethical responsibilities during these sessions. That is, supervisory tasks and training tasks are reviewed conjointly. Audiotape recordings of intervention sessions and case records of each of the clients are brought to these meetings. The supervisor is taught to utilize a standardized form to monitor cases (Exhibit 2.3, Record of Ongoing FBT Training Form) and a prompting checklist to guide the administration of activities during these meetings (Exhibit 2.4, Case Review for Ongoing FBT Training Form). To assist in maintaining client confidentiality, it is recommended that trainers are not provided names or other information that would identify clients, and that appropriate information releases are obtained from clients prior to the release of identifying information, when release of such information is required for training or program purposes. As noted from Exhibit 2.3, the Record of FBT Ongoing Training includes basic descriptive information about each client, as well as important details relevant to legal and ethical issues that may need to be reviewed during the ongoing training meeting, such as incidents or emergencies, court-related activities, outstanding notes, and recommendations. There are also prompts to record information that is relevant to treatment integrity, such as whether treatment integrity feedback was provided for randomly selected session audiotapes, or if session audiotapes were reviewed during the ongoing meeting. Thus, for each client, the supervisor has a record of the MHPs' efforts in providing FBT.

The Case Review for Ongoing FBT Training Form (Exhibit 2.4) focuses on improving implementation of the FBT interventions, including discussion of therapist style, role-playing to teach therapeutic skills, and descriptive feedback on adherence rating forms. It also facilitates positive feedback for successful efforts to implement treatment. Monitoring adherence to treatment protocols is essential when trainees are first learning to implement evidence-based treatments (Madson, Campbell, Barrett, Brondino, & Melchert, 2005), but it is also important for more seasoned MHPs, as there is always the potential for drifting from standardized procedures over time. Therefore, all MHPs receive feedback regarding the quality and extent to which they provided therapy with integrity, with more frequent feedback for those with less experience. As can be seen in Exhibit 2.4, the Case Review for Ongoing FBT Training Form, each therapist reviews the number of cases seen during the past week, and MHPs are encouraged to use structured problem-solving exercises to assist them in generating solutions when clients are not attending therapy sessions as prescribed. The supervisor decides the order of case review with input from MHPs. Priority is typically given to inexperienced MHPs (Morgan & Sprenkle, 2007) or to complicated cases, including those where there is a threat of self-harm or harm to others. MHPs report case feedback using the Case Review for Ongoing FBT Training Form. For cases seen the first time, MHPs disclose basic identifying information, including the client's demographic information; reason for referral; family constellation, including the number of children who may be living in the home and their ages; diagnostic information; drug use history; strengths and areas of growth; a brief conceptualization of how presenting problems developed and are maintained; and a tentative treatment plan. These case presentations last less than 15 minutes. Random sections of session audiotapes are then reviewed for about 5 minutes.

For cases previously presented, only brief descriptive information is provided by the therapist to identify the case to the supervisor. MHPs then present the reason for referral, current session number, estimate of the percentage of scheduled sessions attended, any family members present during the session, the treatment module(s) completed, and plans for the next session. When necessary, the MHPs, supervisor, and trainer, if available, also discuss methods of incorporating other family members into future sessions, and solutions to help resolve problems that occurred during the session. The supervisor initiates a case review that lasts approximately 10 minutes and includes a random review of the session tape, and sometimes a review of clinical records for quality assurance.

In cases where clients were not seen, the supervisor and therapist discuss family support systems that may be recruited, problems that possibly influenced session nonattendance, and strategies to increase attendance at subsequent sessions. This case review supervision format encourages MHPs to be independent and improves their skills in retaining clients in therapy, while allowing for appropriate oversight of cases.

At the end of the supervision session, supervisors place session audiotapes in a locked filing cabinet for evaluation of protocol adherence. Ten percent of these tapes are randomly selected for review by the trainer to assist in the assessment of protocol adherence (see Chapter 1). However, when MHPs are inexperienced or evidence difficulties or low attendance in their treatment sessions, they are also encouraged to review the session audiotapes for treatment integrity utilizing the respective prompting checklists. Of course, conducting treatment integrity checks enhances clinical skill sets by familiarizing MHPs with the intervention protocols.

Booster Workshop   The booster workshop that is performed in the comprehensive training module is similar to the initial workshop, with the exception that the trainer does not model each FBT intervention. Rather, FBT MHPs take turns modeling/practicing in the therapist's role (5-minute blocks) with the trainer serving as the client. The trainer increases the difficulty level of the role-play commensurate with therapist experience level and provides feedback between each role-play. In this way, inexperienced MHPs are able to view senior MHPs implementing the interventions in difficult scenarios, while still practicing FBT at an appropriate level of difficulty. Furthermore, experienced MHPs have opportunities to sharpen their skills at an advanced level.

Record Keeping

It is important to ensure clinic operations and other contextual factors are effectively managed when implementing FBT. Of course, quality assurance is greatly enhanced when treatment is administered with integrity, and some of the methods that were reviewed earlier in this chapter assist in that process. However, case management procedures, such as record keeping, are also extremely important in ensuring quality care for clients. Along these lines, several forms are included in this chapter to assist in efficient record keeping that is relevant to FBT. These forms are standardized, and have undergone several years of revision based on the feedback of MHPs and administrators in both community and clinical research settings. Some agencies and practitioners may prefer to modify these forms, or prefer their own record-keeping system. However, utilization of standardized record-keeping forms may decrease errors and enhance consistency between the persons who complete them. Of course, these forms are legal documents; thus, it is strongly recommended that appropriate program representatives and legal counsel examine each of these forms to ensure that they are legally and ethically appropriate and consistent with the appropriate state laws and relevant licensing boards.

Client records are organized in a folder that includes a Chart Table of Contents Form (Exhibit 2.5) that may be used to guide agency staff through the record. The forms may be easily incorporated into electronic filing systems, and particular forms may be modified or omitted when redundancy occurs within existing systems. The Table of Contents lists the following documents (other documents may be necessary, or when included in the appendix may require revision or exclusion):

1. *Termination Reports:* Completed immediately after the client's case is terminated from the treatment program. The content of these documents varies for a variety of reasons, but generally includes demographic information about the client, reason for referral, type of treatment provided, response to treatment, reasons for program termination, status at the time of termination/discharge, and discharge plans.

2. *Table of Contents Form* (Exhibit 2.5): Show how the client record is organized. Forms on the left side of the chart are listed in numerical order (top to bottom) in the left column, and forms on the right side are listed in numerical order in the right side.

3. *Log of Contacts Form* (Exhibit 2.6): Summarizes all contacts with the client or appropriate others that are in the record, and includes the date, duration of contact, person making the contact, and type of contact.

4. *Monthly Progress Report to Referral Agency Form* (Exhibit 2.7): Sent to referral agents once per month upon consent of clients to show how clients are progressing in therapy. These reports may assist in motivating clients to do well in accomplishing their treatment goals through the establishment of accountability. These standardized reports convey common information typically required by most referral agents, such as the number of sessions attended during the past month and up to that time, promptness to sessions, nonattendance rates, treatments addressed, and compliance/effort of clients during the past month.

5. *Outside Correspondence:* A section in the record that includes all written outside correspondence provided to others, and received from others, such as e-mails, court reports, and letters.

6. *Treatment Plan* (see Chapter 6): Shows which FBT treatments were preferred by clients, and how treatments will be implemented.

7. *Demographic Form:* Shows relevant demographic and contact information. The content of these forms is idiosyncratically determined.

8. *Informed Consent and Releases to/for Information:* The content of all consent forms is determined by state licensing boards, and these forms are required for the protection of clients.

9. *Standard Treatment Session Progress Notes Form* (Exhibit 2.8): A record of content reviewed during each FBT session. The form was designed to be quick and easy to complete, while including relevant information specific to the implementation of FBT. MHPs are prompted to indicate the date and time of the session, who was present, and the session number. To assist in appropriate supervision and safety of clients, MHPs are prompted to record if any "adverse events" (e.g., issues that threaten the safety of the individual) occurred during the session, and if the supervisor was notified within 24 hours. All FBT interventions are listed, permitting them to be circled if they were implemented. Relevant information about each intervention may be quickly recorded in response to standard fill-in-the-blank prompts, such as duration of implementation (which is derived from the start and finish times of each prompting checklist), the protocol

adherence or treatment integrity score (percentage of steps completed as derived from the prompting checklist), helpfulness and compliance ratings (derived from the Ratings section at the bottom of each prompting checklist), and if homework was complete or incomplete, and assigned. Of course, the latter information assists MHPs in maintaining protocol adherence.

10. *Extra-Treatment Session Progress Notes Form* (Exhibit 2.9): All contacts with client excluding the Standardized Treatment Progress Notes, including telephone contacts, court appearances, e-mails, and so forth.

11. *Treatment Session Worksheets:* Include all worksheets that are completed by clients.

12. *Testing Results:* Include all testing results and measures completed by clients.

Method of Checking Quality Assurance of Client Records

To assist in maintaining appropriate records, we have developed a monitoring system to accompany the aforementioned forms (see Exhibit 2.10). In this system, a form is completed by a staff member who is familiar with client record-keeping procedures, such as a therapist or ideally an administrator of the agency. In addition to printing the name of the reviewer and therapist responsible for the chart, the reviewer lists the date of review as well as the date that the necessary revisions to the record are due if errors are determined in the record. Briefly, the reviewer examines each form (listed in the left-most column) to determine if the following errors are present: (1) form is missing, (2) form is sloppy, (3) a required date is not recorded, (4) a time or duration is not recorded, (5) supervisor signature is missing, (6) client signature is missing, (7) there is relevant information missing, and (8) the identification number (or name) of the client is missing. If an error is found in the record, the reviewer indicates the error with a check mark in the appropriate column and row corresponding to the form and error type. If an "NA" is indicated in the column representing the type of error and row representing the form, an error for that form is not applicable.

Several potential errors are not specific to a given form. Rather, these errors are systemic, and include (1) the order of forms is incorrect, (2) the Log of Contacts and Standard Treatment Progress Notes, or (3) Log of

Contacts and Extra Treatment Session Progress Notes do not match, and (4) the Monthly Progress Reports do not include a cover sheet and fax confirmation. These errors are indicated with a "yes" or "no" response.

This overall method of monitoring client records is relatively easy to teach and highly effective in reducing errors that are common to record keeping. However, it is important that MHPs are encouraged to show reviewers how they have corrected errors in the presence of their supervisors or that their supervisors actively support the reviewers to assist in accountability. The time required to monitor client records in this manner will vary depending on a number of issues, such as the extent of treatment received, experience and conscientiousness of the therapist responsible for the record, and involvement of legal entities. However, most record reviews may be completed in about 10 minutes the first time the monitoring system is implemented, and about 5 minutes thereafter. Most records should be monitored on a monthly or every-other-month basis to maintain quality assurance while at the same time minimizing impact on existing resources.

Concluding Remarks

Recognizing challenges inherent in adopting evidence-supported interventions within community settings, FBT was developed to be relatively easy to learn and implement, to be flexible to concurrently address multiple problem areas, and to include interventions that are fun to implement and consumer driven. A relative strength of FBT, as noted in the National Registry of Evidence-Based Programs and Practices (2008), is its inclusion of the many standardized forms reviewed in this chapter. However, we emphasize that these forms may require adjustments to fit individual agencies' unique cultures and reporting and record-keeping requirements. Similarly, some may not be appropriate for all agencies. Additionally, because reporting and record-keeping requirements vary across state and local governments, treatment agency representatives should consider qualified legal representation in the adoption and revision of these forms, including standardized procedures underlying their use.

Supporting Materials for Chapter 2: Infrastructure for Family Behavior Therapy

Exhibit 2.1. Presenter Prompting Checklist for Recruitment Presentation.

FBT PRESENTATION TO ASSIST IN OBTAINING REFERRALS

PRESENTER PROMPTING CHECKLIST

Preparation for Presentation

☐ Establish contact w/referral agency.
- Indicate program building activities can be performed pro bono & distribute program information to administrators (if in person).
  - I've Got Great Co-Workers instead of Family.
  - Positive Request or Self-Control for Co-Workers instead of Family.
- Indicate FBT presentations can also be conducted.
  - Last 10–15 minutes at the end of an existing staff meeting

☐ Obtain address and contact information for presentation:
- Street address (MapQuest if necessary)
- Phone number
- Contact person (typically a supervisor)

☐ Obtain FBT program forms:
- Forms necessary for agencies to make referrals (approx. 5 for each agent)
- Program brochures describing program for agency attendees
- Sign-up sheet for individuals who attend meeting to record names, e-mails, & phone #s
- Personal business cards
  Note: paper clip business cards to program brochures.

☐ Purchase small token gifts to distribute to attendees for answering questions about presentation:
- candy, gum, snacks, costume jewelry, or small toys for clients and their children

☐ Purchase drinks, donuts, snacks, etc., for meeting, if funding permits.

Day of Presentation

☐ Add 15 min. to est. drive time to avoid tardiness.

Presentation Introduction

☐ Introduce self and affiliation (include position held).

☐ State gratitude for invitation to present.

☐ Distribute presentation sign-in sheet.

☐ Provide the following to all presentation attendees:
- Forms necessary for agencies to make referrals (approx. 5 for each agent)
- Program brochure describing program for agency attendees

- Sign-up sheet for individuals who attend meeting to record names, e-mails, & phone #s
- Personal business cards.

☐ State who program targets (e.g., adults w/ drug abuse and their families).

☐ Provide the following list of benefits:

    ☐ Relatively low program costs for participation.

    ☐ Clients & family members choose from list of evidence-based & skills-building interventions.

    ☐ Indicate the typical anticipated # of sessions.

    ☐ Mention client's significant others and sometimes children are involved, as appropriate.

    ☐ Open communication w/ referral agent.
- Monthly progress notes are sent to referral agent if desired, and w/ release from client (attendance, compliance, effort).
- Monthly calls made to referral agent (client attendance, compliance, effort) w/ release.
- Referral agent notified of missed sessions w/in 24 hours if release obtained.

    ☐ Providers advocate for clients in scheduled court hearings.

Treatment Review

☐ Highlight FBT Tx. modules (time is limited so curtail extensive description):

1. **Treatment Planning:** Client and clinician determine which modules are most relevant to client's goals and family's needs.

2. **Behavioral Goals and Rewards:** Determining and monitoring reward contingencies for staying clean and out of trouble.

3. **Environmental Control:** Arranging environment to spend more time w/ people, places, and situations that do not involve drugs & trouble, and less time w/ people, places, and situations that do involve drugs, including management of these situations.

4. **I've Got a Great Family:** Family exchanges things they love, admire, and respect about each other to enhance overall tone in the relationship.

5. **Positive Request:** Teaches appropriate skills in requesting things, and compromising.

6. **Self-Control:** Learning to recognize and manage negative emotions and troublesome behavior through thought stopping, reviewing negative consequences, problem solving, and positive imagery of desired actions.

7. **Job Getting Skills Training:** Assistance getting jobs.

8. **Financial Management:** Assistance lowering expenses and gaining income.

Referral Form Review (refer to the form necessary to make a referral)

☐ State criteria necessary to make a referral.

☐ Show how to complete the referral form.

☐ Tell agents to recommend the referral and call the clinic after referral is faxed.

Referral Process Review

☐ State the process involved once a referral is received.

☐ Solicit questions.

☐ Solicit referrals & sign-up sheet.

After Presentation

☐ Send thank you letter w/ referral forms to contact person (typically supervisor).

Example Letter:

On the behalf of the staff at (AGENCY NAME), we would like to thank you for your support in our treatment program and look forward to working with you in the future. We have enclosed some additional referral forms for your staff. We can be reached at (AGENCY PHONE NUMBER) if you have any questions or need anything.

Sincerely,

TEAM MEMBER'S NAME AND TITLE

☐ Send thank you e-mail w/ an electronic version of the referral form to all attendees of presentation.

Example E-mail:

Thank you for your support of our program. We have attached an electronic version of our referral form that you can conveniently print when you need to and then fax to our office at (AGENCY FAX NUMBER). We can be reached at (AGENCY PHONE NUMBER) if you have any questions or need anything.

We look forward to working with you,

Sincerely,

TEAM MEMBER'S NAME AND TITLE

Exhibit 2.2. Recruitment Brochure.

Contact Information:

INSERT CONTACT PERSON'S NAME AND TITLE HERE

INSERT CONTACT PERSON'S NAME AND CONTACT INFO. HERE

AGENCY NAME AND ADDRESS HERE

Directions:

PUT DIRECTIONS HERE FROM A FEW MAJOR STREETS OR LOCATIONS HERE*

***IN NEXT COLUMN TO RIGHT AT TOP PUT COMPANY LOGO

Please enjoy learning about our program, which includes Family Behavior Therapy, an evidence-based program listed in SAMHSA's National Registry of Evidenced-Based Programs and Practices and other national clearinghouses.

The development of Family Behavior Therapy was funded by grant awards from the National Institutes of Health.

Who Is Eligible?

Any adult who meets the following criteria can be referred for an evaluation to determine program eligibility:

- Adults who have recently been identified to use illicit drugs.

- Adults who have someone who is willing to participate in the client's treatment.

  ADD OTHER CRITERIA HERE

What are the costs? ***PUT COSTS HERE*** OR OMIT SECTION***

How do I make a referral?

INSERT TELEPHONE AND FAX NUMBER HERE

Services Include:

- *LIST # AND MONTHS OF TREATMENT HERE, IF RELEVANT*

- Involvement of family members.

- Evidence-supported Family Behavior Therapy targets:
  - Alcohol & drug abuse
  - Behavior problems
  - Mood disorders
  - Family dysfunction
  - Under/unemployment
  - Poor communication skills
  - Anger management
  - Poor school performance

  ADD MORE INFORMATION HERE THAT IS SPECIFIC TO YOUR PROGRAM

PUT AGENCY LOGO HERE

Exhibit 2.3. Record of Ongoing FBT Training Form.

RECORD OF ONGOING FBT TRAINING

Client identification number:_____

Relationship(s) of adult significant others:_____

Age(s) of children living in the home:_____

Unique or important characteristics about case:_____

Drugs used:_____

Reason for referral:_____

Date & week					
Incidents addressed					
Court activities addressed					
Feedback provided about protocol adherence from someone who listened to an audiotape of session					
Session audiotape reviewed during ongoing session					
Outstanding recommendations made					
Outstanding notes					

Exhibit 2.4. Case Review for Ongoing FBT Training Form.

CASE REVIEW FORM FOR ONGOING FBT TRAINING

Preparation for Case Review meetings

a. Include up to 6 mental health providers and 1 supervisor.
b. Meetings usually last 60 to 75 min. (up to 3 providers) to 90 minutes (up to 6 providers).
c. Require 1 audiotape recorder for audiotape review.
d. Require providers to bring audiotapes for each therapy session during week.
e. May require providers to bring charts for each active client (or have quick access).
f. Require providers to bring copies of this form to guide case review.

Protocol for Case Review

a. Supervisor or lead provider indicates client id# being assessed or scheduled for assessment.
b. Distribute new referrals to providers.
c. Provide summary of enlistment and retention contacts.
    1. Client id# numbers contacted
    2. Outstanding issues
d. FBT trainer or other designated reviewer provides feedback of protocol adherence for session audiotapes since last review.
    1. Provide strengths in style & methods used to accomplish adherence.
    2. Ask provider to state strengths in style & methods of getting adherence.
    3. Solicit things to enhance protocol adherence.
    4. Provide things to enhance protocol adherence (optional).
e. Each mental health provider reports:
    1. Caseload (i.e., how many clients each provider is assigned to treat each week)
    2. # clients seen since last case review
    3. Any incidents (emergencies) that need to be addressed immediately
f. Cases presented by providers for feedback using "CASE REVIEW" format (see below).
    1. Prioritize which cases to review and for how long:
        a. cases that are difficult/evidencing incidents or potential problems
        b. cases that have received relatively less attention in recent past
    2. Supervisor/lead provider completes "Record of FBT Cases" form for each case.
g. Assign 10% of session audiotapes for review by FBT Trainer, prioritizing based on:
    1. Providers attempting to learn intervention
    2. Providers experiencing difficulties w/ protocol adherence
    3. Providers that didn't maintain active caseload during previous week
h. Supervisor completes protocol adherence form in supervision binder.

Note: Monthly Progress Notes should probably be reviewed the last week of every month.

SEE THE FOLLOWING CONTENT ITEMS FOR HOW CASES ARE TO BE REVIEWED (CASE REVIEW FORMAT)

Content for presenting a case for the first time by a provider (10–20 min.)

a. Useful info. about client (i.e., approx. age, # of previous tx. programs attended)
b. Reason for referral
c. #, and ages, of children in home
d. Drug of choice and brief summary of assessment tools/measures administered
e. Synopsis of strengths from assessment
f. Synopsis of weaknesses from assessment
g. Conceptualization of case (i.e., how did probs. develop, how are they maintained)
h. Treatment plan (or tentative treatment plan)
i. Plans for next session
j. Random review of session tape (optional)
   1. Supervisor determines what sections are reviewed, and for how long.

Content for presenting a case that has been presented previously (10–20 min.)

a. Client # and idiosyncratic info about client to jar memory
b. Reason for referral
c. Approximate percentage of scheduled sessions attended
d. Family members present in last session, & methods of including more family in future
e. Treatment modules completed thus far
f. Notable problems that occurred during the session
g. General comments on how client is doing and overall improvement
h. Plans for next session
i. Random review of session tape (optional)
   1. Supervisor/lead provider determines what sections reviewed, and for how long.

Content for presenting a case that has been presented previously, but did not attend scheduled session during past week (10 min.)

a. Client # and idiosyncratic info about client to refresh memory
b. Reason for referral
c. Approximate percentage of scheduled sessions attended
d. Family support available to attempt to bring about session attendance
e. Notable problems that may have influenced nonattendance
f. Plans to increase future attendance

Exhibit 2.5. Chart Table of Contents Form.

TABLE OF CONTENTS

TREATMENT FILE

Client Name:_____

Enlistment Representative (if available):_____

Primary Therapist:_____

Date of Intake:_____

Left Side of Chart (listed from top to bottom)	*Right Side of Chart (listed from top to bottom)*
1. **Termination Report** *(added to chart by treatment provider once client is terminated)*	9. **Standard Treatment Session Progress Notes**
2. **Table of Contents**	10. **Extra-Treatment Progress Notes**
3. **Log of Contacts**	11. **Completed Treatment Session Worksheets**
_____	12. **Testing Results**
4. **Monthly Progress Reports** *(added by treatment provider each month)*	
5. **Outside Correspondence** *(i.e., e-mails, court reports, letters to and from client, etc.)*	
_____	
6. **Treatment Plan** *(added by treatment provider once treatment begins)*	
7. **Demographics Form**	
8. **Consent & Release to/for Information**	

Exhibit 2.6. Log of Contacts Form.

LOG OF CONTACTS

Date of Contact (mm/dd/yy)	Duration of Contact (e.g. 12:00 P.M.–12:30 P.M.)	Outside Person Involved in Contact/Attempted Contact (e.g., client, case worker, probation officer)	Type of Contact	Staff Involved in Contact

Key for type of contacts:

TC = telephone contact   M = meeting   CH = court hearing
E = e-mail   F = fax   Text = text message
LM = left message   TA/NA = telephone attempt,
                                no answer

Exhibit 2.7. Monthly Progress Report to Referral Agency Form.

| MONTHLY PROGRESS REPORT | Client ID:_____
Referral Agent's Name:_____
Client Name:_____ |

PROGRESS REPORT FROM _____ TO _____

Date treatment began: _____

# of Sessions Attended During Month	# of Sessions Late During Month (15 min. or more)	# of Sessions Cancelled or No Showed During Month	# of Sessions Rescheduled During Month	Total Number of Sessions Attended to Date

Treatments performed during month:	Treatment Addressed During the Month (Check = Yes)	Provider Ratings of Client's Compliance for Each Respective Therapy (1 = Needs Improvement 2 = Adequate 3 = Very Good)
Program Orientation (informs client of program policies and briefly reviews communication guidelines)		
Treatment Planning (client and provider determine relevant treatment interventions)		
Behavioral Goals & Rewards (teaches client to develop and manage behavioral goals that are consistent with treatment plan, and establish rewards for their completion)		
Environmental/Stimulus Control (assists client in recognizing triggers to substance use and other problem behaviors and methods of escaping and/ or avoiding such triggers. Also, teaches how to structure environment to be clean and healthy)		
I've Got a Great Family (improves positive exchanges among family members and overall tone in the relationship)		

Self-Control (assists client in terminating thoughts that lead to drug use and other problem behaviors, learning relaxation strategies to reduce stress, and learning to brainstorm and perform alternative actions)		
Positive Request (teaches how to make requests of others that increase likelihood of getting needs met, and also resolving conflicts effectively)		
Financial Planning (assists client in developing financial management skills)		
Job-Getting Skills Training (assists client in gaining satisfactory employment)		
Last Session Review (reviews all modules implemented during treatment with client, and discusses how client plans to use the skills learned)		

Outstanding Notes: _____

_____

_____

_____

_____

_____

Name of Provider(s):_____

Provider Signature/Title:_____

Supervisor Signature/Title:_____

_____

Exhibit 2.8. Standard Treatment Session Progress Notes Form.

STANDARD TREATMENT SESSION PROGRESS NOTES

Client ID:_____Date: ___/___/___Time: from___:___A.M./P.M. to___:___A.M./P.M.   Session Number:_____

Persons present in session:_____

Did any adverse incidents (threats to safety) occur during the session? Yes/No
If yes, was supervisor informed within 24 hrs? Yes/No

Print First and Last Name of all Staff Present: _____

Treatments Implemented

Modules	Duration in Minutes	Percentage of Protocol Steps Completed (e.g., 9 steps completed from a prompting checklist that includes 10 steps = 90%).	Client's Rating of Intervention Helpfulness (1 = extremely unhelpful 7 = extremely helpful)	Provider's Rating of Client's Compliance (1 = extremely noncompliant 7 = Extremely compliant)	Homework Due* (I = incomplete C = complete)	Homework Assigned (Indicate with a check)
Session Agenda						
Program Orientation						
Treatment Planning						
Behavioral Goals & Rewards						
Environmental Control						
I've Got a Great Family						
Self-Control						
Positive Request						
Financial Management						
Job-Getting Skills Training						
Last Session Review						
Specify if Other:						

* If no homework due, leave blank.

Strengths Noted During the Session:

_____

_____

_____

_____

_____

_____

_____

_____

_____

Important Notes Outside of Protocol (if relevant):

_____

_____

_____

_____

_____

_____

_____

_____

_____

Date of Next Session :____/____/____   Time of Next Session: from____:____ A.M. / P.M.
to____:_____A.M. / P.M.

Name of Treatment Provider Completing Session Progress Note (first/last):_____

_____

Signature of Treatment Provider (including degree and title):_____

Exhibit 2.9. Extra-Treatment Session Progress Notes Form.

Client ID:_____

EXTRA-TREATMENT SESSION PROGRESS NOTES

Excluding treatment sessions, this is a summary of all contacts with
client, including e-mails, telephone contacts, court contacts, etc.
Each note should include date/duration of contact, and type of contact made. End all notes by
printing name (first/last), title, degree, and signature of writer.

Date, Time (from-to)	Notes

Exhibit 2.10. Record-Keeping Monitoring Form.

Monitoring Form to Assist in Appropriate Record Keeping

Reviewed by: _____   Client ID #: _____

Review Date: _____   Due Date to fix errors: _____

	Form is missing	Writing is sloppy	Date not recorded	Time not recorded	Supervisor signature missing	Therapist signature missing	Client signature missing	All relevant information not completed	Client ID missing
Table of Contents		NA	NA	NA	NA	NA	NA	NA	
Log of Contacts					NA		NA		
Informed Consent				NA					
Demographics Form			NA	NA	NA	NA	NA		
Authorization to Release				NA					
Authorization for Release				NA					
Treatment Plan				NA	NA	NA	NA		
Standard Tx Session Progress Notes					NA		NA		
Extra-Treatment Progress Notes					NA		NA		
Monthly Progress									
Termination Report*				NA			NA		

NA = not applicable to form listed at left of column

1. Are all the forms in the correct order?   Yes _____ No _____

2. Do the Log of Contacts and Standard Treatment Session Progress Notes match?   Yes _____ No _____

3. Do the Log of Contacts and Extra-Treatment Progress Notes match?   Yes _____ No _____

4. Does the Monthly Client Progress Report include a cover sheet and fax confirmation sheet?   Yes _____ No _____

Signature of Therapist: _____   Date: _____

Therapeutic Style, Techniques, and Implementation Strategies

Overview

As will be demonstrated in subsequent chapters, the content of FBT is well organized, conceptually grounded, and empirically justified, reflecting more than two decades of refinement in clinical research and community settings. However, the successful implementation of FBT is dependent on the therapeutic approach and conduct of FBT providers. Therefore, this chapter underscores the general disposition and style of FBT mental health professionals (MHPs), as well as important guidelines in preparing FBT sessions and methods for organizing and implementing treatment-related materials (i.e., treatment prompting checklists, worksheets, handouts).

Chapter at a Glance

➢ Therapeutic style of FBT MHPs

➢ Techniques and implementation strategies

➢ Method of preparing for FBT sessions

Therapeutic Style of FBT MHPs

Emphasis on Positive Feedback and Encouragement

Initiate All Sessions With Positive Feedback Staff members introduce themselves by their first and last names and professional title. Business cards are distributed upon first contact, and when therapy is conducted outside the office (e.g., client homes), a photo identification card is shown. To demonstrate respect for traditional values, clients and their significant others are addressed formally (e.g., Ms., Mrs.) unless explicitly told otherwise by clients. During introductions, MHPs are trained to immediately compliment family members (e.g., "That's a great handshake," "You've really got a comforting voice"). In difficult circumstances, compliments can be quite powerful and have long-lasting effects in therapy. For instance, upon meeting a therapist for the first time, an adolescent client asserted, "Great, another dump." His comment was directed at the lack of high-end furniture and old pictures used to decorate the nonprofit clinic. The therapist reflexively winked at his mother, told the kid he appreciated his assertiveness, and stated that his mother had raised him well to speak openly. The therapist then offered the son and his mother a soda. In an instant, rapport was established with both family members.

Although praise is certainly important in establishing immediate rapport, its effects may be short lived in the absence of primary reinforcers, such as token gifts (e.g., soda in the previous example). It is also important for MHPs to use a variety of secondary reinforcers, such as being humorous, entertaining, and effective in therapy. For instance, meeting a therapist at the side door of his trailer, an elderly client rudely stated, "So, you're the lady who's going to tell me how to raise my grandkids." The therapist quickly retorted, "No, that's probably your mother. I'm too young to tell people what to do." The client laughed and opened the door. In the latter example, the therapist tactfully indicated that she was not there to tell the client what to do, she deferred wisdom to the client's mother, and subtly indicated that she respected the client enough to avoid judging him.

Implement Positively Focused Agendas Each Session   FBT MHPs avoid asking the family how they're doing, how their week was, and so on at the start of therapy sessions because such queries sometimes lead to long-winded comments that are tangential to the presenting concerns and inconsistent with treatment planning. Instead, MHPs are taught to bias their initial session queries to solicit positive responses that are focused on goal attainment, making it easier to transition into therapy (e.g., "So, tell me how you were able to focus on your goals this past week"). Moreover, a formal agenda is conducted at the beginning of each session in which the MHP transitions into the session format by briefly summarizing achievements that occurred during the past session. The method for determining session agendas is extensively reviewed in Chapter 4.

Descriptively Praise Desired Behaviors and Ignore Undesired Behaviors
Treatment protocols rely heavily on MHPs' utilizing descriptive praise when guiding clients in practicing and reviewing therapeutic skills. For instance, during an initial session, a client told her husband to "please knock it off." The MHP responded, "That was great how you started your request by stating please. You are really making an effort to be polite. Now tell him what you'd like him to do." In this interaction, the MHP recognized that it was unnecessary to draw attention to the undesired tone and content that was demonstrated in the request. Rather, she stated why she thought the client's use of please was timely, and redirected the client to indicate what she specifically desired.

It is also important to descriptively praise pleasant feelings and functional thoughts, as well as the behaviors that led to these feelings and thoughts so the importance of these things are emphasized and thus more likely to recur. In doing so, it may be necessary to solicit *specific* feelings and thoughts that are positive to permit opportunities to *descriptively* praise. The following dialogue between a MHP and her client exemplifies this point:

Diane: I took off work this past Friday to watch my kid's baseball game, and I think it really helped our relationship because he told me he was glad to see me at the game in front of his teammates.

MHP: That was such a great gesture to the commitment of your relationship, especially since your son recently told you that he thinks you spend too much time at work. What kind of positive feelings or thoughts did you have after your son told you that?

Diane: I felt a sense of calmness and it made me think I would like to arrange my work schedule so I can go to his games more often.

MHP: That's absolutely fabulous how you allowed yourself to focus on the feeling of calmness and reinforced this feeling by thinking of plans to accomplish this extremely important activity more often.

Clients may experience FBT MHPs as responding to them with unconditional positive regard (a therapeutic technique originated by Carl Rogers), which is also consistent with the basic tenets of differential reinforcement.

That is, ignoring undesired behaviors and descriptively praising desired behaviors will cause desired behaviors to increase and undesired behaviors to decrease in frequency. Thus, MHPs strategically guide family members in conducting desired behaviors.

Practice Descriptive Praise   It is important to practice descriptive praise so it can be quickly and spontaneously utilized throughout therapy. Along these lines, a culture of positive feedback must be created within the treatment agency. Fortunately, practice exercises are fun and may be performed easily during existing daily activities. One exercise ("catching my coworkers being good") is implemented within regularly scheduled program meetings. A list is passed out requesting all attendees to record something they love, admire, or respect about coworkers. At the end of the meeting, a designated member of the team reads the statements to the group, and discussion of the recorded events naturally occurs. MHPs also practice "catching others being good" throughout the day in spontaneous situations (meeting someone in an elevator). MHPs may record the praiseworthy statements they provide, and subsequently review them with their supervisor once a week. A related exercise involves having MHPs think of hypothetical situations in which they descriptively reinforce clients with various adjectives, particularly ones that are seldom used by others in daily conversations (e.g., exquisite) so praise doesn't get stale. It is helpful to make these imagined scenarios difficult, such as how to descriptively reinforce a person who reports he had a drug relapse, but initially did not want to use. In that situation, a MHP might respond to the client by stating:

I can see you're devastated. You did everything right in going to that grocery store because you've never seen any drug users there before. I'm also very proud of you for not wanting to use initially in that situation. Your intentions were right on, and that's a great step forward. Let's brainstorm a few alternatives so you'll be prepared next time and less likely to use.

In this example, the MHP descriptively praises the client's intentions to remain abstinent while ignoring behaviors, thoughts, and feelings that are associated with drug use, thereby shaping the client into realizing his initial thoughts to maintain abstinence are, indeed, his true intentions. This positive context is also likely to increase the client's receptivity to brainstorming alternatives to drug use.

Initially Blame Problem Behaviors, Including Drug Use, on External Factors in the Situation, Then Generate Solutions   Individuals usually learn poorly, and often become defensive, when their flaws are pointed out. Moreover, the research literature clearly indicates that stress exacerbates psychopathological symptoms. Therefore, when clients err, MHPs are trained to excuse their problem behaviors as having occurred due to situational circumstances that were to some extent out of their control. This approach is consistent with Nate Azrin's Positive Practice intervention. For example, if a client came home late from a party, it would be excused *because his friends didn't want him to come home*, or if a client yelled at her employer, in would be excused *because her stress was especially overwhelming and air conditioning made it difficult for her to be heard in a normal tone of voice*. Upon excusing an undesired behavior, MHPs ask clients what could have been done to solve the problem. If ideas are wanting, MHPs provide solutions or ideally instruct clients to use the Self-Control procedure (see Chapter 10) to generate alternative, problem-free solutions. In this way, clients are more likely to be receptive to learning novel methods of managing problem behaviors. It is sometimes helpful to discount derogatory comments about self and others, and subsequently instruct the person responsible for making these statements to immediately make amends. For example, if a husband were to criticize his wife in therapy by stating, "You don't love me," the MHP could say, "That's ridiculous. She's your wife and she's told me several times how much she loves you. Tell her your statement was made in frustration and that you didn't mean to doubt her love. Then please make a positive request for what you were hoping she'd do for you" (see Positive Request in Chapter 8).

Learn by Doing

Use Role-Playing as an Assessment Strategy   Role-playing is employed as both an assessment and treatment strategy throughout FBT. Relevant to assessment, when MHPs are not confident that a client has mastered a behavioral skill, they may instruct the client to act out hypothetical or, ideally, recently reported scenarios in which these skills were needed. In these scenarios, MHPs portray themselves as confederates (antagonists). For example, a MHP might lead a role-play interaction by stating, "Show me what you'd do if Mary offered you a joint at that party. I'll be her. *(Pause)* This stuff is real good, take a hit." In the aforementioned example, the scene is briefly described to provide a context in which to respond, and the client is subsequently prompted to perform the skill that is of interest to the MHP. The scenarios can be subsequently altered to include important details; for example, "Now, I'd like to see how you could manage a situation where Mary is upset because you don't want to go to a party with her. Show me what you could do in this situation. *(Pause)* I can't believe you're not going to come to the party with me just because I want to have a good time." Instructing significant others to comment on the performance of clients during role-play assessments, or instructing them to be confederates themselves, usually helps with generalization, as significant others are often intimately familiar with various obstacles that may come up when clients attempt to use these skills *in vivo.* For instance, in the earlier stages of therapy, a significant other enthusiastically reported, "I think she'd have a hard time telling her friend that she didn't want to go to the party because that woman has a lot of influence over her. Also, I've seen that lady in action. She'd keep on nagging my wife until she'd give in. I think my wife would just have to tell her she didn't use anymore and didn't want to go." MHPs also make spontaneous adjustments during role-plays so that particular reactions of clients can be observed. For example, a MHP might increase "pressure" to use drugs if a client were able to easily resist a first offer to use drugs.

Use Role-Playing as an Intervention Tool   Most of the FBT intervention components involve skill-building exercises utilizing role-playing. MHPs initially model all intervention skills and encourage and assist clients and significant others in rehearsing these skills. Easy scenarios are modeled first, and the difficulty of scenarios increases as clients and family members enhance their skill level. Role-playing provides an outstanding opportunity to increase self-efficacy, and ultimately increases the likelihood that clients (and their significant others) will attempt the modeled behaviors outside therapy. Role-playing is more likely to be successful when the following steps are employed by MHPs:

1. Generate a realistic scenario that is relevant to the client's concerns.

2. Encourage client to generate skills that may be used to manage problem scenarios, and assist as necessary.

3. Model the generated skills, with the client portraying the role of the confederate.

4. Solicit what was liked about the modeled performance.

5. Solicit what could be done, if anything, to enhance the modeled behavior.

6. Instruct the client to model the skill, with the MHP enacting a compliant confederate.

7. Solicit what was liked about the modeled performance.

8. Solicit what the client could do to enhance modeled behavior.

9. Perform additional role-plays with client modeling the skills in progressively more difficult scenarios.

Each of the aforementioned steps is important to increase the likelihood that clients will be motivated to do well during their role-plays. Indeed, generating problem scenarios that are relevant to clients increases the likelihood that clients will be interested in learning the relevant skills. Motivation is also enhanced when clients participate in the generation of skills that may be used to assist in solving problem scenarios, and this procedure also enhances brainstorming skills to assist in generalization. Clients (and family members) should, of course, be encouraged to generate relevant skills, while MHPs provide prompts to enhance the quality of responses. Also, asking clients to express what they liked about role-plays biases them to assess strengths rather than limitations that may be associated with anxiety. It may be necessary for MHPs to redirect clients (and family members) to focus on strengths, as they often respond quite negatively. Framing limitations as things that can be done to enhance the modeled performance permits family members to focus on a positive *can-do* attitude rather than pointing out things that were insufficient. When MHPs model skills first, they assist in alleviating potential anxieties that clients may have while demonstrating skills as exemplars. Instructing family members to provide positive feedback followed by methods of enhancing skills shows how role-playing can be fun, non-threatening, and constructive. It also shows family members that the role-plays will emphasize positive behaviors. The MHP should then instruct clients to do the modeled skill while the MHP assumes the role of a confederate. For example, the MHP might say, "Great. Now, you're ready for your initial try. Go ahead and ask me for that raise. *(Pause)* Hi, Cardelle, what did you want to talk about?" In the preceding example, the MHP's prompt does not give the client much of a chance to get anxious. Of course, the MHP responds to the client's first attempt with descriptive praise, but unlike the evaluation of the MHP's trial, constructive feedback is usually not solicited. If the client volunteers personal critique, the MHP is usually advised to dismiss the critique. For example, if a client were to say "I was really nervous when I was asked to role-play asking for a raise!" the MHP could dismiss this in a positive way by smiling and saying, "I don't know, if you were nervous you sure hid it well." In the latter example, the client gains very little if the undesired behavior (i.e., nervousness) is verified, while the potential gains in overlooking this behavior are substantial. In later role-plays, when confidence is perhaps better developed and rapport between the MHP and client is high, the MHP may increase difficulty levels in role-play scenarios and solicit constructive feedback from clients (and family members).

Enhance the Effectiveness of Therapy Assignments

Most of the FBT intervention components involve instructions for clients and their family members to practice at home the skills they have acquired during therapy. Of course, this assists in generalizing skill acquisition to *real-world* settings, and permits discussion of these practice trials in subsequent sessions. MHPs may employ a number of strategies to increase the likelihood that these skills will be practiced in a timely manner. First, it is important to make sure all family members know how to perform the skills that will be assigned for practice. Then model the recording process that is involved in completing the therapy assignment for a hypothetical day. Indeed, family members will always be provided a form on which to record their completion of therapy assignments. To ensure that all family members understand the recording process, MHPs instruct each of them to practice the recording process for the current day, after the MHP models or demonstrates how to do this process. It also is important to query family members to indicate where the therapy assignment forms will be located, and to ideally suggest a private location that will be visited on a daily basis, such as a bathroom or bedroom mirror. Other methods of increasing the likelihood of therapy assignment completion include brainstorming solutions to potential obstacles that may make it difficult to complete the therapy assignment when the assignment is prescribed, calling family members a couple of days after the assignment is prescribed to assist in descriptively praising efforts to complete the assignment, as well as determining solutions to problems that may have interfered with therapy completion during the prior week.

MHPs use other strategies when reviewing therapy assignments, such as *instructing* clients to provide their completed therapy assignment forms rather than *asking* if they've completed their assignment. Instructions establish the expectation that assignments have been performed, whereas queries suggest that these assignments are optional and thus may not have been completed. Finally, when therapy assignments are incomplete or not performed, MHPs descriptively praise clients for some aspect of the assignment, such as remembering to bring in the blank assignment form, making an effort to complete some of the assignment form if incomplete, or having the intention to complete the assignment if the form was left at home. It is also usually beneficial to blame homework non-completion on extenuating circumstances (e.g., "Of course, it must have been extremely busy for you this week because I know how important your homework is to you and that you wouldn't miss doing it unless there was a very good reason"), and then to subsequently instruct the client and family members to complete what was originally assigned in retrospect. The retrospective completion of therapy assignments is extremely important for several reasons, including: (1) it provides an opportunity to determine how the recording process is completed, (2) it shows that the assignment is important and must be complete prior to moving forward in the therapy session, and (3) it increases accuracy when reviewing the assignment.

Effectively Manage Significant Others

Solicit Participation From Significant Others   Although decision-making strategies were reviewed in Chapter 1 regarding who is appropriate or inappropriate for inclusion in FBT as significant others, this section describes methods for recruiting significant others when clients indicate that there is no significant other who would be able to participate in FBT. First, it is important to understand some of the factors that may lead clients to be hesitant to include these persons in therapy. Some of the concerns that have been reported to FBT MHPs by clients include they are concerned that:

1. Participation will burden the significant other.
2. They will fail in therapy, and the significant other will know about the failure.

3. The MHP will disclose information to significant other that will be embarrassing or lead to an argument or upset the significant other (i.e., significant other perceives information as the "last straw").

4. Not sure why the significant other should be excluded (i.e., fear of unknown).

5. The significant other will disclose information to MHP that may be embarrassing for the client.

6. The significant other will disclose information or do something that will curtail drug use or other problematic behaviors the client is not ready to give up.

7. The significant other will tell others things that were disclosed in therapy.

8. The significant other will perceive the client's involvement in therapy as a weakness.

9. The significant other will not be interested in therapy.

10. A significant other is truly unavailable or would be a negative influence.

When examining these concerns, it becomes clear that many of them are related to fears of the unknown, embarrassment, and retaliation for disclosure of information. Some of the concerns are encouraging. For instance, when clients indicate that they do not want to burden significant others, this is usually a good sign, as it implies there are significant others available and that these persons are likely to be appropriate support systems. Indeed, it is the ones that have not been burdened that are usually problematic. Nevertheless, assuming they are indeed burdened, clients may be quite accurate in assessing that these persons may have a low tolerance for therapeutic failures if they are unprepared. The preceding concerns are usually effectively managed by asking the client to explain some of the advantages and disadvantages to involving "significant others" in therapy. The MHP should react neutrally, facilitating the natural flow of the brainstorming process and volunteering advantages that other clients have reported. After briefly validating the legitimacy of each of the concerns, the MHP engages the client in generating solutions to each of the potential negative consequences, proceeds to discuss particular individuals who might be involved in therapy, and establishes guidelines for their inclusion while orienting the client to FBT. Indeed, it is usually quite therapeutic to orient clients to the methods that may be used to manage their expressed concerns, such as limits of confidentiality (what may and may not be disclosed), communication guidelines to manage conflict, relapse prevention, the role and responsibilities of significant others, and the type of information that will be disclosed.

The latter strategy is usually very effective in motivating clients to desire significant others' support. However, it is important to carefully assess the appropriateness of significant others, as reviewed in Chapter 1. Fears regarding retaliation, violence, and involvement in illicit behaviors, including drug use, are red flags that need to be extensively assessed. In these situations, it may be particularly important to assess the history of past problematic behavior of significant others and very carefully weigh the risk of their inclusion versus exclusion in the treatment plan. If the risk of including them outweighs the potential benefits, other strategies should be considered.

It is also important to conceptualize the inclusion of significant others as an ongoing process. That is, family may come into town to visit, and an attempt will be made during therapy to establish social networks including family and friends who may be appropriate as significant others. Thus, during telephone calls that occur with the client between sessions, and at the end of each session, clients should be encouraged to consider appropriate significant others they may wish to involve in the next therapy session. Of course, MHPs should be familiar with legal and ethical responsibilities involved in conducting family-based treatment when significant others are involved in therapy.

Managing FBT Without Significant Others   Even in the most motivated families, there will likely be sessions in which significant others are not present. In these cases, MHPs will need to indicate *not applicable* (NA) in all therapeutic steps that involve the significant other on the therapist prompting checklists for each intervention that is implemented. For instance, if a MHP were implementing Environmental Control, "NA" would be marked next to each step that was relevant to gathering information from the significant others. These instructional steps would not be considered when computing treatment integrity (see Treatment Integrity section in Chapter 1). During the next session the significant other attends, the client can be empowered to show the significant other what he or she missed. Although not recommended, it may be appropriate to enroll clients into FBT without having a significant other, provided they have intentions of involving significant others in the near future.

Managing FBT When Significant Others Are Inappropriate   Although rarely encountered when significant others are carefully screened, if significant others become unmanageable, refuse to participate in FBT protocols, and/or become negative influences in treatment protocols of clients (e.g., use drugs, engage in violence), it is advisable to attempt the **HEARD** intervention. The acronym stands for **H**ear, **E**mpathize, prompt client to generate **A**lternatives, **R**eview generated alternatives, and prompt client to **D**ecide what to do based on the generated solutions. This approach can be used to address a variety of noncompliance issues. When significant others appear to be inappropriate, therapists should first instruct clients to indicate how significant others may be a negative influence in treatment. The MHP listens to and empathizes with the client's concerns, and then initiates a review of potential alternatives relevant to the significant other's negative influence in treatment, such as addressing the issue directly with the significant other, or finding another significant other to participate in treatment with the client. Once alternatives are generated and reviewed, the client and MHP decide which of the solutions will be implemented. If this procedure is unsuccessful, it may be useful to encourage significant others to leave the program and come back when they are ready to recommit. Moreover, as indicated in Chapter 1, it is very important that significant others know they are involved in therapy to support clients. This is made clear by telling them that if they desire treatment, MHPs will attempt to get them involved in a treatment program. Of course, significant others should be encouraged to learn skills while assisting clients in FBT, such as learning to perform Self-Control, Positive Request, and Job-Getting Skills. Indeed, this provides them opportunities to be intimately familiar with the treatment of clients, permits them to model skills for clients, and usually enhances family relationships, which, of course, benefits the clients.

Assist Significant Others in Staying Focused on Client Issues   Sometimes significant others become so excited with therapy that they may attempt to shift therapy focus to their issues, rather than the client's. This problem is usually avoided when MHPs follow FBT protocols with integrity. That is, all steps involved in all MHP prompting checklists are focused on clients.

Table 3.1. Communication Guidelines for FBT Sessions.

Communication Guidelines

1. **Avoid interruptions.** Instead, wait for the person to pause, or ask if it is okay to speak.
2. **Avoid talking for more than a minute.**
3. **Avoid saying "no" when someone asks for something.** Instead, tell the person what you can do.
4. **Avoid rolling eyes or using negative facial expressions.**
5. **Avoid swearing, shouting, sarcasm, or statements that are hurtful.**
6. **Avoid talking about past problems or weaknesses.** Instead, suggest solutions and talk about strengths.
7. **Talk about things you want; do not give criticisms about things you dislike.**
8. **Speak in a soft and conversational tone of voice.**

Therefore, if adherence is good, significant others will not have opportunities to dominate intervention sessions. It is also highly recommended that the only time MHPs visit significant others is during FBT sessions with clients. That said, significant others may still attempt to dominate treatment sessions. It is important to indicate approval for their passion for self-improvement, and remind them of their earlier commitment to support clients.

Establish Effective Methods of Communication   Arguments may be prevented by establishing communication guidelines early in therapy and utilizing prompts to engage in communication skills training exercises when triggers for arguments occur, such as anger. Specifically, a list of basic communication guidelines is provided to clients (see Communication Guidelines in Table 3.1). As can be seen, the list includes several guidelines that are important for effective communication. Other guidelines may be added, although the ones that are listed are usually sufficient. MHPs distribute copies of the guidelines and attempt to get commitments from each of the participating family members that they will attempt to comply with each of the guidelines. MHPs then obtain permission from family members to redirect them to correct guidelines when they are broken, and potentially engage them in performing Positive Requests (see Chapter 8) to resolve these potential conflicts.

Enhance Compliance in Therapy

Review Compliance After Each Treatment Is Implemented   As initially described in Chapter 1, MHPs review the compliance of clients after each therapy component is reviewed during each therapy session. The ratings are made using a Likert-type scale (7 = extremely compliant, 6 = very compliant, 5 = somewhat compliant, 4 = neutral, 3 = somewhat noncompliant, 2 = very noncompliant, 1 = extremely noncompliant), which is based on attendance to the treatment session, participation in the respective intervention, and completion of the therapy assignment. The resulting score is recorded in the session progress note, and the referral agent is provided a summary of these scores in a monthly progress note whenever relevant upon permission from clients. There is a standardized prompt to review methods of enhancing compliance at the end of each intervention. Anecdotally, we have found these ratings to be effective as a prescriptive approach in motivating clients and their family members to do well in therapy. The importance of obtaining these ratings becomes apparent when MHPs record these ratings in progress notes and share the ratings with others (upon written release from clients).

Call Clients Between Therapy Sessions to Encourage Attendance and Participation   Telephone calls are routinely utilized to enhance therapy attendance and, as mentioned earlier, to assist in the completion of therapy assignments. Telephone calls usually occur 2 or 3 days prior to the scheduled session. The initial orientation telephone call is made prior to admittance or enrollment in the program. The content of this call usually focuses on briefly describing FBT, discussing how significant others may be involved, generating solutions to obstacles that might interfere with session attendance, having the client report directions to the clinic to ensure they know how to get to the clinic, soliciting positive features associated with FBT, and providing empathy for expressed concerns. Subsequent calls are usually conducted a couple of days prior to therapy sessions and involve positive discussions about the client's progress in therapy, reviewing therapy assignments, and encouraging future session attendance. MHPs sometimes call clients immediately after sessions to review things that were performed admirably in these sessions and to provide encouragement.

Use HEARD to Manage Noncompliance   When family members report having experienced traumatic events or other serious setbacks (e.g., drug relapse, panic attacks, being threatened with divorce), these events may be associated with noncompliance to engage in therapy, including premature termination. These instances of noncompliance are often unpredictable and may be treated with the HEARD intervention (hear, empathize, alternative, review, decide).

For instance, HEARD may be utilized to treat drug relapse. Specifically, clients are instructed to indicate why they are uninterested in abstaining from illicit drug use or other problem behavior at the current time. After listening and empathizing with generated concerns, MHPs facilitate a review of various alternatives that are consistent with being abstinent from drugs or engaging in other problem behaviors (e.g., committing to a reduction in the number of days of use, number of consecutive days in which no drugs will be used). This is very important because several of the FBT interventions depend on clients being committed to goals that are relevant to eliminating illicit drug use, at least initially. Once the decision to reduce drug use is made (even if it was one day per week), MHPs praise clients for this commitment and attempt to shape them into setting goals that are focused on abstinence. Throughout the HEARD process, it is important for MHPs to actively listen and descriptively praise behaviors, thoughts/intentions, and feelings that are associated with abstinence while empathizing with expressed concerns.

Organization of Treatment Materials for MHPs

To assist in preparing for FBT sessions, MHPs can create a three-ring binder that includes MHP prompting checklists, handouts, and worksheets for each of the FBT intervention components. The best order in which to list the interventions in this binder is consistent with the order in which these interventions are reviewed in this book. Each intervention would represent a section in the binder. Each section would first include an initial prompting checklist, followed by a future sessions prompting checklist (if relevant), followed by its worksheets and handouts (if relevant). For example, the first section of the binder would be for the Agenda. This intervention has only one prompting checklist, and there are no forms for this intervention, so there would be no worksheets or handouts listed in this section. The next section would be Behavioral Goals and Rewards. This section includes both initial and future session prompting checklists, and two worksheets. Therefore, the two prompting checklists would be followed by the two worksheets in this section of the binder. This manner of presentation would continue until the conclusion of treatment (see Chapter 13).

Once organized, MHPs make multiple copies of each of the forms in the binder. The number of copies will depend on the number of sessions performed each week, although most MHPs prefer to have a balance of approximately 5 to 10 copies of each form in their binders. The binders permit MHPs to rapidly obtain materials they need during treatment sessions, and are essential when therapies are implemented in the homes of clients or other off-clinic locations. An alternative strategy to using binders is to create a similar system in a filing cabinet.

Concluding Remarks

It becomes clear reading this chapter that the style of FBT is uniquely positive, making it particularly refreshing for clients who have come from or live in aversive environments. Although insufficient by itself, descriptive praise and other therapeutic strategies reviewed in this chapter complement the therapeutic effects of the FBT interventions described later, and increase the effectiveness of FBT. Therefore, the style, techniques, and implementation strategies of FBT MHPs are superimposed onto its content, which is extensively reviewed in each of the remaining chapters.

CHAPTER 4

Establishing Effective Agendas for Treatment Sessions

Rationale and Overview

A structured agenda is developed at the start of each treatment session. In doing so, positive comments are made about the family's performance during the previous session, and the mental health professional (MHP) discloses the intervention components to be considered during the current session. To assist in time management, the MHP provides an estimate of the expected duration of each intervention component that is prescribed. Family members are encouraged to suggest potential modifications to the agenda, including the order in which therapies are implemented as well as the omission or addition of therapies. This prescriptive approach helps to reduce spontaneous dialogue that is irrelevant and poorly integrated into treatment planning. This strength-based approach helps family members to stay focused on processes that are likely to facilitate goal accomplishment. Although session agendas usually require 5 or 10 minutes to implement, their absence may result in a relative lack of flow and general inefficiency when implementing the FBT intervention components.

Goals for Intervention

➤ Review positive efforts that occurred during the preceding session.

➤ Determine the upcoming session agenda.

Materials Needed

➤ Session Agenda Therapist Prompting Checklist (Prompting Checklist 4.1, also located on the CD that accompanies this book)

Procedural Steps for Implementation

Preparing an Initial Draft for the Session Agenda

Immediately prior to each treatment session, MHPs review what happened during the past session. This information is usually derived from progress notes. Of course, MHPs acknowledge behaviors that are consistent with treatment planning, such as improvements in behaviors that may have been indicated in objective testing (e.g., negative drug urinalyses) or reports from reliable others (e.g., probation officers). Outstanding accomplishments might also include extreme effort during one of the therapies, accomplishing a difficult goal, family members exchanging meaningful positive comments, honesty in reporting substance use, and desire to learn new methods of relapse prevention. MHPs record goal directed behaviors and outstanding accomplishments in the Session Agenda Prompting Checklist (Prompting Checklist 4.1) so these positive points are available for review at the start of the next session.

The next step is to select the interventions that will be implemented in the session. To determine which interventions to implement, MHPs utilize the general guidelines that are specified in Table 4.1. As the table indicates, an agenda is always implemented at the beginning of each session. Behavioral Goals and Rewards is implemented during the first session after the agenda. Importantly, Behavioral Goals and Rewards is implemented during most of the remaining sessions to some extent because the established contingencies need to be monitored on an ongoing basis. I've Got a Great Family is usually only implemented three to five times throughout treatment to assist in maintaining its novelty when family members exchange positive compliments with one another. To permit the I've Got a Great Family intervention to be implemented during the second session, Behavioral Goals and Rewards must be implemented swiftly and the session may need to be extended (most treatment sessions are about 60 minutes). Treatment Planning is implemented during the third session to assist the client and adult significant others in determining when the remaining intervention components are to be introduced, and reviewed during subsequent sessions. After the treatment plan is established, the core or primary interventions are implemented based on the preference of the client and adult significant others. These interventions usually include Environmental

Control and Self-Control because these directly target the elimination of illicit substance use and other target behaviors. Throughout therapy, these interventions will be revisited as needed, as the skills taught in these interventions are not typically mastered during the course of one session. Treatments are selected by the client and adult significant others based on their specific needs as identified through behavioral goals. Of course, the last session review always occurs during the last scheduled session. Thus, MHPs are guided by the aforementioned guidelines, but are free to make adjustments on a session-by-session basis during the agendas. MHPs are encouraged to record scheduled interventions, and their anticipated times of implementation, in the Session Agenda Therapist Prompting Checklist prior to each session.

Establishing the Session Agenda (Usually With Client and Adult Significant Others)

MHPs initiate each agenda by reporting and soliciting outstanding efforts and accomplishments that may have occurred since the last session. The family is always recruited to participate in the provision of affirmative comments. It is within the MHPs' discretion to determine how long the positive reviews occur, although they are usually limited to a few minutes.

MHPs then report the interventions that have been planned for the session, including a brief explanation of why the interventions were selected, and an estimate of how much time it will take to implement each therapy. Potential modifications to the agenda are solicited, although family members usually agree with the prescribed agendas. When clients or family members disagree with the proposed agenda (most often because negative life experiences occurred since the last session), MHPs are advised to listen to expressed concerns and provide empathy. Most intervention components are capable of assisting in the management of spontaneously reported problems. Therefore, MHPs should attempt to clarify how the planned therapies might be adjusted to accommodate expressed concerns prior to changing prescribed agendas.

The example dialogue that follows presents a typical exchange among MHPs, clients, and significant others in completing the session agenda.

Table 4.1. Usual Order of Interventions and Estimated Times for Implementation.

Intervention	When Implemented	Approximate Duration (based on 60-min. session)
• Agenda	Start of every FBT session	<5 min.
• Behavioral Goals and Rewards	First FBT session, and every session thereafter	First time implemented (goal construction, assigning goals) = 55–65 min. Remaining sessions (reviewing goal assignments) = 10–30 min.
• I've Got a Great Family	First FBT session, and occasionally thereafter	First time implemented (exchanging several pos. statements) = 20–30 min. Remaining sessions (exchanging 1 positive statement) = 15–30 min.
• Treatment Plan	Second FBT session only	20–25 min.
• Environmental Control	Influenced by Treatment Plan	First time implemented (setting up the lists) = 45 min. Remaining sessions (reviewing lists) = 20–50 min.
• Self-Control	Influenced by Treatment Plan	First time implemented (initially teaching steps) = 45 min. Remaining sessions (reviewing steps for real problem behaviors) = 15–60 min.
• Positive Request	Influenced by Treatment Plan or spontaneously to prevent argument	First prescribed time implemented (initially teaching steps w/ rationale) = 25–55 min. Remaining sessions (reviewing steps to assist in communication) = 15–30 min.
• Job-Getting Skills Training	Influenced by Treatment Plan	First time implemented (reviewing interviewing and job-getting skills) = 40 min. Remaining sessions (calling prospective employees) = 20–35 min.
• Financial Management Skills	Influenced by Treatment Plan	35–50 min.
• Last Session Review	Last session only	40–50 min.

MHP: I can't wait to start today. I've got some great stuff planned, but before I tell you about it, I wanted to point out a few things I'm particularly proud of regarding your efforts to accomplish your goals. First, Robby, this past week I appreciate your calling me to let me know you had a relapse. Although you wanted to cancel our session today, you're here and ready to learn from the experience. I'm also proud of your mom for coming here today, as well. This is only your third intervention session, and being present today is a step in the right direction. You managed to stay sober for 2 weeks prior to this relapse, which is 2 weeks more than you had during the entire past year. Tell me some positive things you felt in accomplishing this feat.

Robby: I felt really great about my progress until I relapsed, and then I felt really bad. I did not want to come back to treatment 'cause I was embarrassed.

MHP: I understand, but you didn't answer my question fully. What positive things did you feel after remaining sober for 2 weeks?

Robby: I felt like I was someone who could accomplish anything I set my mind to accomplishing. I felt a sense of pride, and I think my mom felt the same way.

Mom: I was proud of you, and I'm particularly proud of you being here today. However, I'm concerned this will lead you to go back in the wrong direction.

MHP: I think that is a healthy thought. You obviously love him dearly and want to do everything within your power to assist him, but only if he shows effort. I also agree that he needs to be carefully supported during the next few weeks when he is most apt to relapse. I thought it would be good to start out with the Self-Control intervention using the situation that brought about the relapse. This will permit Robby to closely examine triggers that may have been avoided using some of the strategies we've been working on in the Environmental Control intervention. If we practiced two or three trials during the first 25 minutes or so, we could probably initiate Environmental Control during the remainder of the session to cover new strategies to be reviewed within the context of his day-to-day activities. Do you feel this agenda is a good one, or should we modify it?

Robby: Sounds good to me.

Mom: Yes, that sounds like a good plan for today.

Concluding Remarks

The agenda assists in establishing a positive, focused tone for each treatment session, and is necessary for several reasons. It ensures busy MHPs do not underestimate the importance of therapeutic preparation. Positive statements at the start of each session assist in putting treatment progress into proper perspective, and often aid in the prevention of negative tangents that proliferate in unstructured therapies. In our interviews with clients and their families, they have told us that they very much appreciate the specification of treatments in the agenda and the invitation to change the protocols after rationales have been provided. This latter point reflects consumer driven therapy, as MHPs and their clients share in the determination of FBT implementation.

Supporting Materials for Chapter 4: Establishing Effective Agendas for Treatment Sessions

Prompting Checklist 4.1. Session Agenda Therapist Prompting Checklist.

SESSION AGENDA
THERAPIST PROMPTING CHECKLIST

Client ID:_____ Clinician:_____ Session #:_____ Session Date:_____

Begin Time:_____

Establishing the Session Agenda (usually the client and adult significant others)

___1. State/solicit outstanding efforts and/or accomplishments occurring during last session.
___2. State planned interventions to be implemented in session, & how long each will take.

Scheduled Interventions	Estimated Time
1. _____	_____
2. _____	_____
3. _____	_____
4. _____	_____
5. _____	_____
6. _____	_____

Note. Complete aforementioned table prior to session.

___3. Provide opportunity for client and significant others to modify proposed agenda.

End Time: _____

5

Establishing Goals and Rewards for Maintaining a Drug-Free Lifestyle

Rationale and Overview

Clients establish goals for therapy with the aid of participating adult family and friends whenever appropriate. In doing so, the Drug-Incompatible Goals Worksheet is utilized to assess the extent to which potential antecedent stimuli or "triggers" have been associated with drug use in the client's past. Triggers are rapidly converted to goals when clients are interested in targeting the elimination or management of these triggers in therapy. Mental health providers (MHPs) also have the option of behaviorally objectifying each of the selected generic goals so they can be monitored easily. Developed goals are recorded in the Primary Goals Worksheet, where clients can indicate which goals will be targeted at home each week throughout therapy. Significant others are encouraged to provide rewards when clients accomplish their goals, with more substantive rewards being provided for goals that are harder to accomplish. Similarly, clients are encouraged to establish rewards for participating friends and family each week for their provision of support. In this way, family members reciprocally reinforce one another for their efforts in working together to establish a drug- and trouble-free lifestyle. Each week, MHPs assist in managing the contingencies set forth in the contract.

Goals for Intervention

➤ Determine goals for therapy that are specific to drug use reduction.

➤ Establish a contingency in which clients are rewarded for their efforts to maintain sobriety.

➤ Successfully monitor the developed contingency.

Materials Needed

> Behavioral Goals Therapist Prompting Checklist for Initial Session (Prompting Checklist 5.1, also located on the CD that accompanies this book)

> Behavioral Goals Therapist Prompting Checklist for Future Sessions (Prompting Checklist 5.2, also located on the CD that accompanies this book)

> Drug-Incompatible Goals Worksheet (Worksheet 5.1, also located on the CD that accompanies this book)

> Primary Goals Worksheet (Worksheet 5.2, also located on the CD that accompanies this book)

Procedural Steps for Implementation

Preparing for Behavioral Goals and Rewards

Prior to implementing Behavioral Goals and Rewards for the first time, MHPs obtain a copy of the Drug-Incompatible Goals Worksheet (Worksheet 5.1). It is helpful to review the list of generic goals that are included in this worksheet prior to the session, including potential obstacles that may make it difficult for the client to accomplish these goals in case they are selected as treatment targets.

Rationale (Usually With Client and Adult Significant Others, When Appropriate)

When first presenting Behavioral Goals and Rewards, MHPs use the Behavioral Goals Therapist Prompting Checklist for Initial Session (Prompting Checklist 5.1) to introduce the rationale and implement the intervention. For the rationale, MHPs first report how goals for therapy will be focused on avoiding things that have been associated with drug use and other problem behaviors in the past. It is explained that goals are initially chosen from a generic list of antecedent stimuli (i.e., triggers) that have been identified to precede drug use, and chosen goals may be individualized based on input from the MHP, client, and appropriate adult supportive others. The importance of establishing a system in which the client and significant others exchange rewards for goal accomplishment is underscored—the client for accomplishing goals, and supportive others for supporting the client in doing so. The client and significant others are encouraged by indicating how, specifically, the intervention is expected to be particularly effective for them. For instance, a client may be told that family support is unusually strong, or that the client has a good grasp of which triggers need to be targeted in therapy. Finally, the client and significant others should be prompted to report how behavioral goals and contingency management are likely to be successful. Such prompts help to instill hope and motivation.

Reviewing Drug–Incompatible Goals Worksheet (Usually Client and Adult Significant Others, When Appropriate)

The heart of this intervention concerns the establishment of goals utilizing the Drug-Incompatible Goals Worksheet (Exhibit 5.1). First, it is explained that other drug users have indicated that there are emotions, images, thoughts, and things in the environment that "trigger" drug use due to their past associations with drug use. Therefore, it is explained that a list of such triggers in the Drug-Incompatible Goals Worksheet will be used to determine which specific triggers have occurred prior to the client's past use of drugs. It also mentioned that the client will have the opportunity to set goals to prevent these triggers. In doing so, a card is provided to the client that indicates "almost never, sometimes, almost always."

Exhibit 5.1 contains three items listed in the Drug-Incompatible Goals Worksheet (i.e., smoking trigger only). As can be seen in the exhibit, the top of the first column for each page of the Drug-Incompatible Goals Worksheet includes the standardized prompt "HOW OFTEN HAVE YOU (POTENTIAL DRUG TRIGGER BELOW) BEFORE USING DRUGS?" Below this prompt is a list of drug use triggers. MHPs read the prompt with the first trigger (i.e., smoking cigarettes) inserted. Clients are instructed to respond using the distributed card. If the trigger is reported to have occurred "almost never," MHPs mark the box as such and proceed to the next trigger listed below (i.e., stashed or hidden drugs). If the trigger is said to have occurred sometimes or almost always, MHPs read the prompt at the top of the second column: "WOULD YOU LIKE TO SET (DRUG-INCOMPATIBLE BEHAVIOR BELOW) AS A GOAL?" with the respective "drug-incompatible behavior" (i.e., avoiding cigarettes) inserted as indicated. When goals are undesired,

Exhibit 5.1. Drug-Incompatible Goals Worksheet.

DRUG-INCOMPATIBLE GOALS WORKSHEET			

- Review Drug-Incompatible Goals Rationale before completing the Drug-Incompatible Goals Worksheet

HOW OFTEN HAVE YOU (POTENTIAL DRUG TRIGGER BELOW) BEFORE USING DRUGS?	"WOULD YOU LIKE TO SET (DRUG-INCOMPATIBLE BEHAVIOR BELOW) AS A GOAL?"	"WHAT WOULD MAKE IT EASIER FOR YOU TO (DRUG-INCOMPATIBLE BEHAVIOR)?" (Empathize, Solicit info, Volunteer Help)	ASSIST IN DEFINING GOALS BEHAVIORALLY/ SPECIFICALLY.
Smoked cigarettes ❏ almost never (proceed to next trigger) ❏ sometimes ❏ almost always	**Avoid cigarettes** ❏ no (proceed to next trigger) ❏ yes		
Stashed or hidden drugs ❏ almost never (proceed to next trigger) ❏ sometimes ❏ almost always	**Keep secret stashes of drugs away from you** ❏ no (proceed to next trigger) ❏ yes		
Drunk alcohol ❏ almost never (proceed to next trigger) ❏ sometimes ❏ almost always	**Avoid alcohol use** ❏ no (proceed to next trigger) ❏ yes		

the MHP has discretion to present information that would suggest the goal should be targeted in therapy, attempt to persuade the client to target the goal, and/or proceed to the next trigger. When goals are desired, the MHP may proceed to the next trigger (usually if there is not much time left in the session and/or the client has endorsed many goals) or, if time permits, read the prompt at the top of the third column: "WHAT WOULD MAKE IT EASIER FOR YOU TO (DRUG-INCOMPATIBLE BEHAVIOR)?," inserting the respective "drug-incompatible behavior" where appropriate. As noted at the top of the third column, the MHP records relevant information in the

Drug-Incompatible Goals Worksheet, and empathizes, solicits information, and generates solutions whenever possible. In this way, MHPs get a clearer understanding of obstacles that may threaten goal accomplishment while establishing rapport and opportunities to conduct therapeutic techniques consistent with motivational interviewing. MHPs may then proceed to the next trigger if time is limited and the respective goal is specific, or read the prompt at the top of the fourth column for the respective goal: "ASSIST IN DEFINING GOALS BEHAVIORALLY/SPECIFICALLY." Along these lines, MHPs may include specific target dates or observable actions that would objectively indicate that the respective goal was accomplished. Of course, MHPs then proceed to the next trigger and continue in a similar manner until all triggers are reviewed. MHPs may solicit feedback from significant others throughout the process.

Although many of the antecedent triggers listed in the Drug-Incompatible Goals Worksheet are often targeted in dually diagnosed adults who abuse drugs (e.g., anger, sadness, arguments), there are, of course, many other problems that have been found to coexist with drug abuse (e.g., obesity, tension headaches, gambling, fears, domestic violence, child maltreatment, HIV risk behaviors). Many of these problems can be targeted in Behavioral Goals and Rewards, although these problem behaviors are not listed in the Drug-Incompatible Goals Worksheet form. These problems can usually be treated utilizing FBT components (e.g., obesity can be treated within Environmental Control).

An example of typical dialogue among MHP, client, and significant other in completing the Drug-Incompatible Goals Worksheet is provided below, as well as an example of a partially completed Drug-Incompatible Goals Worksheet based on this dialogue in Exhibit 5.2.

MHP: Jessica, people sometimes experience emotions, thoughts, and images that trigger drug urges or desire to use drugs. Usually, this occurs because these things have been so associated with drug use in the past that they later trigger memories about drugs. Although triggers affect people differently, we put together a list of some of these things, and I'm now going to read them to you to determine which of these things may be triggers for you. When you respond to me I want you to answer with one of the responses that are on this card. *(Client is provided the card with responses "almost never," "sometimes," almost always.")* For each trigger you have experienced, I'll ask if you'd like to set a goal to prevent or manage the trigger. I may also work with you to brainstorm ways of accomplishing the goals you set for yourself, including ways of making these goals specific. Let's begin. How often have you smoked cigarettes before using drugs?

Jessica: Sometimes.

MHP: Would you like to avoid cigarettes as a goal?

Jessica: Yes.

MHP: What would make it easier for you to avoid cigarettes?

Jessica: Well, if I avoided that convenience store where I usually get my cigarettes, and only smoked when I was outside of my house. I also think it would help if I asked other family members not to smoke in my house.

MHP: That's wonderful. I'm going to write those down. I'd also like you to tell me how many cigarettes you'd like to smoke each day as a goal because specific goals are better accomplished.

Jessica: I guess I could try to smoke five cigarettes each day, which would be an improvement from a whole pack.

MHP: Great, I've written that note down in your Drug-Incompatible Goals Worksheet.

The MHP would continue in this manner for the remaining triggers until the Drug-Incompatible Goals Worksheet was complete. Exhibit 5.2 depicting the partially completed Drug-Incompatible Goals Worksheet shows that Jessica identified "Smoking Cigarettes" as a trigger for drug use in column 1, and indicated in column 2 that she would like to target this as a behavioral goal. In column 3, she indicated that not smoking inside her house and avoiding the convenience store would make it easier for her to cut down on her smoking. In column 4, she set a specific goal of smoking five cigarettes a day, down from her current pack a day.

Exhibit 5.2. Example of Partially Completed Drug-Incompatible Goals Worksheet.

DRUG-INCOMPATIBLE GOALS WORKSHEET

- Review Drug-Incompatible Goals Rationale before completing the Drug-Incompatible Goals Worksheet

HOW OFTEN DO YOU (POTENTIAL DRUG TRIGGER BELOW) BEFORE YOU USE DRUGS?	"WOULD YOU LIKE TO SET (DRUG-INCOMPATIBLE BEHAVIOR BELOW) AS A GOAL?"	"WHAT WOULD MAKE IT EASIER FOR YOU TO (DRUG-INCOMPATIBLE BEHAVIOR)?" (Empathize, Solicit info, Volunteer Help)	ASSIST IN DEFINING GOALS BEHAVIORALLY/ SPECIFICALLY.
Smoke Cigarettes ❏ almost never (proceed to next trigger) ☒ sometimes ❏ almost always	**Avoid Cigarettes** ❏ no (proceed to next trigger) ☒ yes	Avoid convenience store. No smoking in house.	Smoke < 5 cigs. a day from pack.

Creating Goals for the First Time (Usually Client and Adult Significant Others)

After completing the Drug-Incompatible Goals Worksheet, MHPs record all endorsed goals in the Primary Goals Worksheet (Worksheet 5.2), where they become a written contract among the client, significant other, family members, and MHP. A portion of the Primary Goals Worksheet is presented in Exhibit 5.3. Goals on the Primary Goals Worksheet may be recorded as written in the Drug-Incompatible Goals Worksheet, or as modified by the client from the prompt listed in the last column of the Drug-Incompatible Goals Worksheet. For instance, if the goal to avoid cigarettes was endorsed and it was later determined that the client would specifically reduce cigarette use by 5 cigarettes, the broad goal (i.e., avoid cigarettes) and specific goal (i.e., reduce cigarette use to 5 per day) would be included in the same row of the Goals Worksheet. The Primary Goals Worksheet also includes the mandatory goals of attending therapy sessions, staying clean from drugs, completing therapy practice assignments, and ensuring that adult significant others attend treatment sessions. Mandatory goals are those

Exhibit 5.3. Example of Partially Completed Primary Goals Worksheet.

PRIMARY GOALS WORKSHEET

GOAL	FOCUS GOAL FOR THE WEEK	INDICATE How GOAL WAS COMPLETED	GOAL	FOCUS GOAL FOR THE WEEK	INDICATE How GOAL WAS COMPLETED
Attend treatment sessions	X		Ensure an adult significant other attends treatment sessions	X	
Stay clean from drugs	X		Complete practice assignments: _____ _____ _____	X	
*Maintain psychotropic medications	X		Arrange for paychecks to be direct deposited into savings account		
Reduce cig. to 5 a day	X				

goals that are determined by persons other than clients, including MHPs or referral agents. For example, in treating a client with a substance use disorder and schizophrenia, a psychiatrist may suggest medication compliance as a mandatory goal if the client had a history of noncompliance (see Exhibit 5.3). These mandatory goals are marked with an "X" in their respective rows under the Primary Goals Worksheet column "Focus Goals for the Week" because these goals will be targeted during each week of therapy (see Exhibit 5.3).

The Primary Goals Worksheet is shown to the client and significant other. An attempt is made to determine which of the client-generated goals will be a focus until the next treatment session (mandatory goals will always be a focus in treatment). Next to each goal the client wishes to target (denoted a "focus goal") in the Primary Goals Worksheet, an "X" is marked. The MHP reviews how each goal will be accomplished and modifies these goals as necessary. Lastly, the MHP instructs the client to record notes that are relevant to depicting how the respective goals were accomplished in the third column of the Primary Goals Worksheet. The client is encouraged to also target goals that are not a focus whenever possible. After focus goals are chosen, the significant other(s) is encouraged to commit to the provision of a reward for the client if all goals are achieved. It sometimes helps to suggest rewards that will be inspiring. The reward is recorded in the Primary Goals Worksheet, and the client is encouraged to commit to the provision of an inspirational reward for the significant other(s) as a demonstration of appreciation. The client and significant other(s) sign the Primary Goals Worksheet, and indicate where the Primary Goals Worksheet will be posted to facilitate daily review prior to the next treatment session. The dialogue below continues the intervention with Jessica, transferring goals from the Drug-Incompatible Goals Worksheet to the Primary Goals Worksheet.

MHP: Jessica, last session we developed a number of goals for you. Since the time I last saw you, I took the liberty of putting these goals in this form *(hands Jessica a copy of Primary Goals Worksheet).* This is called the Primary Goals Worksheet. As you can see, I listed all your goals in this form. Some of the goals include other more specific goals. For instance, you indicated that one of your goals is to reduce your cigarette use to five cigarettes a day instead of one pack, and in the Primary Goals Worksheet box for this goal, I also wrote to avoid going to the convenience store. As you can see, there are many goals. Therefore, each week you will choose which goals you would like to focus on for the week. Some of the goals listed at the top of your Primary Goals Worksheet will always be a focus because when these goals are accomplished, our clients have found it much easier to achieve success. These goals include attendance at your therapy sessions and staying clean from drugs, completing therapy practice assignments, and ensuring that adult significant others attend treatment sessions. I also included the nonoptional goal of monitoring your medications because it would be dangerous if you didn't do so, and your psychiatrist highly recommends this oversight. These goals are marked with a large "X" in their respective rows under the Primary Goals

Worksheet column Focus Goals for the Week. What is your understanding of what I've said?

Jessica: You wrote down my goals, and some goals that are for my own good, although I didn't choose them. These goals I'll need to focus on each week, but I can choose which additional goals I attempt each week.

MHP: Great. So, today, we will need to determine which of the goals we developed that you would like to focus on until I see you next treatment session. Obviously, I want you to focus on as many of your goals as possible, but I also understand you have a lot to do this week, and I want to make sure you do not get overwhelmed by taking on too many goals. Next to each goal you wish to target, I will mark a big "X." So take this form and tell me which goals you would like to focus on for this upcoming week. Kelsey, feel free to provide suggestions whenever you like.

Jessica: I think I would like to try to do all of these goals *(marks all goals).*

MHP: This is quite ambitious. Kelsey, you must be very happy with her intentions. I would, however, like to review your goals and make sure they are all realistically achievable for this week. I really want to start off with success.

(Jessica and Kelsey discuss options to assist in accomplishing the goals with the MHP. However, they indicate that they will save a few goals for the following week.)

MHP: This looks great. You've marked decreasing your smoking to five cigarettes a day, as well as managing your finances. I wonder if you can add a little to your goal of effectively managing your savings by adding to make arrangements to have your paycheck sent into your account via direct deposit. I think this would be particularly important this week because Kelsey will be out of town, and it is very early in your sobriety.

Jessica: Well, I could have my check directly deposited into our bank account, which might help me not be tempted to go out and spend it on drugs on payday.

Kelsey: That sounds like a good idea. I could try that, too, if it would help.

MHP: Yes, that does sound like a great idea. When would you like to get that done?

Jessica: I couldn't do that for another 2 weeks 'cause I just got paid.

MHP: That sounds good. Now, when you complete your goals throughout the week, I want you to write a few very brief notes about how you accomplished each goal in the last column of your Primary Goals Worksheet. You can also spontaneously focus on nonfocus goals throughout the week if you like, but remember to focus on the ones with the "X" next to them. *(Jessica and Kelsey agree.)* Kelsey, if Jessica accomplishes all of the goals with an "X" next to them in the Primary Goals Worksheet, what special reward could you provide her at the end of the week?

Kelsey: I could take her out to her favorite movie and maybe dinner, then a back rub.

MHP: I love it. What do you think, Jessica? Is this something you'd like to receive?

Jessica: That does sound nice, but I don't really need a reward when I am trying to achieve these goals—they are things I should be doing anyway and I really want to do them for myself.

MHP: Yes, I understand. However, I insist. You need to let your body experience pleasure for accomplishing these very important goals. Besides, it will also be important for you to reward Kelsey for his efforts to support you in accomplishing your goals this week, such as keeping you busy with that wonderful evening he just mentioned he'd set up. What could you do for him along these lines?

Jessica: Well, I could buy the popcorn and soda at the movies.

MHP: I love how you're both offering to do something you do not usually do. I just need you both to sign your names to the bottom of this Primary Goals Worksheet, and we're done for today. I'll make a copy of your Primary Goals Worksheet, and give you a copy to keep track of things. By the way, where can you put your Primary Goals Worksheet so you won't forget?

Exhibit 5.4 shows that, in addition to the nonoptional goals, Jessica identified "Smoking Cigarettes" as a focus goal for the week, but will not make arrangements for her check to be directly deposited into her bank account until the following week (i.e., not a focus this upcoming week).

Exhibit 5.4. Example of Completed Primary Goals Worksheet.

PRIMARY GOALS WORKSHEET

GOAL	FOCUS GOAL FOR THE WEEK	INDICATE HOW GOAL WAS COMPLETED	GOAL	FOCUS GOAL FOR THE WEEK	INDICATE HOW GOAL WAS COMPLETED
Attend treatment sessions (1)	X	ON TIME	Ensure an adult significant other attends treatment sessions (2)	X	GAVE REMINDER CALL
Stay clean from drugs (3)	X	FOCUSED ON WORK AND KIDS	Maintain contact with client service representative (4)	X	SCHEDULED APPT. AFTER WORK
Maintain medications as prescribed (5)	X		Arrange for paychecks to be direct deposited into savings account		
Decrease smoking to 5 cigarettes per day	X	Avoided smoking in house and convenience store			

Reward for client from significant other if all focus goals are completed: <u>GO TO DINNER, MOVIES, BACK RUB.</u>

Reward for significant other from client if significant other supports client: <u>BUY POPCORN AND SODA AT MOVIE.</u>

I agree to complete all my focus goals for the week and reward my significant other if I receive support:

_____.
      Client's Signature

I agree to support client in focus goals and provide a reward if they are completed:

_____.
      Significant Other's Signature

Reviewing Goals in Future Sessions (Usually Client and Adult Significant Others)

The steps for reviewing goals established in the initial session are summarized in the Behavioral Goals Therapist Prompting Checklist for Future Sessions (Prompting Checklist 5.2). To start the review of goals and maintenance of contingencies, the client and adult significant others are instructed to provide a completed copy of their Primary Goals Worksheet. The client is descriptively praised for accomplishing goals, particularly the goal that is relevant to remaining drug free. If all focus goals are completed, MHPs ensure that the significant others provided the rewards, and if not, MHPs attempt to arrange a makeup reward in which the significant other promises to do something "extra special" for the client. If the goals were not accomplished, MHPs ensure that the significant other withheld established rewards. Similar assurances are made regarding the client's contingent rewarding of the significant other. MHPs also query the client to report potential accomplishment of goals that were not a focus since last contact, and consequently praise efforts in doing so. Similarly, both the client and significant other are encouraged to discuss methods of achieving future goals in therapy, including goals that are not listed in the Primary Goals Worksheet. The client is instructed to put an "X" next to goals that will be a focus until the next therapy session. Rewards are established for both the client and significant other for their efforts in accomplishing goals and providing support. Signatures are obtained, and the client and significant other arrange a place to put the completed Primary Goals Worksheet. All future sessions are reviewed in a similar manner.

MHP: Great to see you both today. Go ahead and let me see your Primary Goals Worksheet. Wow! I'm so impressed to see that almost all of your goals were accomplished this week. Let's start with avoiding cigarettes. It says here you avoided the convenience store where you usually buy cigarettes and stopped smoking in your home. Tell me how you were able to get the motivation to accomplish such an important but difficult task.

Jessica: Well, I took a new route to work to avoid the convenience store. I also spoke with my family and told them I was trying to quit smoking so was not going to smoke inside anymore. I asked them if they would do that, too, and they said they would.

MHP: Fantastic! I like how you don't even go by the same street where the convenience store is located, and that you asked your family to help you in cutting down on your smoking. (*This pattern of responding would continue until all obtained focus goals were discussed.*)

MHP: Kelsey, what did you like about her attempts to accomplish her goals this week?

Kelsey: Well, I was disappointed because she did not get all focus goals accomplished.

MHP: I understand how you might feel disappointed. After all, you worked hard to assist her this past week. Did you withhold the dinner, movie, and back rub?

Kelsey: No, I gave her the movie, dinner, and back rub because even though she did not do all her goals, she did better than usual.

MHP: I understand you wanted to reinforce her relative efforts. However, you agreed to withhold these rewards if she did not accomplish all of her focus goals. Jessica, if this happens again, you need to tell him to be strong, and fight his good-natured personality. You also need to withhold your reward for him. I still think you accomplished a lot this past week, and want to mention that you both should continue to support one another. Just don't share the rewards in this contract so you'll really appreciate them when you earn them. I just looked at the time and wanted to move on to Self-Control today. Sorry to rush our Goals and Rewards this week. Here's a new Primary Goals Worksheet. Let's determine what goals you'd like to focus on for the upcoming week, and get some rewards established like we did last week. . . .

Concluding Remarks

The standardized method of establishing goals discussed in this Chapter to address drug use and other commonly evidenced comorbid problems distinguishes FBT from many existing treatment programs. These goals have been standardized to specifically target drug use, and each goal is anchored to a contingency management system in which adult significant others provide rewards for goal accomplishment. The method allows great flexibility in addressing the needs of these often complicated cases, and assists in establishing motivation to pursue goal accomplishment. The method of permitting clients to choose which goals to focus on prior to the upcoming session is also seldom utilized in clinical practice and extremely important, as it more closely corresponds to *real-world* scenarios, is client centered, and takes advantage of the client's social ecology.

Supporting Materials for Chapter 5: Establishing Goals and Rewards for Maintaining a Drug–Free Lifestyle

Prompting Checklist 5.1. Behavioral Goals Therapist Prompting Checklist for Initial Session.

BEHAVIORAL GOALS
THERAPIST PROMPTING CHECKLIST
Initial Session

Client ID:_____Clinician:_____Session #:_____ Session Date:_____

Materials Required

- Drug-Incompatible Goals Worksheet (DIGW)
- Primary Goals Worksheet (PGW)

Begin Time:_____

Rationale (Client and Adult Significant Others)

___a. Next intervention involves setting goals regarding staying clean.
___b. Client will choose goals from a list.
___c. State how client expected to benefit from intervention, and/or solicit how behavioral goals will help.
___d. Solicit questions and provide answers.

Reviewing Drug-Incompatible Goals Worksheet (Client, Adult Significant Others When Appropriate)

- State or review the following:
___a. Other drug users have indicated there are things that trigger drug use.
___b. Client will be asked to indicate which triggers have occurred prior to drug use from a list.
___c. Client will have opportunity to set goals to prevent triggers that have been experienced in past.
___d. Provide "almost never, sometimes, almost always" response card, and indicate how it will be used.
___e. Determine if triggers in 1st column of DIGW have occurred.
   ___1. For each trigger endorsed "sometimes" or "almost always," ask if goal should be set.
       - For each desired goal, the therapist has <u>the *option of doing the following*</u>:
         - Assess how to make goal easier & record client's response.
         - Generate beneficial alternatives to inappropriate responses.
         - Assist in stating the goal more specifically.
         - Record specific goal in last column of Drug-Incompatible Goals Worksheet.

___f. State all goals will be included in Primary Goals Worksheet, which helps identify focus goals in future.

• Put all endorsed goals in the Primary Goals Worksheet, including nonoptional goals, such as attending therapy sessions, staying clean from drugs, completing therapy practice assignments, ensuring adult significant others attend treatment sessions, ensuring children complete practice assignments (if assigned), and maintaining contact w/client services representative (if assigned).

Creating Goals for the First Time (Client and Appropriate Adult Significant Others)

___a. Provide a completed copy of the completed Primary Goals Worksheet (PGW).

___b. Review program goals client is expected to complete each week (those w/pre-determined "X").

___c. Solicit which of the additional listed goals client would like to focus on during upcoming week.

    ___1. Review how each goal can be accomplished.

        • If client made/makes a more specific or elaborate goal, place this goal next to generic goal.

        • Record a check in the corresponding box of each focus goal on therapist copy of PGW.

    ___2. Instruct client to put a check next to each focus goal on client copy of PGW.

___d. Solicit reward sig. other can provide if all focus goals are completed & client is drug free.

    ___1. Solicit from client if reward provided by sig. other would be inspiring.

        • If not, attempt to get a more inspiring reward.

___e. Record promised reward in Primary Goals Worksheet.

___f. Solicit reward client can provide if sig. other supports client in completing focus goals.

    ___1. Solicit from sig. other if reward would be inspiring.

        • If not, attempt to get a more inspiring reward.

        • Record promised reward on the PGW.

___g. Obtain signature & commitment from client.

___h. Obtain signature & commitment from sig. other.

___i. Disclose that goal sheet will be reviewed next week.

___j. Query place to put client's copy of Primary Goals Worksheet so it won't be lost.

Client's Assessment of Helpfulness of the Intervention

___a. After stating client should not feel obligated to provide high scores, as an honest assessment helps better address client needs, solicit how helpful client thought intervention was using 7-point scale:

    7 = extremely helpful, **6** = very helpful, **5** = somewhat helpful, **4** = not sure, **3** = somewhat unhelpful, **2** = very unhelpful, **1** = extremely unhelpful

• **Record Client's Rating Here:** _____

___b. Solicit how rating was derived, & methods of improving intervention in future.

Therapist's Rating of Client's Compliance with Intervention

___a. Disclose therapist's rating of client's compliance using 7-point scale:

7 = extremely compliant, **6** = very compliant, **5** = somewhat compliant, **4** = neutral,
3 = somewhat noncompliant, **2** = very noncompliant, **1** = extremely noncompliant
- Factors that contribute to compliance ratings are:
  - Attendance.
  - Participation and conduct in session.
  - Homework completion.
- **Record Therapist's Rating of Client's Compliance Here:** _____
___b. Disclose client's compliance rating.
___c. Explain how rating was derived, and methods of improving performance in future.

End Time:_____

Prompting Checklist 5.2. Behavioral Goals Therapist Prompting Checklist for Future Sessions.

BEHAVIORAL GOALS
THERAPIST PROMPTING CHECKLIST
Future Sessions

Client ID:_____ Clinician: _____ Session #: _____ Session Date: _____

Materials Required

• Primary Goals Worksheet (PGW), 2 copies

Begin Time:_____

Review Goals for Future Sessions (Client and Adult Significant Others Should Be Present)

___a. Ask client to provide copy of completed PGW.
    • Provide PGW if client is unable to do so.
___b   Praise client for completing focus goals.
___c. Query how client completed goals and remained drug free.
___d. Query if sig. other provided reward for focus goals & do following:
    • If **all** focus goals were performed, & **reward provided**, praise sig. other.
    • If **all** focus goals were performed, & **reward not provided**, instruct sig. other to provide, or arrange to provide, a makeup reward.
    • If all **focus goals were not performed**, & **reward was provided**, inform sig. other to avoid rewards unless all focused goals were completed.
    • If all **focus goals were not performed**, & a **reward was not provided**, inform sig. other this is a good thing because a reward should not be provided if goals not met & client was not drug free.
___e. Query if client provided reward to sig. other for supporting client & do the following:
    • If client provided reward for support given, praise client.
    • If client didn't provide reward & support was given, instruct client to provide a makeup reward.
    • If client provided a reward, but no support was given, instruct client not to provide reward.
    • If client didn't provide a reward, and support not given, inform all this is appropriate.
___f. Assess/praise for completion of non-focus goals.
___g. Assist client in arranging to do more focus and non-focus goals, or do them more efficiently.
___h. Query if client would like to modify and/or add goals.
    • If yes, modify or develop goals & record in blank section of client & therapist copies of PGW.
___i. Solicit from client which of the listed goals will be focus during upcoming week.
___j. Instruct client to put a check mark next to goals that will become a focus during the next week.

___k. Instruct client to fill out how she has completed/made significant effort to complete a goal.

___l. Solicit and record a reward from sig. other if focus goals are completed.

___m. Record reward to be provided to sig. other.

___n. Obtain signature & commitment from client to complete focus goals during week.

___o. Obtain signature & commitment from sig. other to provide support & reward.

___p. Tell client & sig. other the goal sheet will be reviewed next week and query place to put form.

Client's Assessment of Helpfulness of the Intervention

___a. After stating client should not feel obligated to provide high scores, as an honest assessment helps better address client needs, solicit how helpful client thought intervention was using 7-point scale:

   7 = extremely helpful, 6 = very helpful, 5 = somewhat helpful, 4 = not sure,
   3 = somewhat unhelpful, 2 = very unhelpful, 1 = extremely unhelpful

- **Record Client's Rating Here:_____**

___b. Solicit how rating was derived, & methods of improving intervention in future.

Therapist's Rating of Client's Compliance with Intervention

___a. Disclose therapist's rating of client's compliance using 7-point scale:

   7 = extremely compliant, 6 = very compliant, 5 = somewhat compliant, 4 = neutral,
   3 = somewhat noncompliant, 2 = very noncompliant, 1 = extremely noncompliant

- Factors that contribute to compliance ratings are:
  - Attendance
  - Participation and conduct in session
  - Homework completion
- **Record Therapist's Rating of Client's Compliance Here:_____**

___b. Disclose client's compliance rating.

___c. Explain how rating was derived, and methods of improving performance in future.

End Time:_____

Worksheet 5.1. Drug-Incompatible Goals Worksheet.

DRUG-INCOMPATIBLE GOALS WORKSHEET

Client: _____ Clinician: _____ Session #: _____ Session Date: _____

- Review Drug-Incompatible Goals Rationale before completing the Drug-Incompatible Goals Worksheet

"HOW OFTEN HAVE YOU (POTENTIAL DRUG TRIGGER BELOW) BEFORE USING DRUGS?"	"WOULD YOU LIKE TO SET (DRUG-INCOMPATIBLE BEHAVIOR BELOW) AS A GOAL?"	"WHAT WOULD MAKE IT EASIER FOR YOU TO (DRUG-INCOMPATIBLE BEHAVIOR)?" (Empathize, Solicit info, Volunteer help)	ASSIST IN DEFINING GOALS BEHAVIORALLY / SPECIFICALLY.
Smoked cigarettes ❑ almost never (proceed to next trigger) ❑ sometimes ❑ almost always	**Avoid cigarettes** ❑ no (proceed to next trigger) ❑ yes		
Stashed or hidden drugs ❑ almost never (proceed to next trigger) ❑ sometimes ❑ almost always	**Keep secret stashes of drugs away from you** ❑ no (proceed to next trigger) ❑ yes		
Drunk alcohol ❑ almost never (proceed to next trigger) ❑ sometimes ❑ almost always	**Avoid alcohol use** ❑ no (proceed to next trigger) ❑ yes		

"HOW OFTEN HAVE YOU (POTENTIAL DRUG TRIGGER BELOW) BEFORE USING DRUGS?"	"WOULD YOU LIKE TO SET (DRUG-INCOMPATIBLE BEHAVIOR BELOW) AS A GOAL?"	"WHAT WOULD MAKE IT EASIER FOR YOU TO (DRUG-INCOMPATIBLE BEHAVIOR)?" (Empathize, Solicit info, Volunteer help)	ASSIST IN DEFINING GOALS BEHAVIORALLY / SPECIFICALLY.
Kept drug paraphernalia like papers, foil, needles, & pipes close to you ☐ almost never (proceed to next trigger) ☐ sometimes ☐ almost always	**Keep drug paraphernalia away from you** ☐ no (proceed to next trigger) ☐ yes		
Gotten angry ☐ almost never (proceed to next trigger) ☐ sometimes ☐ almost always	**Effectively manage anger** ☐ (proceed to next trigger) ☐ yes		
Gotten bored ☐ almost never (proceed to next trigger) ☐ sometimes ☐ almost always	**Stay busy doing things that do not involve drugs** ☐ no (proceed to next trigger) ☐ yes		
Gotten stressed ☐ almost never (proceed to next trigger) ☐ sometimes ☐ almost always	**Effectively manage stress** ☐ no (proceed to next trigger) ☐ yes		

Gotten sad ❑ almost never (proceed to next trigger) ❑ sometimes ❑ almost always	**Stay happy and satisfied** ❑ no (proceed to next trigger) ❑ yes
Gotten anxious or excited ❑ almost never (proceed to next trigger) ❑ sometimes ❑ almost always	**Effectively manage anxiety or excited** ❑ no (proceed to next trigger) ❑ yes
Experienced bad memories or images ❑ almost never (proceed to next trigger) ❑ sometimes ❑ almost always	**Effectively manage or stop bad memories or images** ❑ no (proceed to next trigger) ❑ yes
Experienced urges or cravings ❑ almost never (proceed to next trigger) ❑ sometimes ❑ almost always	**Effectively manage/stop cravings, urges to use drugs** ❑ no (proceed to next trigger) ❑ yes
Experienced tension in your muscles ❑ almost never (proceed to next trigger) ❑ sometimes ❑ almost always	**Relax when you feel tense** ❑ no (proceed to next trigger) ❑ yes
Experienced arguments ❑ almost never (proceed to next trigger) ❑ sometimes ❑ almost always	**Effectively manage conflicts with others** ❑ no (proceed to next trigger) ❑ yes

"HOW OFTEN HAVE YOU (POTENTIAL DRUG TRIGGER BELOW) BEFORE USING DRUGS?"	"WOULD YOU LIKE TO SET (DRUG-INCOMPATIBLE BEHAVIOR BELOW) AS A GOAL?"	"WHAT WOULD MAKE IT EASIER FOR YOU TO (DRUG-INCOMPATIBLE BEHAVIOR)?" (Empathize, Solicit info, Volunteer help)	ASSIST IN DEFINING GOALS BEHAVIORALLY / SPECIFICALLY.
Attended parties, events, get-togethers, or celebrations where drugs are present ☐ almost never (proceed to next trigger) ☐ sometimes ☐ almost always	**Avoid parties, events, get-togethers, or celebrations where drugs are present** ☐ no (proceed to next trigger) ☐ yes		
Spent time with other drug users ☐ almost never (proceed to next trigger) ☐ sometimes ☐ almost always	**Meet and spend time with people who do not use drugs** ☐ no (proceed to next trigger) ☐ yes		
Had lots of cash available ☐ almost never (proceed to next trigger) ☐ sometimes ☐ almost always	**Effectively manage savings and avoid having large sums of cash easily available** ☐ no (proceed to next trigger) ☐ yes		
Is there anything else that has triggered drug use for you that I did not ask you about: _____ . ☐ almost never (assessment completed) ☐ sometimes ☐ almost always	**(INDICATE SOMETHING THAT IS INCOMPATIBLE WITH THE MENTIONED DRUG TRIGGER HERE):** ☐ no (assessment completed) ☐ yes		

Worksheet 5.2. Primary Goals Worksheet.

PRIMARY GOALS WORKSHEET

Client ID:_____ Clinician: _____ Session #: _____ Session Date: _____

Goal	FOCUS GOAL FOR THE WEEK	INDICATE HOW GOAL WAS COMPLETED	Goal	FOCUS GOAL FOR THE WEEK	INDICATE HOW GOAL WAS COMPLETED
Attend treatment sessions	X		Ensure an adult significant other attends treatment sessions	X	
Stay clean from drugs	X		Complete practice assignments: _____ _____ _____	X	

Reward for client from significant other if all focus goals are completed: _____

Reward for significant other from client if significant other supports client: _____

I agree to complete all my focus goals for the week and reward my significant other if I receive support:

_____.
Client's Signature

I agree to support client in focus goals and provide a reward if they are completed:

_____.
Significant Other's Signature

Makeup rewards for the week_____

_____

*Note: If significant other is not present, therapist has option to either ask client to identify a reward to be provided by the significant other or to include a self-reward.

CHAPTER 6

Developing a Successful Treatment Plan

Rationale and Overview

Treatment planning is a critical component in all interventions for substance abuse, but the process for developing the treatment plan often is not clearly explicated. FBT utilizes a well-specified and collaborative approach to treatment planning that engages the client and adult significant others in the process. The intent is to tailor the treatment plan to the unique needs and circumstances of the client while at the same time motivating clients to actively participate in treatment.

Treatment planning is implemented in the session after Behavioral Goals and Rewards are introduced for the first time. MHPs begin the process by instructing the client and adult significant others to prioritize the interventions that have yet to be implemented (e.g., Environmental Control, Self-Control, Positive Request). In doing so, clients and their adult significant others separately rank the interventions in regard to their perceived importance, and the MHP subsequently sums their rank scores. In subsequent sessions, the order in which these interventions are introduced for the first time is based on the summed rankings. For instance, if Self-Control is ranked as the preferred number one choice, it is introduced prior to all other interventions. If Job-Getting Skills Training is ranked second, it is the second intervention implemented, and so on. Once an intervention is introduced, it is generally reviewed during many of the remaining treatment sessions, albeit to a progressively lesser extent because the client will eventually master the targeted skills. Interventions that are implemented earlier in the treatment process, therefore, are usually reviewed in therapy to a greater extent than later implemented interventions. Of course, MHPs and clients further negotiate intervention prioritization during the development of each of the session agendas. Thus, treatment planning is consumer driven and dynamic, which increases buy-in from the clients and allows flexibility so that interventions target the most pressing needs of the client and family as therapy progresses.

Goal for Intervention

> ➤ Assist client and adult significant others in prioritizing FBT interventions.

Materials Needed

> ➤ Treatment Planning Therapist Prompting Checklist (Prompting Checklist 6.1, also located on the CD that accompanies this book)

> ➤ Intervention Priority Worksheet (Worksheet 6.1, also located on the CD that accompanies this book)

Procedural Steps for Implementation

Developing the Treatment Plan (Client and Adult Significant Others)

The steps for developing a successful treatment plan are provided in the Treatment Planning Therapist Prompting Checklist (Prompting Checklist 6.1). To begin, the MHP distributes a copy of the Intervention Priority Worksheet included at the end of this Chapter (Worksheet 6.1) to the client and adult significant others, and reads what each intervention involves. The MHP then solicits how the client and significant other believe each of the interventions might be helpful (the MHP may summarize the solicited ideas in the appropriate cell of the Intervention Priority Worksheet). When clients and their significant others indicate an intervention will not be helpful, the MHP reports how other clients have benefited from the respective intervention, and subsequently attempts to get a commitment from the client that the respective treatment would be helpful to some extent. If the client again indicates that the therapy would not be helpful, the MHP states that the treatment will not be considered in the client's treatment plan. Of course, clients are praised when they make statements that indicate the interventions are likely to be helpful.

Clients and significant others separately rank all interventions they expect will be helpful according to the priority they should be given in treatment. The MHP sums the client and significant other rankings for each intervention in the appropriate cell of the last column of the Intervention Priority Worksheet, and discloses the rankings, starting with the lowest sum and progressing to the highest sum. The MHP tells the family that the interventions will be introduced in this order. It often helps to explicitly disclose which intervention will be administered first, second, third, and so on. The MHP should also indicate that the order in which therapies are introduced may be modified during session agendas, and in this way treatment planning is flexible to address spontaneous concerns that are likely to influence goal-oriented behavior. Table 6.1 shows an example of the interventions that were administered in the first 12 weeks of therapy for a person who abused cocaine. As can be seen, the first three sessions were prescribed in the customary order (i.e., Behavioral Goals and Rewards, I've Got a Great Family, Treatment Planning), with the remaining nine sessions being determined by the treatment plan. As seen in the table, the duration of time spent in each intervention varies, with time allocated to each specific intervention lessening as therapy progresses across time. In session 1, for example, 55 minutes was allocated to Behavioral Goals and Rewards, which is implemented in each of the remaining sessions but decreases in time to 15 minutes by session 7. Similarly, Self-Control is first implemented in session 5, and is successively administered until session 11, where only 20 minutes is allocated.

In some sessions, treatments were spontaneously implemented based on extra-treatment factors. For instance, the agenda was modified during session 10 to emphasize family relationships rather than job-getting skills training, as there was an argument between the client and his mother the night prior to the therapy session. Self-Control was revisited in session 11, due to increased urges toward substance use. The following dialogue illustrates implementation of the treatment plan using the Intervention Priority Worksheet.

MHP: Here's a copy of the Intervention Priority Worksheet *(hands a copy of the Intervention Priority Worksheet to James and his wife Karen).* It summarizes the interventions we have available to assist you in achieving your goals. In a moment I will read a summary that

Table 6.1. Example of Interventions Conducted for a Client During the First 12 Weeks of FBT.

Session Number	List of intervention components implemented and duration of time each intervention required	How were interventions determined?
1	• Session Agenda: 5 min. • Behavioral Goals and Rewards: 55 min.	Fully Prescribed
2	• Session Agenda: 3 min. • Behavioral Goals and Rewards: 27 min. • I've Got a Great Family: 30 min.	Fully Prescribed
3	• Session Agenda: 4 min. • Behavioral Goals and Rewards: 26 min. • Treatment Planning: 30 min.	Fully Prescribed
4	• Session Agenda: 14 min. • Behavioral Goals and Rewards: 16 min. • I've Got a Great Family: 30 min.	Influenced by Treatment Planning
5	• Session Agenda: 3 min. • Behavioral Goals and Rewards: 13 min. • Self-Control: 44 min.	Influenced by Treatment Planning
6	• Session Agenda: 3 min. • Behavioral Goals and Rewards: 15 min. • Self-Control: 42 min.	Influenced by Treatment Planning
7	• Session Agenda: 4 min. • Behavioral Goals and Rewards: 15 min. • Self-Control: 20 min. • Positive Request: 21 min.	Influenced by Treatment Planning
8	• Session Agenda: 3 min. • Behavioral Goals and Rewards: 15 min. • Self-Control: 22 min. • Positive Request: 25 min.	Influenced by Treatment Planning
9	• Session Agenda: 2 min. • Behavioral Goals and Rewards: 15 min. • Job-Getting Skills Training: 43 min.	Influenced by Treatment Planning
10	• Session Agenda: 5 min. • Behavioral Goals and Rewards: 10 min. • Positive Request: 15 min. • I've Got a Great Family: 30 min.	Influenced by Treatment Planning, with I've Got a Great Family occurring instead of Job-Getting Skills Training as negotiated during agenda
11	• Session Agenda: 2 min. • Behavioral Goals and Rewards: 15 min. • Self-Control: 20 min. • Positive Request: 15 min. • Job-Getting Skills Training: 20 min.	Influenced by Treatment Planning, with Self-Control being administered due to drug urges that came up during agenda.
12	• Session Agenda: 3 min. • Behavioral Goals and Rewards: 13 min. • Environmental Control: 45 min.	Influenced by Treatment Planning

describes what each of the interventions are all about in this column (*points to FBT Interventions column of Intervention Priority Worksheet*). I'll then ask you both to prioritize these interventions for their expected usefulness to you both, and we'll introduce these interventions in that order. That is, the one that averages out as the most useful will be reviewed first. Then we'll introduce the intervention you both feel is next most important, and so on. So the ones you feel are most important will be prioritized. The first intervention listed is relevant to controlling your environment. In this intervention you will learn to control the stimuli or things you sense in your environment that are associated with drug use, so that you can avoid situations that might make you feel like using drugs, and spend more time with people, places, and situations that do not involve drug use or trouble. How might this intervention be useful to the family?

James: I have not thought about it that way, but it does make sense. I know that I have the most difficult time avoiding drugs when I go out with my friends after work for a couple drinks.

Karen: Yeah, you usually end up spending the whole night with them and coming home drunk or high.

James: Hmmm (*somewhat annoyed and embarrassed*) . . . I guess I have to say that is true.

Karen: It would also be great if you did not go out so much. Then you could spend more time around the house. The kids always want to spend more time with you and worry when you are not here.

James: Well, maybe this would be an important one for us, 'cause it would help me spend more time with the kids and less time doing stuff that gets me into trouble.

MHP: Those are some great ideas about how this one might really help you and your family. It sounds like you would like to spend more time with your kids, James, and who needs more trouble in life?

James: That's right—true enough.

MHP: Okay, so let's keep those in mind and take a look at this next intervention. (*The MHP would continue to review the remaining interventions in a similar manner. After reviewing all the interventions, the MHP would say . . .*) That was wonderful. I really liked how you were able to identify the ways in which these interventions would be helpful to you and your family. Now, based on our discussion, I'd like James (client) to rank these interventions in terms of their expected usefulness to you and your family and record your rankings here *(points to second column of the Intervention Priority Worksheet)*. A "1" is what you think will be most useful, a "2" is what you would consider the second most useful intervention, and so on. Start with the most useful, and put your numbers in this second column. After you're done, Karen will rank what she thinks would be most useful. We'll then add them together and we'll do the intervention with the lowest resulting number first in therapy, the intervention with the second lowest number next, and so on. Of course, you both will always be able to change the intervention plan during each agenda at the start of our sessions. *(The MHP would then assist James and Karen in ranking the interventions, and later review the rankings.)* Good. After all interventions are attempted, we can again reprioritize them based on your needs at that time.

Concluding Remarks

This method to treatment planning addresses a shortcoming in many treatment approaches that do not consider the clients' thoughts, desires, and circumstances in the treatment planning process. The collaborative approach presented here has the advantage of allowing the client and family members to choose those interventions that are most relevant and amenable to their current circumstances, and in this way creates intrinsic motivation to actively engage in therapy. For clients who are court referred or otherwise compelled to participate in treatment, collaborative treatment planning may be of particular benefit, as these clients are often not interested in treatment and resistant to intervention. For these clients, even when open resentment of the treatment process is not expressed, passive behaviors can undermine engagement, such as failing to show up for scheduled appointments, failing to complete assigned homework, or disingenuous reporting of the successes and challenges since last contact. Actively engaging clients early on in the treatment planning process can help ward off these active or passive resistances, allow for more engagement as treatment progresses, and improve overall outcomes.

Supporting Materials for Chapter 6: Developing a Successful Treatment Plan

Prompting Checklist 6.1. Treatment Planning Therapist Prompting Checklist.

> ## TREATMENT PLANNING
> ### THERAPIST PROMPTING CHECKLIST
> #### Initial Session
>
> Client ID: _____ Clinician: _____ Session #: _____ Session Date: _____
>
> ### Materials Required
>
> * Intervention Priority Worksheet (IPW)
>
> ### Begin Time: _____
>
> ### Developing the Treatment Plan (Client and Adult Significant Others)
>
> ___ a. Distribute IPW to client and significant other(s).
> ___ b. State what each treatment targets as per 1st column in IPW, & solicit how each tx. would be useful.
>   * If family indicates tx. will not be helpful, assist in explaining how it has helped others.
>   * If family continues to believe the tx. will not be helpful, disclose it will not be implemented.
>   * Notes regarding perceptions of usefulness may be recorded in 2nd column.
> ___ c. State txs. will be introduced according to summed ranking of client & adult sig. others.
> ___ d. Instruct client & significant others to each rank interventions in order of priority (expected usefulness).
>   * Rankings can be determined w/client and adult sig. others together or separately.
>   * Record their rankings in the IPW 3rd and 4th columns.
> ___ e. Instruct client & adult significant others to disclose how they arrived at their rankings & praise their decisions.
> ___ f. Sum rank scores & state txs. will be introduced according to derived ranking (lowest to highest).
>   * Therapist has discretion to adjust order of implementation.
>   * Record sum of rank scores in the IPW.
> ___ g. State order of implementation may be adjusted during session agendas.
> ___ h. State order of treatments can be changed in future sessions once all interventions are attempted.
>
> ### Client's Assessment of Helpfulness of the Intervention
>
> ___ a. After stating client should not feel obligated to provide high scores, as an honest assessment helps better address client needs, solicit how helpful client thought intervention was using 7-point scale:

7 = extremely helpful, **6** = very helpful, **5** = somewhat helpful, **4** = not sure,
3 = somewhat unhelpful, **2** = very unhelpful, **1** = extremely unhelpful
- **Record Client's Rating Here:_____**

___ b. Solicit how rating was derived, & methods of improving intervention in future.

Therapist's Rating of Client's Compliance with Intervention

___ a. Disclose therapist's rating of client's compliance using 7-point scale:
     7 = extremely compliant, **6** = very compliant, **5** = somewhat compliant, **4** = neutral,
     3 = somewhat noncompliant, **2** = very noncompliant, **1** = extremely noncompliant
- Factors that contribute to compliance ratings are:
  - Attendance
  - Participation and conduct in session
  - Homework completion
- **Record Therapist's Rating of Client's Compliance Here:_____**

___ b. Disclose client's compliance rating.

___ c. Explain how rating was derived, & methods of improving performance in future.

End Time:_____

Worksheet 6.1. Intervention Priority Worksheet.

INTERVENTION PRIORITY WORKSHEET

Client ID: _____ Clinician: _____ Session #: _____ Session Date: _____

FBT Interventions	How Helpful?	Priority Rank for Client (lowest # is the top priority)	Priority Rank for Significant Other (lowest # is the top priority)	Priority Rank Sum (lowest # is the top priority)
Eliminating Substance Abuse and Other Problem Behaviors				
a) Environmental Control = Learning to arrange your life so you can spend more time with people, places, and situations that do not involve drug use or trouble. - How might this be useful?	a)	a)	a)	a)
b) Self-Control = Learning to control impulses, urges, & thoughts that increase drug use and other problems. - How might this be useful?	b)	b)	b)	b)
Improving Communication & Relationships				
a) I've Got a Great Family = Family members learn to communicate things they love, admire, respect, or appreciate about each other. - How might this be useful?	a)	a)	a)	a)
b) Positive Request = Learning how to best make requests so people are more likely to do what you want, and how and when it's best to settle disagreements. - How might this be useful?	b)	b)	b)	b)

Show Me the Money!				
a) Job-Getting Skills Training = Learning ways to find satisfying job opportunities and to learn job interviewing skills. - How might this be useful?	*a)*	*a)*	*a)*	*a)*
b) Financial Management = Learning how to reduce expenses and increase income. - How might this be useful?	*b)*	*b)*	*b)*	*b)*

CHAPTER 7

Enhancing Relationships

Rationale and Overview

Poor communication and critical comments are often present in families where substance abuse is a problem, leading to negative emotions and stressors that often trigger drug use. Poor communication also impedes reinforcing comments directed at increasing behaviors that are incompatible with substance use. Thus, developing effective positive communication patterns is likely to help reduce stimuli that often precede drug use, and increase positive behaviors that are incompatible with continued drug use.

The I've Got a Great Family intervention was developed to enhance family relationships through improved communication, and was originated from Nate Azrin's Reciprocity Counseling. I've Got a Great Family's theoretical underpinnings are based on the assumption that positive relationships occur because there is reciprocity in the exchange of reinforcement between individuals. I've Got a Great Family builds on this theoretical framework in family members by teaching them to acknowledge their appreciation of one another. Indeed, family satisfaction is associated with positive interactions, and the amount of positive affect present when exchanging reinforcement (Carruth, Tate, Moffett, & Hill, 1997).

In the I've Got a Great Family intervention, all significant others, including children, are invited to participate. During the intervention, each participating family member is prompted by the mental health provider (MHP) to disclose qualities and behaviors that are loved, admired, or respected about all other participating family members. Family members respond to these positive statements with expressions of appreciation and reassure that the acknowledged qualities and behaviors will continue to occur. In this way, family members feel appreciated for the things they do, and are more likely to reciprocate desired behaviors. I've Got a Great Family includes therapy assignments to practice these skills at home between therapy sessions, and these prescribed interactions are reviewed during subsequent treatment sessions to reinforce these positive encounters. This intervention usually requires 20 to 30 minutes to complete the first time, and less than 20 minutes in subsequent sessions. I've Got a Great Family is implemented multiple times through the course of treatment, but it is best to implement it only periodically to maintain its novelty and freshness. Also, I've Got a Great Family is usually implemented early in FBT treatment, to create a positive atmosphere in the family and encourage family members to work together in addressing the substance use of the client.

Goals for Intervention

➤ Teach family members to provide compliments.

➤ Teach family members to receive compliments and show appreciation.

Materials Needed

➤ I've Got a Great Family Therapist Prompting Checklist for Initial Session (Prompting Checklist 7.1, also located on the CD that accompanies this book)

➤ I've Got a Great Family Therapist Prompting Checklist for Future Sessions (Prompting Checklist 7.2, also located on the CD that accompanies this book)

➤ Things I Love, Admire, or Respect About My Family Session Worksheet (Worksheet 7.1, also located on the CD that accompanies this book)

➤ Things I Love, Admire, or Respect About My Family Assignment Sheet (Worksheet 7.2, also located on the CD that accompanies this book)

Procedural Steps for Implementation

Providing Rationale (Client and All Available Significant Others)

The steps necessary to implement the I've Got a Great Family when initially presented to the family are contained in the I've Got a Great Family Therapist Prompting Checklist for Initial Session (Prompting Checklist 7.1). The prompting checklist begins with the rationale that is provided to family members for the

I've Got a Great Family intervention. This rationale must be simple, positive, and quick because children are encouraged to participate in this intervention and their attention is limited. MHPs explain to the family that people who say positive things to one another are more likely to have good relationships, so I've Got a Great Family helps family members feel comfortable saying positive things to one another and makes them feel appreciated. MHPs also state why they believe I've Got a Great Family is expected to be effective with the family, and the family is asked to indicate how I've Got a Great Family will be useful. The following dialogue provides an example of a rationale for I've Got a Great Family.

MHP: Today is going to be a great day! In a moment you're each going to say something that you love, admire, or respect about each other. The reason we're going to do this is that it feels wonderful to have people appreciate the things you are great at! Saying positive things to those in your family also helps build strong relationships. I think this is going to be the perfect thing for this family because there are a lot of positive things going on in your family that need to be brought out into the open. How do you all think this will be helpful?

Positive Statement Exchange (Client and All Significant Others)

Sometimes, family members are hesitant to initially engage in this intervention with the client due to long-standing resentment resulting from negative behaviors associated with substance abuse. In these situations MHPs may encourage the family that it may be necessary to think of things they *used to* admire, love, and respect about each other.

After discussing the positive benefits of I've Got a Great Family with the family, each family member is then provided a copy of the Things I Love, Admire, or Respect About My Family Session Worksheet (Worksheet 7.1). The MHP tells everyone to record the names of participating family members in the top row of the form, and then instructs each person to record at least one thing that is loved, admired, or respected about each of the other family members. Younger children often have a difficult time understanding the directions, and are often hesitant to record information. Therefore, the MHP usually walks around the room assisting small children in recording pictures that represent positive behaviors and pointing out how busy everyone is recording their responses. The latter strategy assists in prompting people to write more information on their papers because they want to make sure they have just as many positive things on their papers as the others. MHPs prompt additional responses by telling family members what parents and children in other families have reported. It is sometimes necessary for MHPs to remind their families to record one remark for each family member in the first row prior to recording additional positive statements in the second row. This prevents hurt feelings from family members who may otherwise receive relatively fewer compliments.

When two or three responses are recorded for each family member, MHPs instruct one family member to tell one of the other family members something that is loved, admired, or respected about that person from the list. The one who receives the compliment is instructed to respond as follows: (1) express how it felt to hear the positive statement; (2) express that the comment was appreciated; (3) express that an attempt will be made to continue the desired behavior; and (4) reciprocate with a compliment of something loved, admired, or respected about the other person. Early in the process, the MHP can prompt the family members in what types of things to say, and it is sometimes necessary to remind family members of the four steps if they leave one out when providing feedback. The dialogue below provides an example of this process.

MHP: Okay, everyone, here's a copy of a worksheet for you to record things you love, admire, or respect about each of your family members in this room. As you look at this form, the top row has a space available where you can write the name of each person in this room. After you record everyone's name, I want you to write something you love, admire, or respect about each person here in the second row. When you finish this row, do the same for the third row. I'm going to help Roberto with his form because he's just learning to write *(Roberto is 7 years old)*. Let's see your form, Roberto. What could we put down for your mother? I'll write it where it needs to be.

Roberto: *(Whispers to the MHP)* My mom cooks good spaghetti.

MHP: That's fantastic! Hey mom, wait until you hear what Roberto said about you! *(After about 5 or 10 minutes)* Suzanne, go ahead and tell Roberto how you love, admire, or respect him.

Suzanne: Roberto, I really love it when you help me pack your lunch in the morning.

MHP: That's so beautiful! Roberto, you're the man! That must have felt so good to hear. Please tell your mom how that made you feel.

Roberto: That made me feel happy, Mom.

MHP: Of course, I could see how that would make you feel happy. It would make me happy, too. Go ahead and let her know you will keep making your lunch!

Roberto: I will keep helping you pack my lunch.

MHP: Great, now tell your mom something she does that you love. *(Roberto looks at the ground, and the MHP whispers in his ear that he indicated that his mother makes great spaghetti.)*

Roberto: Mom, you make great spaghetti.

MHP: Oh, my. That must have made you feel amazing. Is that right, Mom?

Suzanne: Yes, Roberto, that made me feel really good. I did not know you liked my spaghetti that much. Thanks for telling me.

MHP: Now, Mom, remember the next step?

Suzanne: Oh, yes. I will keep making spaghetti for you, Roberto. Is there anything else that I cook that you especially like?

MHP: This is great, you guys. . . . *(The positive exchange would continue much like the preceding dialogue for the third row of responses, or other responses that are spontaneously made by the family members).*

Homework (Client and All Significant Others)

When assigning homework, the MHP provides each family member a copy of the Things I Love, Admire, or Respect About My Family Assignment Sheet (Worksheet 7.2), and assists each person in recording the participating family members' names in the left column. The MHP then assigns each person to tell each family member how they are loved, admired, or respected throughout the week. If necessary, the MHP may assign adults or older children to assist in the recording process for younger children. Of course, they should also indicate that each family member should record at least one compliment in the Assignment Sheet for each of the other family members, and remind family members to respond positively when compliments are provided, for example, stating "thank you" or some other appreciation in response to the comment. Also, the MHP reminds family members to assure that they will continue in that complimented behavior, after the compliment is given.

Review Assignment (Client and All Significant Others)

Steps for reviewing the I've Got a Great Family homework assignments are included in I've Got a Great Family Therapist Prompting Checklist for Future Sessions (Prompting Checklist 7.2). The MHP initiates all homework reviews by first collecting the completed Things I Love, Admire, or Respect About My Family Assignment Sheet from each participating family member. When the assignments are performed, the MHP praises homework completion.

The review of homework involves the MHP first pointing out positive comments that were performed during the past week and descriptively praising these efforts. MHPs ask family members to describe how it felt to be the recipient of positive statements. MHPs have discretion in choosing which of the recorded responses to review. After therapy assignments are reviewed, based on clinical impressions and the treatment plan, MHPs decide when, and if, future I've Got a Great Family assignments will occur. The following dialogue shows how an I've Got a Great Family therapy assignment is reviewed when the assignment recording forms are missing.

MHP: Okay, I'm so excited to look at your I've Got a Great Family therapy assignments. Go ahead and pass them to me!

Suzanne: I did them, but I forgot them at home this week (*appears uncomfortable*).

MHP: Well, I'm so glad you found the time to do I've Got a Great Family this past week. What about you, Roberto?

Roberto: I did not do my forms this week with my mom.

MHP: I'll bet your mom did them but forgot to show them to you. Mom, what would make it easier for you to bring the assignments to counseling?

Suzanne: Well, I could keep them by the front door so I saw them when I was leaving the house. Or I could put them in my purse. Maybe if I just put them on the front of the refrigerator, that would help remind me.

MHP: All those sound like good ideas. Which one of those plans could you try this week?

Suzanne: Well, I think putting them on the refrigerator would be good because Roberto and I both could be reminded throughout the day.

MHP: Great—go ahead and try that plan. But since we don't have them this week, let's do the assignment in retrospect. Go ahead and fill out one positive thing each of you remember telling everyone else in the room this past week in your Assignment Sheet. *(After 3 or 4 minutes)* Mom, what is one positive thing you said about Roberto this past week, or maybe you wished you said about him during the past week?

Suzanne: I told Roberto that I appreciated his hard work studying for a math exam.

MHP: That's absolutely fantastic, Roberto. That must have felt great. Mom, please tell Roberto how you showed him that you appreciated him for doing this. I'd like to see his reaction.

Suzanne: *(Compliments Roberto)* Roberto, I am so proud of the way that you are studying for your math test. You are a really smart boy and a good student.

MHP: Wow, I can see from your smile, Roberto, that you liked being recognized. Go ahead and tell your mother how it felt to hear that, and also that you will continue to work hard doing your school assignments.

Roberto: I love you, Mom. I felt really happy when you said that. Sometimes when you say I am not doing a good job, it makes me feel bad.

MHP: Well, that's important information to know, Roberto. Mom, did you know that your praise was that powerful? *(This process would be repeated for the remaining family members.)*

In Exhibit 7.1, a partially completed worksheet is presented for Suzanne, who is the client, based on the preceding dialogue. Other family members are also listed on the form, including her husband, Brendon, and two daughters, Roo and Kendra. These individuals would also participate in the intervention, even though her interactions with Roberto are the only ones presented in the dialogues, so they are included in Exhibit 7.1. The exhibit shows Suzanne's positive statement for Roberto, her son, that he helps pack his lunch in the morning, as well as positive statements for her other family members. Ideally, more than one comment is recorded for each of the family members, although only one is presented in the exhibit.

Exhibit 7.1. Example of a Partially Completed Things I Love, Admire, or Respect About My Family Worksheet.

THINGS I LOVE, ADMIRE, OR RESPECT ABOUT MY FAMILY WORKSHEET

Instructions: In the top row of the form, list names of each of the family members with one family member per column. Fill in the rows with things your family members do that you love, admire, or respect.

☺	Family Member 1 Brendon	Family Member 2 Roberto	Family Member 3 Kendra	Family Member 4 Roo	Family Member 5 _____
Write something you love, admire, or respect about each person.	WORKS HARD AND BRINGS HOME A GOOD WAGE	HELPS ME PACK HIS LUNCH IN THE MORNING	KEEPS HER ROOM CLEAN WITHOUT ME REMINDING	HELPS ME SET THE TABLE FOR DINNER EACH NIGHT	
Write something you love, admire, or respect about each person.					

Concluding Remarks

The I've Got a Great Family intervention is simple but powerful. We find that families referred for substance abuse treatment have developed negative communication patterns, and the structured approach to positive communication provided by I've Got a Great Family often results in deep-felt, positive emotions, with some members crying in appreciation by the end of the intervention and others exchanging hugs, spontaneous compliments, tears, or other signs of encouragement and affection. For many of these family members, it has been a long time since others in the family have focused on their positive qualities and behaviors, and to do so in this intervention brings a sense of family unity and a renewed hope for the future.

Supporting Materials for Chapter 7: Enhancing Relationships

Prompting Checklist 7.1. I've Got a Great Family Therapist Prompting Checklist for Initial Session.

I'VE GOT A GREAT FAMILY

THERAPIST PROMPTING CHECKLIST
Initial Session

Client ID:_____ Clinician: _____ Session #: _____ Session Date: _____

Materials Required

- Things I Love, Admire, or Respect About My Family Session Worksheet (TILW)
- Things I Love, Admire, or Respect About My Family Assignment Sheet (TILAS)

Begin Time:_____

Rationale (Client and All Significant Others)

- State (or solicit) the following:
___a.   People who say positive things to each other are more likely to have good relationships.
___b.   I've Got a Great Family (IGGF) helps family members recognize good things they do for each other.
___c.   IGGF helps family members say more positive things to each other, so they can feel appreciated.
___d.   State why IGGF is expected to be effective w/the family.
___e.   Solicit why the family thinks IGGF will be helpful.
___f.   Solicit questions.

Positive Statement Exchange (Client and All Significant Others)

- Provide each family member a copy of the TILW.
___a.   Assist each person in completing session worksheet.
  - Record names in the top row.
  - Each person should record at least 1 thing that is loved, admired, or respected about all others.
  - Walk around room, comment how good things are being written, and provide prompts.
___b.   Instruct family member in taking turns telling each other what they love, admire, or respect about one another.
___c.   Instruct family members to respond to the positive statements by expressing:
  ___1.   How the comment was appreciated.
  ___2.   An attempt will be made to continue the desired behavior.
  ___3.   Something loved, admired, or respected about the other person.

Homework (Client and All Significant Others)

- Give each a copy of the TILAS.
- ___a.   Assist family in recording each family member's name in the left column.
- ___b.   Assign each to demonstrate how listed family members are loved, admired, or respected throughout the week.
    - State at least 1 statement should be recorded in the Assignment Sheet per person during the week.
    - Remind family each positive statement should be reciprocated.

Client's Assessment of Helpfulness of the Intervention

- ___a.   After stating client should not feel obligated to provide high scores, as an honest assessment helps better address client needs, solicit how helpful client thought intervention was using 7-point scale:

    7 = extremely helpful, 6 = very helpful, 5 = somewhat helpful, 4 = not sure,
    3 = somewhat unhelpful, 2 = very unhelpful, 1 = extremely unhelpful
    - **Record Client's Rating Here:_____**
- ___b.   Solicit how rating was derived, and methods of improving intervention in future.

Therapist's Rating of Client's Compliance with Intervention

- ___a.   Disclose therapist's rating of client's compliance using 7-point scale:

    7 = extremely compliant, 6 = very compliant, 5 = somewhat compliant, 4 = neutral,
    3 = somewhat noncompliant, 2 = very noncompliant, 1 = extremely noncompliant
    - Factors that contribute to compliance ratings are:
        - Attendance
        - Participation and conduct in session
        - Homework completion
    - **Record Therapist's Rating of Client's Compliance Here:_____**
- ___b.   Disclose client's compliance rating.
- ___c.   Explain how rating was derived, and methods of improving performance in future.

End Time:_____

Prompting Checklist 7.2. I've Got a Great Family Therapist Prompting Checklist for Future Sessions.

I'VE GOT A GREAT FAMILY
THERAPIST PROMPTING CHECKLIST
Future Sessions

Client ID:_____ Clinician: _____ Session #: _____ Session Date: _____

Materials Required

• Things I Love, Admire, or Respect About My Family Assignment Sheet (TILAS)

Begin Time:_____

Review Homework (Client and All Significant Others)

___a. Solicit completed TILAS.
   • Praise homework completion or instruct family to complete assignment in retrospect.
___b. Solicit or point out what efforts were done to make positive statements.
___c. Praise efforts in providing positive statements & solicit how it felt to receive them.
   • Provide each person w/a new copy of TILAS, and assign family to complete TILAS, if clinically indicated.

Client's Assessment of Helpfulness of the Intervention

___a. After stating client should not feel obligated to provide high scores, as an honest assessment helps better address client needs, solicit how helpful client thought intervention was using 7-point scale:
   7 = extremely helpful, **6** = very helpful, **5** = somewhat helpful, **4** = not sure,
   3 = somewhat unhelpful, **2** = very unhelpful, **1** = extremely unhelpful
   • **Record Client's Rating Here:_____**
___b. Solicit how rating was derived, and methods of improving intervention in future.

Therapist's Rating of Client's Compliance with Intervention

___a. Disclose therapist's rating of client's compliance using 7-point scale:
   7 = extremely compliant, **6** = very compliant, **5** = somewhat compliant, **4** = neutral,
   3 = somewhat noncompliant, **2** = very noncompliant, **1** = extremely noncompliant
   • Factors that contribute to compliance ratings are:
     • Attendance
     • Participation and conduct in session
     • Homework completion
   • **Record Therapist's Rating of Client's Compliance Here:_____**
___b. Disclose client's compliance rating.
___c. Explain how rating was derived, and methods of improving performance in future.

End Time:_____

Worksheet 7.1. Things I Love, Admire, or Respect About My Family Session Worksheet.

THINGS I LOVE, ADMIRE, OR RESPECT ABOUT MY FAMILY WORKSHEET

Client ID:_____ Clinician: _____ Session #: _____ Session Date: _____

Instructions: In the top row of this form, list the names of each member of your family in the room. For each of the remaining rows write something you love, admire, or respect about each member.

☺	Name of Family Member: _____	Name of Family Member: _____	Name of Family Member: _____	Name of Family Member: _____	Name of Family Member: _____
Write something you love, admire, or respect about each person.					
Write something you love, admire, or respect about each person.					
Write something you love, admire, or respect about each person.					
Write something you love, admire, or respect about each person.					

Worksheet 7.2. Things I Love, Admire, or Respect About My Family Assignment Sheet.

THINGS I LOVE, ADMIRE, OR RESPECT ABOUT MY FAMILY ASSIGNMENT SHEET

Client ID:_____ Clinician: _____ Session #: _____ Session Date: _____

Instructions: Write the name of each member of your family in the far left column. Then write how you showed these persons that you love, admire, or respect them. At least one positive statement should be made for each person each week.

Family Member	Monday	Tuesday	Wednesday	Thursday	Friday	Saturday	Sunday
How did you show that you love, admire, or respect _____?							
How did you show that you love, admire, or respect _____?							
How did you show that you love, admire, or respect _____?							
How did you show that you love, admire, or respect _____?							
How did you show that you love, admire, or respect _____?							

8

Enhancing Communication Skills

Rationale and Overview

Poorly stated requests increase the likelihood of drug use and other problem behaviors by negatively altering the appropriate distribution of reinforcement among family members and friends. That is, when people perceive their requests as being ineffectual, they may become frustrated and angry. To relieve upset, these persons may use illicit drugs to eliminate these negative emotional states. Negative emotions and arguments also distract individuals from effectively solving interpersonal problems. The Positive Request intervention is designed to improve positive communication among family members, thereby assisting in the prevention of substance abuse and other problem behaviors.

The Positive Request procedure involves teaching the client and relevant others to effectively and appropriately solicit desired reinforcers. Through modeling and behavioral rehearsal, participants are taught to diplomatically resolve differences of opinion, resulting in perceived equity of reinforcement among family members. Components include politely requesting specific actions (i.e., when, what, where), reporting benefits that are likely to occur if requests are completed, stating why requested actions might be difficult or inconvenient to perform, offering to assist in accomplishing what is being requested, offering to reciprocate reinforcement if the request is accomplished, and suggesting alternative actions. After positive request components are effectively performed in simulated scenarios, participants are assigned to practice positive requests at home. Therapy assignments are reviewed during subsequent sessions.

Goals for Intervention

➤ Increase positive reinforcement between the client and family.

➤ Improve the equitable exchange of reinforcement among family members.

➤ Assist in resolving conflicts calmly.

Materials Required

➤ Positive Request Therapist Prompting Checklist for Initial Session (Prompting Checklist 8.1, also located on the CD that accompanies this book)

➤ Positive Request Therapist Prompting Checklist for Future Sessions (Prompting Checklist 8.2, also located on the CD that accompanies this book)

➤ Positive Request Handout (Worksheet 8.1, also located on the CD that accompanies this book)

➤ Positive Request Practice Assignment (Worksheet 8.2, also located on the CD that accompanies this book)

Procedural Steps for Treatment Implementation

Rationale (Client and Adolescent and Adult Significant Others)

Steps for initially implementing the Positive Request intervention are contained in the Positive Request Therapist Prompting Checklist for Initial Session (Prompting Checklist 8.1). As in other FBT interventions, the prompting checklist begins with a rationale, which is designed to instill motivation for clients and their significant others to learn the Positive Request Procedure. The mental health professional (MHP) initiates the rationale by stating that people who are skilled in requesting things from others usually get what they want without arguments. The Positive Request Procedure is described as a technique aimed at improving communication. It is reported that the Positive Request Procedure increases the likelihood that family members will be relatively motivated to do what is requested. It is also stated that anger and arguments will probably decrease because family members will be more likely to arrive at mutually satisfying solutions. Of course, the client and significant others are told specific reasons the Positive Request Procedure is expected to be successful for them, and questions are solicited. The following dialogue demonstrates a rationale for the Positive Request Procedure.

MHP: "People who are able to ask for things positively and convincingly usually get more of what they want without arguments. Therefore, today you are all going to learn to positively request things to improve communication in your family and increase the likelihood that each of you will get more of what you desire from other family members without arguments. The Positive Request procedure has been shown to increase compliance with requests. Anger that results from arguments will probably decrease because you will all learn to achieve mutually satisfying solutions. I am really confident that learning to make positive requests will work in your family because there is a lot of love here. How do you think this skill can help your family?"

MHP Models Positive Request (Client and Adolescent and Adult Significant Others)

After providing the rationale and obtaining feedback from the family, MHPs distribute a copy of the Positive Request Handout to all participating family members (Worksheet 8.1). The MHP states that the Positive Request Handout is used to remind family members how to make positive requests whenever things are desired, whether at home or during treatment sessions. The MHP brings copies of the Positive Request Handout to subsequent therapy sessions to positively resolve arguments if they spontaneously occur during sessions, so that family members practice appropriately asking for what they want. Prior to modeling a Positive Request, the MHP explains that all steps will be practiced in the order listed in the Positive Request Handout, but that in real-life situations it is not necessary to state all steps in the listed order. Moreover, it is unnecessary to state all steps in real-life situations. However, during sessions, all steps are conducted so the family members can practice.

MHP: Here is a handout that reveals several things that have been shown to increase the likelihood of getting others to do what you want. I want each of you to use this handout when problems are encountered in your home throughout the week, or when it is necessary to make a request for something during our sessions. We will also use Positive Request when there is an argument or someone is dissatisfied with something. You'll learn to request what you want, not what you don't want. In real-life situations, you don't have to say all the steps, and you don't have to say them in the order that is listed in your handout. However, we will practice all of these steps in the order that is listed so that it will be easier for you to learn them.

The MHP then asks for an example of something desired by one of the family members. If the MHP determines that the request has a poor likelihood of being accepted because it is unrealistic, or that the request is associated with a great deal of negative emotion, the MHP may instead initiate a hypothetical, non–emotionally laden request and attempt the more difficult scenario later. The MHP then role-plays the steps listed in the Positive Request Handout. In this role-play, the person who provided the request usually serves as the recipient of the request. This person is instructed to listen to the entire request prior to responding. The steps modeled in the role-play include the following:

1. Request a specific action using "please," and specify when the action is desired.

2. State how it would be difficult for the recipient do the action.

3. State how it would be good for the recipient if the request were performed.

4. State how it would be good for the person making the request if the request were performed.

5. Offer to help the person get the action done.

6. Offer to do something for the recipient.

7. Tell the recipient you would appreciate the action being done.

8. Suggest something that would be acceptable as an alternative action.

9. Ask the recipient to suggest an alternative in case the action can't be done.

The following exemplifies the MHP modeling a Positive Request.

MHP: Who has a request for one of the members in your family?

Brendon: Well, I would like someone to wash my car sometime this week.

MHP: Great, Dad. That sounds like a great request, so I am now going to model the Positive Request Procedure for the request you just provided me. Brendon, since you made the request, you will be the one who gets asked to wash the car. While requesting the action, I am going to attempt all the steps in the Positive Request handout. Okay, here I go. (1) Brendon, please wash my car tomorrow anytime before I go to work at 5 P.M.? (2) I know it will be difficult to wash the car because you work the day before, (3) but I also know you like driving around in a clean car. Washing the car would also give you a chance to get outside and get some fresh air, (4) and it would save me a lot of time this week so I can do my work. I know that you might be really busy, (5) so maybe we can do it together. We could spend some time together. (6) Afterwards, I'll make you a large ice tea because you'll probably be hot. (7) If you washed the car, it would mean so much to me. (8) If you can't wash it tomorrow, it would still be great if you could wash it Monday. (9) Can you think of something else that can be done to get the car washed?

After the modeled performance, the recipient should be asked to first indicate what was liked about the request, and then either accept the request or make a counter positive request. That is, an attempt to compromise by making a positive request to the MHP. The MHP should also inform the family that this is the basis of compromise.

MHP: Brendon, what did you like about the request I just made?

Brendon: I get what you are trying to do, but that request was pretty unrealistic. I don't think my car is going to get washed.

MHP: Well, that's not what I asked you. What did you like?

Brendon: Oh . . . I guess I liked the fact that when you asked me to wash the car, you were not angry—you were nice.

MHP:	You're so right. Why should I get angry? You wouldn't be very interested in responding positively to me or granting my request if I raised my voice with an angry face, would you? This is a really important point. Remember, when responding to a positive request, it is important to first indicate what was liked about the request, and either accept it or make a counter request for something different. This shows interest in compromising. That's how people are able to come to agreements, making everyone happy and helping to assure things are right for everyone, without getting angry or fighting with each other.

Client/Family Members Role-Play Positive Request
(Client and Adolescent and Adult Significant Others)

Each participating family member should practice making at least one positive request. It is best to solicit who would like to attempt the positive request first. If the MHP feels that the family understands and is willing to follow the Positive Request steps during sessions, it is best to have family members make a request that is genuinely desired by one of the family members. However, if the MHP perceives that the family is uncontrollable and unable to follow the Positive Request steps due to problems with emotional regulation or other issues, the MHP instructs the family to utilize hypothetical requests, such as requesting the other family member to buy a soda at the end of the session. Another method of managing uncontrollable clients is to have the MHP model the role of a compliant recipient. Later in therapy, after clients have had opportunities to practice Positive Request and anger has diminished, the requests may be shifted to things that are more difficult. The person making the request in the role-play scenario should be prompted to perform one step at a time, utilizing the Positive Request Handout while the recipient listens. The MHP provides descriptive praise throughout practice requests. The following dialogue demonstrates an MHP leading clients in a role-play scenario.

MHP:	I'd like you guys to practice the request now. Who would like to perform a request first?
Suzanne:	I'll give it a try.
MHP:	Fantastic! Very briefly, what is it that you'd like?

Suzanne: I'd like to have more free time.

MHP: Okay, so go ahead and use your handout to make this request. After you do each step, look at your handout to see what you need to say for the next step. I'll help you if you get stuck. Do you have any questions?

Suzanne: No questions!

MHP: Great! Let's get started. Request free time using "please" and when you want it done. Remember to state exactly what you mean by free time. *(The MHP will help Suzanne as necessary as she completes these steps for the first time, offering praise for those steps that are completed effectively, and suggestions for improvement when needed.)*

Homework Assignment

For Positive Request to generalize to the home environment, the family is given homework to practice Positive Request. For homework, MHPs provide all family members with the Positive Request Practice Assignment (Worksheet 8.2) and Positive Request Handout, and are instructed to practice making positive requests prior to next session. The family is not assigned to conduct a set number of requests, but rather to utilize the handout anytime something is desired and record one of their Positive Requests in the Positive Request Practice Assignment form. As therapy progresses, and communication skills improve, the number of practice trials decreases. However, family members are told to practice Positive Request throughout therapy when difficult interpersonally based problems are experienced. They are instructed to inform recipients when they need more time to make positive requests, and recipients are encouraged to never refuse requests outright. Rather, they are instructed to attempt compromises.

Homework Review (Client and Adolescent and Adult Significant Others)

Steps for reviewing Positive Request homework are outlined in the Positive Request Therapist Prompting Checklist for Future Sessions. MHPs initiate future Positive Request sessions by gathering completed Positive Request Practice Assignment worksheets from all participating family members (Worksheet 8.2). The Positive Request Practice Assignment worksheets are reviewed, with MHPs descriptively praising positive responses, and encouraging performance of behaviors that are not performed or performed incorrectly. Role-playing may be necessary to address particularly difficult requests, or to clarify aspects of Positive Request that appear problematic. Family members are encouraged to role-play these Positive Requests with each other, utilizing the Positive Request Handout.

Concluding Remarks

The Positive Request Procedure is the basis for all communication skills training within FBT. It may be utilized to quell arguments during sessions, or may be implemented as a prescribed therapy to address an underlying problem. When used spontaneously to circumvent arguments, the MHP can usually skip the rationale and possibly MHP modeling to practice emotional regulation. In doing so, the MHP, upon first recognition of upset (i.e., voice raised), should pass the Positive Request Handout to the person who is upset and instruct this person to make a request one step at a time. Doing so usually assists in lowering anger because the focus of conversation shifts to very manageable solution-oriented tasks. The recipient of the request is instructed to either accept the request outright or use the Positive Request Handout to make a responding request. This process continues until the issue is successfully negotiated.

Supporting Materials for Chapter 8: Enhancing Communication Skills Using Positive Request

Prompting Checklist 8.1. Positive Request Therapist Prompting Checklist for Initial Session.

POSITIVE REQUEST (PR)
THERAPIST PROMPTING CHECKLIST
Initial Session

Client ID:_____Clinician:_____ Session #:_____ Session Date:_____

Materials Required

- Positive Request Handout (PRH)
- Positive Request Practice Assignment (PRPA)

Begin Time:_____

Rationale (Client and Adolescent and Adult Significant Others)

- State each of the following:
___a. People who are skilled in requesting things from others usually get what they want w/out arguments.
___b. Positive Request (PR) is designed to improve communication.
___c. PR increases likelihood the recipient will do what is requested.
___d. Anger associated w/arguments will probably decrease due to mutually satisfying solutions.
___e. Disclose why PR will be beneficial for family.
___f. Solicit how PR will be beneficial to family.
___g. Solicit questions and provide answers.

Therapist Models Positive Request (Client and Adolescent and Adult Significant Others)

- Distribute copies of the PRH to family members.
___a. Instruct family to use PRH when things are desired from others at home or in tx. sessions.
___b. Explain all steps will be practiced in sessions as listed, but all may not be necessary at home.
___c. Solicit example of something that is desired by a family member.

___d. Model PR for solicited example, using each of the following steps w/person who gave example.

  ___1. Request specific action using "please" and saying when action is desired.
  ___2. State how it would be difficult for other person to do action.
  ___3. State how it would be good for other person if request was performed.
  ___4. State how it would be good for you if the request was performed.
  ___5. Offer to help the other person get the action done.
  ___6. Offer to do something for other person if request is performed.
  ___7. Tell other person you would appreciate the action being done.
  ___8. Suggest something that would be acceptable as an alternative action.
  ___9. Ask other person to suggest an alternative action in case the request can't be fully done.

___e. Tell recipient to state what was liked about the request.
___f. Tell recipient to either accept the request or do PR as a compromise.
  • When motivation is low, to increase client buy-in, query why each step is important.

Client/Family Members Role-Play Positive Request (Client and Adolescent and Adult Significant Others)

___a. Solicit who would like to attempt positive request first.
___b. Solicit example of something desired by the person who volunteered to do PR.
  • If request is too emotionally laden, therapist may instruct client to use a hypothetical request.
  • Client may role-play PR w/therapist first, rather than a family member.
___c. Tell recipient not to respond until all steps are finished.
___d. Tell requester to initiate PR for solicited example using each of the following steps in handout:

  ___1. Request specific action using "please" and saying when action is desired.
  ___2. State how it would be difficult for other person do action.
  ___3. State how it would be good for other person if request was performed.
  ___4. State how it would be good for you if the request was performed.
  ___5. Offer to help the other person get the action done.
  ___6. Offer to do something for other person if request is performed.
  ___7. Tell other person you would appreciate the action being done.
  ___8. Suggest something that would be acceptable as an alternative action.
  ___9. Ask other person to suggest an alternative action in case the request can't be fully done.

___e. Tell recipient to indicate what was liked about PR to requester.
___f. Tell recipient to either accept request or attempt compromise using PRH as guide.
___g. Repeat preceding steps w/client and/or family members until the steps are performed well.

Homework Assignment

• Distribute PRPA.
___a. Inform family to practice PR prior to next session whenever requests are desired.
___b. Review how to complete PRPA.

Client's Assessment of Helpfulness of the Intervention

___a.   After stating client should not feel obligated to provide high scores, as an honest assessment helps better address client needs, solicit how helpful client thought intervention was using 7-point scale:

> 7 = extremely helpful, 6 = very helpful, 5 = somewhat helpful, 4 = not sure,
> 3 = somewhat unhelpful, 2 = very unhelpful, 1 = extremely unhelpful

- **Record Client's Rating Here:** _____

___b.   Solicit how rating was derived, and methods of improving intervention in future.

Therapist's Rating of Client's Compliance with Intervention

___a.   Disclose therapist's rating of client's compliance using 7-point scale:

> 7 = extremely compliant, 6 = very compliant, 5 = somewhat compliant, 4 = neutral,
> 3 = somewhat noncompliant, 2 = very noncompliant, 1 = extremely noncompliant

- Factors that contribute to compliance ratings are:
  - Attendance.
  - Participation and conduct in session.
  - Homework completion.
- **Record Therapist's Rating of Client's Compliance Here:** _____

___b.   Disclose client's compliance rating.

___c.   Explain how rating was derived, and methods of improving performance in future.

End Time: _____

Prompting Checklist 8.2. Positive Request Therapist Prompting Checklist for Future Sessions.

POSITIVE REQUEST (PR)

THERAPIST PROMPTING CHECKLIST
Future Sessions

Client ID:_____Clinician:_____ Session #:_____ Session Date:_____

Materials Required

- Positive Request Handout (PRH)
- Positive Request Practice Assignment (PRPA)

Begin Time:_____

Homework Review (Client and All Family Members Aged 13+ Years)

- Distribute PRH
___a. Instruct family to provide completed PR homework
___b. Review homework and instruct family to role-play how PR was used   OR   if PR was not used, instruct family to role-play PR using hypothetical situation following steps in PRH.
   ___1. Request specific action using "please" and saying when action is desired.
   ___2. State how it would be difficult for other person do action.
   ___3. State how it would be good for other person if the request were performed.
   ___4. State how it would be good for you if the request were performed.
   ___5. Offer to help the other person get the action done.
   ___6. Offer to do something for other person if request is performed.
   ___7. Tell other person you would appreciate the action being done.
   ___8. Suggest something that would be acceptable as an alternative action.
   ___9. Ask other person to suggest an alternative action in case the request can't be fully done.
___c. Provide descriptive praise/corrective feedback.
___d. Instruct family to use PR prior to next session and distribute new PRPA.

Client's Assessment of Helpfulness of the Intervention

___a. After stating client should not feel obligated to provide high scores, as an honest assessment helps better address client needs, solicit how helpful client thought intervention was using 7-point scale:
   7 = extremely helpful, **6** = very helpful, **5** = somewhat helpful, **4** = not sure, **3** = somewhat unhelpful, **2** = very unhelpful, **1** = extremely unhelpful
- **Record Client's Rating Here:** _____
___b. Solicit how rating was derived, and methods of improving intervention in future.

Therapist's Rating of Client's Compliance with Intervention

___a.   Disclose therapist's rating of client's compliance using 7-point scale:

      7 = extremely compliant, **6** = very compliant, **5** = somewhat compliant, **4** = neutral,

      3 = somewhat noncompliant, **2** = very noncompliant, **1** = extremely noncompliant

- Factors that contribute to compliance ratings are:
  - Attendance.
  - Participation and conduct in session.
  - Homework completion.
- **Record Therapist's Rating of Client's Compliance Here:** _____

___b.   Disclose client's compliance rating.

___c.   Explain how rating was derived, and methods of improving performance in future.

End Time: _____

Worksheet 8.1. Positive Request Handout.

POSITIVE REQUEST HANDOUT

1. Request a specific action using "please" and specify when action is desired.

2. State how it would be difficult for other person to do action.

3. State how it would be good for other person if the request was performed.

4. State how it would be good for you if the request was performed.

5. Offer to help other person get the action done.

6. Offer to do something for other person.

7. Tell the other person that you would appreciate the action being done.

8. Suggest something that would be acceptable as an alternative action.

9. Ask other person to suggest an alternative in case the action can't be done.

Worksheet 8.2. Positive Request Practice Assignment.

POSITIVE REQUEST PRACTICE ASSIGNMENT

Client ID:_____Clinician:_____ Session #:_____ Session Date:_____

Instructions: Write a description of what was requested and how you used each step of Positive Request.

What was requested:	_____ _____ _____ _____
Did you say please: (check one)	☐ Yes ☐ No
Did you state when the action was desired: (check one)	☐ Yes ☐ No
How would it be difficult for the person to do:	_____ _____ _____
How would it be good for the other person:	_____ _____ _____ _____
How would it be good for you if action was performed:	_____ _____ _____ _____
How did you offer to help the other person get the action done:	_____ _____ _____
What did you offer to do for the other person:	_____ _____ _____
Did you tell the other person you would appreciate the action being done?	☐ Yes ☐ No
What did you suggest as an alternative action:	_____ _____ _____ _____
How did you ask the other person to provide an alternative action:	_____ _____ _____
What was the result of the request:	_____ _____ _____

Restructuring the Environment to Facilitate a Drug-Free Lifestyle

Rationale and Overview

There are stimuli or things in the environment that make drug use more, or less, likely to occur (e.g., people, places, objects, odors, tastes). For instance, people may encourage drug use or prime drug urges due to their past associations with drug use. Some stimuli contribute to negative emotional states, such as increased stress or anxiety, which in turn may lead to drug use as a means of removing these aversive states. Time spent in places such as bars, nightclubs, or friends' apartments are notorious "triggers" for drug use, as is contact with objects that have become associated with drug use, such as drug use paraphernalia. Other common situational antecedents to drug use include arguments and aversive confrontations, traumatic experiences, unemployment, sudden loss of loved ones, boredom, ill health, chronic pain, visceral excitement, celebrations, and having cash. Conversely, people who are associated with abstinence from drugs usually act to buffer against drug use, as these individuals are more likely to engage in non-drug-associated activities (e.g., jogging and other sport activities, employment, child care). Places that act to buffer drug use often include churches, schools, and employment agencies, where drug use is relatively difficult. Similarly, there are stimuli that increase the likelihood of other problem behaviors, such as nightmares (e.g., a veteran watching war-related movies), obesity (e.g., leaving a cake on the counter), stealing (e.g., visiting a store that has very little security), unemployment (e.g, stress), depression (e.g., marital arguments), violence (e.g., living with a violent partner), child neglect (e.g., being distracted due to presence of stressors), contracting HIV (e.g., going on a date with a sexually promiscuous stranger), and so on. Conversely, there are stimuli that prevent, or are incompatible with, such behavior (e.g., not leaving "taboo" foods on the counter, communicating things that are desired in a positive manner, monogamous sexual partners). Therefore, the aim of Environmental (Stimulus) Control is to identify, monitor, and eliminate or control stimuli that have led to or influenced drug use or problem behaviors in the past and assist clients in spending more time with drug-incompatible "safe" stimuli doing "safe" activities. In doing so, it is important to teach skills that will assist clients to avoid or escape from at-risk stimuli and plan ways to spend more time with safe stimuli. Given that at-risk stimuli often occur unexpectedly, clients are taught to identify where and when at-risk stimuli are likely to occur, and develop plans for managing such stimuli when avoidance is impossible.

In conducting Environmental Control, the mental health professional (MHP) first assists the client and adult significant others in creating a comprehensive list of behavioral stimuli that decrease the likelihood of drug use and other problem behaviors (safe list). Later, a list of behavioral stimuli that increase the client's likelihood of drug use and other problem behaviors is developed (at-risk list). Once the lists are obtained, the client, participating significant others, and the MHP review the amount of time spent with safe and at-risk stimuli. In this review, the MHP attempts to identify behaviors the client demonstrated that increased time spent with safe stimuli, encourages those behaviors, and further assists the client in spending more time with safe stimuli. The MHP also attempts to identify behaviors that were performed to avoid or escape from at-risk stimuli. MHPs then utilize various specified behavioral interventions to encourage and teach clients and significant others repertoires to spend more time with safe stimuli, and to avoid or escape from at-risk stimuli. These interventions include descriptive praise, behavioral rehearsal, self-control, job interviewing skills training, and communication skills training. While reviewing the safe and at-risk lists, MHPs may spontaneously add goals to their Goal Worksheet (see Chapter 5), and a family activity is always scheduled at the end of the session in "safe" environments and subsequently reviewed during the next session. Although children are not involved in most aspects of Environmental Control, they are involved in the scheduling and review of family activities.

Goals for Intervention

➤ Assist the client and participating adult significant others in identifying stimuli that increase (at-risk stimuli) and decrease (safe stimuli) the likelihood of drug use and other problem behaviors.

➤ Assist the client in increasing time spent with safe stimuli and decrease time with at-risk stimuli.

Materials Required

➤ Environmental (Stimulus) Control Therapist Prompting Checklist for Initial Session (Prompting Checklist 9.1, also located on the CD that accompanies this book)

➤ Environmental (Stimulus) Control Therapist Prompting Checklist for Future Sessions (Prompting Checklist 9.2, also located on the CD that accompanies this book)

➤ Safe and At-Risk Association List (Worksheet 9.1, also located on the CD that accompanies this book)

➤ Things To Do and Places I Like to Visit Worksheet (two copies) (Worksheet 9.2, also located on the CD that accompanies this book)

➤ Things That May Lead to Drug Use and Other Problem Behaviors (two copies) (Worksheet 9.3, also located on the CD that accompanies this book)

➤ Family Invitation for Fun (Worksheet 9.4, also located on the CD that accompanies this book)

Procedural Steps for Treatment Implementation

Initial Session

Rationale for Environmental (Stimulus) Control (Client and Adult Significant Others) The steps required to initiate the Environmental Control intervention are contained in the Environmental Control Therapist Prompting Checklist for Initial Session (Prompting Checklist 9.1). The rationale for Environmental Control begins by explaining to clients and significant others that there are things in the environment that make drug use and other problem behaviors more likely and less likely to occur. They are informed that they will be assisted in developing a list of people, places, and situations that have involved drug use and other problem behaviors (an "at-risk" list) and another list of people, places, and situations that have not involved drug use and other problem behaviors (a "safe" list). If specific problem behaviors have been identified (e.g., stealing, unemployment), these behaviors can be included as potential targets in this intervention. It is further explained that items in these lists will be extensively reviewed so that appropriate interventions may be planned and implemented. As usual, the MHP underscores the effectiveness of this intervention, and provides the client with an explicit reason the intervention is expected to be effective. Most clients are intimately familiar with the preceding information and easily understand the idea that certain stimuli in the environment increase their risk for drug use, making the rationale for this intervention quick and easy to implement. The client and adult significant others are present when MHPs present this rationale. The following is an example of a rationale conducted with a client, who had drug abuse and sexual promiscuity as problem behaviors.

MHP: There are people, places, and situations that make it easier to stay clean from drugs and avoid dangerous sexual activities, which are both problem behaviors you identified on the Behavioral Goals Worksheet. Of course, there are also people, places, and situations that make it more difficult to stay clean from drugs and avoid behaviors that put you at increased risk of contracting HIV or other sexually transmitted diseases. Together, you will both help me construct a list of people, places, and situations that have been associated with Nina's drug use and sexual promiscuity in the past, which we'll call an "at-risk" list. During separate interviews, you will each help me develop this at-risk list of people, places, and situations that have been associated with Nina's drug use and sexual promiscuity. You will also both help me to develop a "safe" list for Nina. That is, a list that includes people, places, and situations that decrease the chances that she will engage in drug use or promiscuous sexual behaviors. These lists will be reviewed in future sessions to assist in developing skills to help Nina spend more time with things that are listed in the safe list and less time with things in the at-risk list. In reviewing these lists, we'll also have opportunities to set new goals that will help Nina eliminate drug use and undesired sexual behaviors, and develop plans to accomplish these goals. This intervention has shown great success with others who have complicated problems, and I think it will be especially effective with you, Nina, because your sister is available to spend an extended amount of time with you in the evenings. Do either of you have any questions before we begin?

Obtaining "Safe" Associations (Client and Adult Significant Others)

After the rationale is provided, the MHP, in a neutral and nonjudgmental manner, prompts the client and adult significant others to report all people, situations, and activities (stimuli) for which the client has had repeated contact without drug use. If other problem behaviors are being targeted (e.g., stealing, depression), the MPH should additionally ensure that the obtained stimuli have not been associated with these target behaviors. Thus, stimuli in the safe list are likely to bring about healthy goal-directed behavior. MHPs may need to query about stimuli that have not been a part of the client's recent life in developing this list. For instance, clients may have had old friends who were abstinent from substances many years ago. Another strategy in obtaining safe stimuli is to assess abstinent people (and activities) that clients think would be enjoyable but have yet to experience. These stimuli will be listed in the safe associations column of the Safe and At-Risk Associations List at the end of this chapter (Worksheet 9.1).

While attempting to generate safe stimuli, clients and significant others may mention that a stimulus has preceded or has been associated with past drug use or other targeted behaviors. When this occurs, the stimulus should be immediately listed in the At Risk column of the client's at-risk associations list. After the MHP has exhausted all possibilities, the List of Things to Do and Places I Like to Visit worksheet is provided to the client to prompt additional safe associations (Worksheet 9.2). This worksheet contains commonly reported safe associations that are helpful to prompt clients when developing their safe lists. It is advisable to check to ensure all generated stimuli have never been associated with drug use or other target behaviors. It is appropriate to separate risk factors from safe stimuli. For instance, if a client indicated that she argued with her husband only when he came home late, "husband coming home after 8 P.M." could be recorded as an at-risk item, whereas "being with husband prior to 8 P.M." could remain on the safe list. If time permits, it is always good to solicit things that are liked and disliked about safe stimuli to facilitate an understanding of potential obstacles to spending more time with safe situations, and conceptualize values that are desired by clients so these can be pointed out in subsequent treatment when they occur. Knowing what is not liked about safe stimuli provides MHPs opportunities to assist clients in appropriately making attempts to rectify them. For instance, if a client indicated that she didn't like how her mother nags her for eating too much, effective solutions could be generated, such as requesting the mother to make supportive comments when weight goals were accomplished, involving the mother in her weight loss program, and so on. In situations where the client and participating adult significant others disagree about which list to put a person into, the person should conservatively be moved to the at-risk list, or if left in the Safe Associations List, an asterisk may be put next to the respective stimulus to ensure the stimulus is reviewed with enhanced sensitivity. The following example dialogue with Nina and her sister Heather illustrates how to generate a list of safe stimuli relating to Nina's goals of decreasing substance use and decreasing episodes of child neglect.

MHP: Who are some people who do not use drugs and distract you away from effective parenting?

Nina: Well, there is my brother Jim and my best friend Jessica.

Heather: What about Mom? She is a good influence and really wants to help.

MHP: Okay, those sound like three good choices. Nina, to the best of your knowledge, would you say these people are clean from drugs and benefit your children in some way?

Nina: I think all of them are drug free, and they all want me to be a better parent.

Heather: But what about Jessica? She just stopped smoking pot and drinking a few weeks ago, when you did.

MHP: That is a good point, Heather. Let's put all of these people in the Safe column of the Safe and At-Risk Associations List, except Jessica. We'll put her in the At-Risk column of the Safe and At-Risk Associations List. Nina, it may be that Jessica doesn't use drugs anymore, but I want to put her there so we can be more ready to manage risky situations that may occur when you spend time with her, since she is early on in her own attempts to eliminate her substance use. *(The MHP would attempt to solicit more persons in a similar manner as the preceding.)* Now, let's generate some positive activities or places you like to visit that do not involve drug use or other problem behavior.

Nina: I like to play tennis at the park with Jessica. Also, I like playing my guitar. I remember going on vacations with my mom and the kids, and those were always fun.

Heather: When I used to come over more, we played board games with the kids, and I think we all liked that.

Nina: That's right. You always seem to get all the property and money by the end! *(laughs)*

MHP: What a job! I like how you provided me a lot of things that you can do with your children that do not involve drug use. Nina, have you ever used drugs or been unable to effectively parent in these situations?

Nina: The only thing is that when we used to go on family vacations, my mom would often spoil the kids, which bugged me and we usually ended up arguing about it in front of the kids. Also, sometimes after playing tennis with Jessica, we would smoke pot together.

MHP: I'm glad you're sensitive to these concerns. I can see how arguments would not be good for your daughter and son. Let's keep your mother on the safe list, but put arguments with mom and mom spoiling children as potential targets. Also, let's put playing tennis with Jessica on the at-risk list for now because you did use drugs after that activity in the past. I am also interested in knowing places you like to take your children that do not involve drug use and are good for their development in some way.

Nina: We used to go to church more than we do now, and that always felt safe. I don't use drugs at my mom's house.

Heather: You don't use drugs at my house, either!

MHP: Great, I'll list these places in your Safe column. Now Nina, tell me some things that Heather likes to do, or places she and you like to go that do not involve drug use or other problem behaviors.

Nina: We like to go shopping together at the mall.

MHP: Great, I recorded that in your safe list. Just to be sure, none of these things have occurred before drug use or during drug use, right?

Nina: Yes, that is correct.

Heather: Yes, that is true.

Exhibit 9.1 presents an example of a Safe and At-Risk Associations List that is completed based on some of the dialogue reviewed above thus far. The exhibit contains the safe people, activities, and places in the Safe column, including Nina's brother Jim and her mom; playing the guitar and board games; and her mom's and sister's homes, among others. Because three at-risk associations came up during the course of the dialogue (her friend Jessica, arguing with her mother, and playing tennis with Jessica), these were listed in the At-Risk column. The MHP will return to the At-Risk list column later in the interview, when specifically focusing on identification of at-risk stimuli with Nina and Heather.

The following dialogue demonstrates how the MHP is able to use the Things to Do and Places I Like to Visit Worksheet with Nina and Heather after they no longer are able to generate safe people, activities, and places:

MHP: You were able to get a lot of safe items. Here is a list of things to do and visit that are usually not associated with drug use or problem behaviors *(hands the worksheet to client and significant other)*. Read this list and check off which ones you'd enjoy and that have never been associated with drug use or other problem behaviors.

Nina: I like going to movies and restaurants and playing with my dog.

MHP: Great, Nina, I just recorded those in your safe list. *(The therapist would continue to generate safe items from this list in a similar manner.)* We were able to get a lot of safe items quickly, and so, Nina, tell me a few things that you like and do not like about some of the stimuli we recorded. This will assist me in getting a better

Exhibit 9.1. Example of Partially Completed Safe and At-Risk Associations List for Nina.

SAFE AND AT-RISK ASSOCIATIONS LIST

Instructions: Please indicate each day you spent time with each item on your safe list and at-risk list over the past week.

Safe List	Mon	Tues	Wed	Thur	Fri	Sat	Sun	At-Risk List	Mon	Tues	Wed	Thur	Fri	Sat	Sun
Jim (brother)						X		Jessica							
Mom								Argues with Mom							
Playing guitar								After Tennis							
Family vacations															
Board games															
Church															
Mom's house															
Heather's house															

145

understanding of some of the things you enjoy and don't enjoy in life. Let's start with your mom.

Nina: I love that I can trust my mom, but I don't like arguing with her.

MHP: That is great that she can be trusted. Maybe she can hold onto your paychecks until you're able to establish sobriety. Should I add that as a goal in your Behavioral Goals and Rewards Recording form?

Nina: Yes, that would be great.

MHP: Great, so I'll add that to your Behavioral Goals and Rewards form as a goal. I'll also put giving paychecks to your mother in the safe list. We already have arguments in your at-risk list. *(MHP goes on to review things that are liked and disliked about other generated safe stimuli.)*

Exhibit 9.2 presents a part of the Things to Do and Places I Like to Visit Worksheet that Nina completed. The boxes for "Going to restaurants," "Going to movies or attending plays," and "Playing/Walking with a pet" are checked. Once completed, the MHP transfers these safe list items to the Safe and At-Risk Associations List Worksheet.

"At-Risk" Associations Rationale—Optional (Client and Adult Significant Others)

Although not necessary, it is often helpful to provide a rationale relevant to transitioning from the generation of safe stimuli to the generation of at-risk stimuli. For instance, the MHP may alleviate potential defensiveness by blaming the client's past time with at-risk stimuli on environmental circumstances that may have been out of the client's control. It is also important to let the client and participating adult significant others know that outcomes are usually best when significant others are involved in developing, and subsequently reviewing, the at-risk list. Along these lines, they are told that the MHP usually meets with the client and adult significant others separately to gather at-risk items so that the reporting of one does not bias or otherwise influence the reporting of the other, which often increases the number of at-risk items identified. While MHPs strongly encourage clients and significant others to be forthright with each other throughout the process, each will be asked while alone if there is any information that should remain confidential. MHPs explain that they will attempt to identify methods of discussing confidential information to the extent possible when it is directly relevant to the Environmental Control intervention.

Exhibit 9.2. Sampling of "Safe" Items from the Things to Do and Places I Like to Visit Worksheet.

THINGS TO DO AND PLACES I LIKE TO VISIT

Instructions: Put a check mark next to each thing you like to do and place you like to visit that does not involve drug use and benefits your family.

Leisure Activities

- ❏ Going to parks
  - ○ Fishing in the local ponds
  - ○ Feeding the ducks
  - ○ Playing tennis/volleyball
- ☑ Going to restaurants
- ❏ Visiting museum/historical landmarks
- ❏ Visiting Visitor Center for local lakes or state or federal parks
  - • Kids can become Jr. Rangers and earn badges.
  - • Nature walks/hikes.
  - • Guided tours or learning workshops.
- ☑ Going to the movies or attending plays
  - • Free movies at local libraries
  - • Inexpensive plays at schools/universities
- ❏ Gardening
- ☑ Playing/Walking with a pet
- ❏ Doing arts/crafts
  - • See attached sheet for fun family craft ideas and resources.
- ❏ Active recreation: Participating in sport leagues, bicycling, dirt bike riding, ice-skating, skateboarding
  - • Review newspaper for community events sponsoring these types of free or discounted events.
  - • Community centers often have inexpensive swimming pools.
  - • Community centers may have free dance classes.

It is almost always the case that clients will agree to these procedures, but in some cases clients or their significant others request that they develop the lists together. In such cases, we recommend that they develop the lists separately to facilitate candid responses, but also to facilitate effective brainstorming that is not biased by input from the other. MHPs may use the following dialogue as a model to transition from generation of safe stimuli to generation of at-risk stimuli with Nina, who has also listed stealing as one of her problem behaviors.

MHP: Now, we will compile an at-risk list that will help me to identify all the people, places, and situations that put you at risk to use drugs, and increase the chances of you stealing something. Nina, for most of your life you were exposed to other drug users and people who approved of stealing, and this exposure was initially out of your control. Of course, it is extremely hard to sever these relationships, but I'm so happy with your commitment to talk about some of these influences with Heather and me. We've found best results when both our clients and their significant others are involved in the development of the at-risk list. However, I'd like to work with each of you individually in developing these at-risk lists so I can take advantage of both of your individual perspectives. We have found that we can identify more at-risk items when we do this separately because you don't bias each other's reports.

Heather: I think it is great that she is going to talk about these things, since they have troubled her and our family for a long time.

MHP: If there are no questions, let's start with you, Nina.

Obtaining "At-Risk" Associations (Client)

MHPs begin generating at-risk associations with clients. In a neutral and nonjudgmental manner, MHPs prompt clients to provide a list of people with whom they have used drugs and may have future contact, or who in some way influence drug use or other problems indirectly, such as by increasing stress or other negative emotional states. A similar at-risk list is generated for other problem behaviors. These stimuli are recorded in the At-Risk column of the Safe and At-Risk Associations List (Worksheet 9.1). In some cases, clients may indicate that they do not want to put people on the at-risk list due to fears that significant others or MHPs will prevent them from spending time with these persons once their names are disclosed. In such cases, it should be explained that these persons may elicit strong visceral cravings or desires for drug use if they have used drugs with the client in the past, particularly if these persons are still using drugs or engaging in other risky problem behaviors. MHPs should also emphasize that these persons are not considered "bad" people and may, in fact, benefit them in some ways. However, MHPs further explain that since clients ultimately determine whom they spend time with, if they decide to spend time with these persons, they are at risk to use drugs or experience other problems, so they should take precautions to prevent these things from happening when spending time with these at-risk individuals. Examples of preventative measures might include having at least one safe person present in activities involving at-risk persons, and limiting contacts to safe places. Clients are also told that persons who have an extended history and commitment to drug abstinence and healthy living (e.g., sponsor of Alcoholics Anonymous) may be recorded in the safe list if there is no history of past drug use with client. When clients do not want to mention names because they are concerned these people will get into trouble, MHPs may replace their names with unique, and ideally derogatory, characteristics that describe them (e.g., gold-toothed pusher), or include at-risk persons in safe lists with asterisks next to their names. During the generation of at-risk items, MHPs may also suggest goals for therapy.

After clients respond with all the at-risk people, places, and situations they can think of, MHPs provide them with the Things That May Lead to Drug Use and Other Problem Behaviors list, which is included at the end of this chapter (Worksheet 9.3). This list may prove useful to assist clients in identifying other at-risk items that either they forgot to mention, or that they had not previously associated with drug use or other problem behavior. MHPs ask clients to indicate items from this list that have been found to be associated with drug use or other problem behaviors in the past. MHPs subsequently query how these stimuli put clients at risk, and summarize these circumstances in the At-Risk column of the Safe and At-Risk Associations List. Whenever time permits, clients are queried to discuss the things that are liked and disliked about the at-risk items to identify potential reinforcers that may be stressed during reviews of safe stimuli. That is, if a client indicates he likes hanging out with one of his at-risk friends because this friend makes him laugh, the MHP can point out when persons on his safe list are humorous and assist the client in finding safe friends with a good sense of humor. MHPs provide empathy when clients report things that are disliked about at-risk stimuli and attempt to solicit things in the safe list that might help to replace or satisfy desired aspects of at-risk stimuli.

The following dialogue depicts implementation of the at-risk list generation with a client who is resistant to disclosing the identity of an at-risk person.

MHP: Nina, who are all the people in your life with whom you have used drugs, or who have influenced you to use drugs?

Nina: I guess there are lots of people. A bunch of my friends—Marvina, Justin, Jackie. Some of my family members influence my drug use, too, like my dad and my sister Heather. Then, of course, the guy

	who gets me my drugs, but I can't tell you his name because he wouldn't like that. I guess there are also all those people I meet when I go out partying, but I don't know half their names anyway.
MHP:	That's a great start. I'm proud of you for being so candid. Can you tell me why you put your father on the list?
Nina:	Because he stresses me out.
MHP:	I'd like to record specific things that stress you out about your father.
Nina:	Okay, so like whenever I go over to his house, he pressures me to drink with him. And when I say I can't or even if I do it, we always end up arguing about stuff—I can't even remember what exactly.
MHP:	I'll record these specific stressors in your at-risk list. Pressuring to drink and arguing. Later we'll practice strategies to help cope with them. I'm familiar with why you put the others in your list, but I thought your sister Heather doesn't have a history of drug use. Why is she on the list?
Nina:	You know I love Heather and love to have her around, but we don't see eye to eye on how to discipline my kids. She is pretty tough, and I think she sometimes oversteps her boundaries. We end up arguing about that, sometimes in front of the kids. It really stresses me out, and I often end up smoking pot afterwards to try to relax.
MHP:	I agree that is not a good thing for the kids to see you and your sister arguing. Heather is on your safe list because she doesn't use drugs and cares for your children while you're at work. However, this is a legitimate concern that must be addressed. I should have recognized this as a problem when we reviewed your safe list. I'll keep Heather in the safe list and put arguments about disciplining in your at-risk list. I wanted to remind you that everything is confidential if you want it to be, but I think it would be good for us to work on this with Heather because I think she is probably unhappy about the situation, too. What do you think?
Nina:	I think that would be a big relief if we could stop arguing about this crap.

MHP: That's great—so I'll put "Argue with Heather" in your at-risk list. Now, I remember that you did not want to identify your drug dealer. Like I said before, everything is confidential if you want it to be. However, I wonder if you would permit me to record a code name or some characteristic to describe this person. In this way, I can discuss important issues that put you at risk, while maintaining confidentiality.

Nina: Just put down Sam.

MHP: Great, I'll put Sam on your at-risk list. Now, let's identify some other people for your at-risk list.

Nina: You can put my supervisor on there. He swears at me, which stresses me out and makes me angry!

MHP: Well, you probably won't be able to avoid your boss, unless you want to get another job. However, we can write "boss criticizing" in your at-risk list. Later, we'll practice methods of effectively responding to these situations. Tell me some places you have used drugs in the past.

Nina: There is the park because I used to smoke pot there after tennis and would buy drugs there sometimes. Also, the bar two blocks down was a major place where I used.

MHP: I'm putting these places in your list. Tell me some situations that have influenced you to use drugs or have been associated with your use of drugs.

Nina: It seems like whenever I go to a party at someone's house, I end up using drugs.

The MHP would continue to identify at-risk items in a similar manner. The following dialogue shows how the MHP shifts to using the worksheet to identify more items.

MHP: Outstanding job! This is a great list so far. Now, look at the Things That May Lead to Drug Use and Other Problem Behaviors form and try to use it to think of additional at-risk stimuli.

Nina: Here are two I did not think of—being alone or lonely and being bored. When that happens, I start thinking about using drugs.

If I'm shopping and this happens, I also think about stealing as a challenge.

MHP: Great, now let's talk about what you like and dislike about each of these stimuli. First, what do you like and dislike about your boss?

Nina: I like that he is smart, works hard, and gets a lot done. He also gives me lots of overtime hours. But he can really be insensitive and gets angry sometimes, which is really hard to deal with.

MHP: It is just like you to recognize the positive qualities in others. It also shows how you're a hard worker. I'm sorry to learn he's insensitive. That is always a tough thing to experience, but you need the work just the same. Later we'll learn to manage these situations.

Nina: I usually just shut up as soon as he starts raising his voice.

MHP: That makes sense because you don't want to get fired. However, perhaps we can spend some time reviewing methods of making positive requests as an alternative. Oh, look at the time. I need to meet with your sister Heather to determine if she can tell me any additional at-risk items. I'd like to review more things you like and dislike about the items in your list later. I like to be up front with significant others about your list, but wanted to ask if there is anything that you want me to keep confidential?

Nina: My friend Cardelle is Heather's ex-boyfriend, and she used to get really jealous when I used drugs with him, but I think it might be okay to mention he is on the at-risk list.

MHP: I will keep that in mind, although I bet she will like his being on the at-risk list.

Obtaining "At-Risk" Stimuli (Adult Significant Other)

After the MHP completes the at-risk list with the client, the client is then excused and the adult significant other is asked to come into the room. All at-risk stimuli are reported to the significant other, with the exception of stimuli that were requested to be confidential by the client. The significant other is then asked to list additional persons, places, and situations that have been associated with the client's drug use or other problem behaviors.

The methods of soliciting, recording, and reviewing these stimuli are the same as those utilized with the client.

Reviewing "At-Risk" and "Safe" Associations List (Client and Adult Significant Others)

After completing the at-risk list with the significant other, the client is instructed to come back into the room, and both the client and significant other are descriptively praised for their work in developing the lists, including their honesty. The MHP solicits how they can increase more enjoyable time with safe stimuli. In this regard, it is very important that MHPs solicit specific details involved in these strategies. Whenever possible, goals are recorded in the Goals Worksheet (see Chapter 5, Behavioral Goals and Rewards Worksheet), and MHPs provide solutions to assist the practical implementation of time spent with safe stimuli. For the at-risk list, MHPs spend time discussing how more time can be spent avoiding or managing at-risk stimuli, and goals are recorded in the Goals Worksheet, whenever possible. The following dialogue contains an excerpt of a typical review of items on the at-risk and safe lists.

MHP: You were both fabulous in developing a lot of safe and at-risk stimuli. As far as I can tell, you were both honest and very straightforward. This will go a long way in the upcoming sessions involving this intervention. How can you both spend more time this upcoming week with safe stimuli?

Nina: We could try to avoid arguments *(referring to her and her sister)*.

MHP: That is a great idea. How will you two avoid arguments?

Nina: I could try to use the handout you gave us, the Positive Request Handout, and see if that helps.

MHP: I'm so proud of you. I'll put that on your Behavioral Goals and Rewards Worksheet. What other things can you do to stay clean and problem free?

The MHP would continue to review additional safe items, and then do the same for the at-risk list, as indicated in the following dialogue.

MHP: Let's review some things you can both do to avoid or manage at-risk stimuli.

Heather: We could take the kids and the dog for a walk after dinner.

MHP: That is absolutely fantastic! I especially like that one because it will keep you busy and improve your family relationships. What will you do to control your impulses if you spontaneously decide to change your plans?

The MHP would continue to assist the client and her significant other in the identification of strategies to decrease time with at-risk stimuli for the upcoming week. To the extent possible, MHPs should problem-solve with clients and significant others for "hypothetical" situations that might arise. This is particularly important if the MHP suspects, based on information gained from the session, that some situations might prove particularly challenging in the upcoming week. For example, while Nina and Heather have set a goal of walking after dinner, Nina sometimes stays late at work to get extra pay or has visited the local bar for drinks after work if stressed. Given this knowledge, the MHP would problem-solve these potential difficulties with Nina and Heather to help ensure that they meet their goals.

Planning a Family Activity (Client and All Significant Others, Including Children if Available)

The last part of the initial session of Environmental Control involves scheduling a pleasant family activity that is relatively novel. All family members, including small children and infants, are encouraged to attend. When children are available, they are usually very excited to participate, and should be chiefly involved in generating the activity. It is helpful to emphasize activities that are inexpensive, fun, interactive, educational, and involve physical activity. Families can use the Things to Do and Places I Like to Visit Worksheet to help generate activities. Once an activity is identified, the Family Invitation for Fun form (Worksheet 9.4) is completed to assist in increasing the likelihood the activity will be performed as prescribed. This form requires family members to record what the activity will involve, when it will occur, and who will participate. It is important to let the family members know the activity will be reviewed during the next session to promote accountability.

Future Sessions

Reviewing Safe and At-Risk Associations List (Client and Significant Others) As indicated in the Environmental Control MHP Prompting Checklist for Future Sessions (Prompting Checklist 9.2), all future sessions involving Environmental Control involve first instructing clients to complete the Safe and At-Risk Associations worksheet. Clients are instructed to record a check mark in the column and row corresponding to each safe and at-risk stimulus in which time was spent since the last session. Thus, as indicated in Exhibit 9.1, if a client spent time with her "safe" brother Jim on Saturday, a check is recorded in the column marked Saturday and the row that includes the name of the brother. Prior to completing the form, it is critical for MHPs to explicitly state that they will focus their discussions on clients' strengths and positive behaviors (rather than on weaknesses or negative behaviors). With this assurance, clients feel less defensive about potential negative events and behaviors that occurred during the prior week, such as substance use, and so are more willing to candidly report and discuss these matters. MHPs typically review all endorsed safe stimuli prior to reviewing endorsed at-risk stimuli. However, MHPs are free to alternate in their review of safe and at-risk stimuli based on priority or preference. For instance, an MHP may wish to review all endorsed at-risk items first, and finish with a review of safe items to end on a positive note. Regardless of the approach used for review, for each endorsed item, MHPs first solicit actions that were performed to avoid drug use or other problem behaviors (in reviews of at-risk and safe stimuli), and then descriptively praise performance of these actions. If drug use or other problem behavior is indicated, clients are asked to indicate how they intended or attempted to stay drug free or problem free. Again, the responses of clients are descriptively praised, and they are encouraged to make and assisted in making plans to stay clean and avoid behavior problems in the future. Therefore, mistakes and efforts to use drugs or engage in other problem behaviors are essentially ignored. Rather, the client is encouraged to report plans that are relevant to spending more time with safe stimuli in the future.

FBT interventions are initiated during the review to assist in solving problems that are likely to occur in the future. For instance, MHPs may encourage or facilitate the generation of goals for inclusion on the Behavioral Goals and Rewards Worksheet (see Behavioral Goals and Rewards, Chapter 5), teach clients to respond in a job interview (see Job-Getting Skills Training, Chapter 11), create or balance a financial budget (see Financial Management, Chapter 12), practice a request (see Positive Request Procedure, Chapter 8), or manage a negative impulse (see Self-Control, Chapter 10). Therefore, the focus of the review is on the prevention of future undesired behaviors through encouragement and practice of desired behaviors. The number of items reviewed in any session is ultimately determined by the client and MHP and guided by practical considerations, such as time constraints. However, significant others are included in this process whenever possible. Indeed, significant others are prompted for assistance and support throughout the review, as indicated in the following dialogue.

> *MHP:*   Last week we obtained lists of items that either increase or decrease your risk for using drugs and experiencing other difficulties, such as problems effectively caring for your children. We put them on this form. In going over these for this session, if you spent time with one of the people, places, or situations listed, I want you to put a check in the row that includes that item and the column that represents the day you spent time with it. Do the same for the remaining items. It is important for you to know that when we review your responses, I will emphasize your strengths and things you do that are positive. Together, we will generate solutions to problems you may have experienced in staying clean from drugs and free from other troubles.

After the MHP permits the client to complete the form, the MHP may either select items to review that are contemporaneously important and/or permit the client and significant others to determine items to emphasize in the review.

> *MHP:*   Tell me something that is listed in your safe list that you would like to review first. I'm particularly interested in knowing what you did to stay clean from drugs and benefit your children.

> *Nina:*   I spent a lot more time with my kids and Heather, and got more exercise than I had in a long time because of our family walks after dinner.

> *MHP:*   That's wonderful! Exercise is so incompatible with drug use, and if you do it hard enough you can even get what has been coined a runner's high.

Nina: Well, I don't think I exercised that hard, but I really enjoyed watching the kids have fun and talking with Heather. She was really great watching the kids this week.

MHP: Heather, way to go! You guys are starting to really work as a team with the kids. I wonder if you guys could work out together at home sometimes. Heather, I know you'd be interested, and it would be good for your kids to see you modeling exercise.

Heather: I'd like to work out with Nina, but after Nina comes home from work and we have dinner, I am pretty tired and it is getting pretty late, so I am not sure if I would be able to do it.

Nina: It does sound like a pretty big commitment. I don't think it is realistic, although it would be great to do this together.

MHP: Nina, remember you both agreed you'd encourage each other. I have another way I'd like you both to resolve this dilemma. Two weeks ago you both practiced Positive Request. Nina, I'd like you to please make a request of your sister to exercise. Let me get out my Positive Request Worksheets from my files. . . .

In the preceding example, the MHP goes on to implement the Positive Request Procedure. The MHP puts aside the Safe and At-Risk Associations List and takes out all materials necessary to implement the Positive Request Procedure. After this intervention is completed, the MHP again takes out the Safe and At-Risk Associations List and resumes the review of this form.

While the review focuses on the strengths and positive behaviors of the client and significant others, it is often the case that negative behaviors occur between sessions, and MHPs need to address these in the review process. The following dialogue demonstrates the review of a common negative behavior in which the client used drugs when spending time with Jessica, a person on her at-risk list.

MHP: I absolutely love how you tried to invite your sister to be around when you hung out with Jessica. How did your actions keep you clean from using drugs?

Nina: I just kept suggesting we go to the restaurant, and when Jessica brought up drugs I used the broken record technique to say I didn't use anymore. I also told my sister to never let her get us to go down-town. I knew she respected my sister too much to go against her.

MHP: I'm really proud of you. Did you get any urges to use, and if so, how did you handle these?

Nina: Well *(looking embarrassed and sad)*, I did get them. In fact, I should mention that behind my sister's back I told Jessica to meet me out-side the house. Later, we smoked a couple of joints.

Heather: I knew you used! What a fool I was to believe your lies again!

MHP: I can see how both of you are very upset. First, Nina, I'd like to say I'm glad you had the courage to tell us you used, and I know you must be disappointed you won't be able to take advantage of the re-ward trip to the play that Heather planned for next week in celebra-tion of being clean for your first month in over 2 years. However, the important thing is that you learn to respond better to urges in the future. Although it wasn't selected in your treatment plan until much later, I think practicing the Self-Control intervention will help you manage your urges. We'll do that in a few minutes. However, this experience shows that Jessica is too big a trigger to spend time with, even with trusted, safe people. Last week, Heather told you she thought Jessica was a problem, and her instincts were correct. Are there any ways Jessica can be eliminated from your life?

Heather: Nina is like putty in Jessica's hands. I've got no problem letting Jessica know she's not welcome here anymore.

MHP: I think that's a good idea for now. Your family needs you now more than ever. However, Nina, you will eventually have to learn to be more assertive with people like her. Nina, let's do the Self-Control intervention now for the situation with Jessica. This interven-tion will give you a chance to brainstorm options to do instead of spending time with Jessica for the scenario you just mentioned. One of the options you might think about during this trial might be assertively telling Jessica you can't spend time with her. This might be an option we can do on the phone in our session after the Self-Control. I know severing relationships with drug-using friends is difficult, but maybe we should make it one of your goals.

Nina: I think you are right. Thanks.

Reviewing Family Activity (Client and All Significant Others, Including Children, if Available)

Each review of the Environmental Control ends with a review of the family activity that was prescribed during the past session. The MHP invites all family members into the room, and asks the family to provide a copy of the completed Family Invitation for Fun form. Family members are encouraged to discuss what they liked about the activity they performed, and they are descriptively praised and encouraged to do similar activities in the future. When the prescribed activity is not performed, MHPs discuss methods of ensuring prescribed family activities will occur in the future. This discussion typically includes a review of solutions to potential obstacles. The family is then provided another copy of the Family Invitation for Fun form, and a new activity is scheduled for the next week, including what it will be, when it will occur, and who will participate. All family members are invited to indicate what they can do to ensure that the activity is performed, and they are informed that the activity will be reviewed during the next session.

Concluding Remarks

Environmental Control is often conceptualized as the control center of FBT, as all interventions may be initiated during its review. For instance, if an MHP recognized a skill deficit while reviewing Environmental Control, all forms that are relevant to Environmental Control might be put on the desk, and another skill-based FBT component could be implemented immediately (e.g., Job-Getting Skills Training could be implemented to assist in gaining employment if a job interviewing skill deficit was recognized while reviewing "work" in Environmental Control). Upon completion of the skill-based intervention, the MHP would terminate the other FBT component as prescribed, and return to Environmental Control if sufficient time remained in the session. Environmental Control would resume where the therapist left off.

Supporting Materials for Chapter 9: Restructuring the Environment to Facilitate a Drug-Free Lifestyle

Prompting Checklist 9.1. Environmental Control Therapist Prompting Checklist for Initial Session.

ENVIRONMENTAL (STIMULUS) CONTROL

THERAPIST PROMPTING CHECKLIST
Initial Session

Client ID:_____ Clinician: _____ Session #: _____ Session Date: _____

Materials Required

- Safe and At-Risk Associations List (SARAL)
- Things Like to Do and Places I Like to Visit list (TDPLV)
- Things That May Lead to Drug Use and Other Problem Behaviors (TLDOPB)
- Family Invitation for Fun form (FIFF)

Begin Time:_____

Rationale for Environmental Control (Client and Adult Significant Others)

- State the following:
___a. Things in environment make drug use and problem behaviors more or less likely to occur.
___b. Client & sig. others will together develop safe list of people, places, and situations that increase likelihood of staying clean from drugs & avoiding problem behavior.
___c. Client & sig. other will separately develop at-risk list of people, places, and situations that decrease likelihood of staying clean from drugs, and avoiding problem behavior.
___d. Lists will be reviewed each session to discover how to enjoy more time w/safe items & avoid risky items.
___e. Intervention has been successful w/other clients.
___f. Indicate how intervention is expected to be successful w/client.
___g. Solicit questions.

Obtaining "Safe" Associations (Client and Adult Significant Others)

___a. Solicit enjoyable people who do not use drugs or problem behavior.
___b. Solicit enjoyable <u>activities/places</u> that do not involve drugs or problem behavior.
___c. Solicit enjoyable activities that have not involved drug use or problem behavior from TDPLV.
   - Record solicited safe stimuli in the Safe column of the SARAL.
___d. Assure all generated items have not involved drug use or problems.
   - If time permits, solicit things liked about safe items.

Obtaining "At-Risk" Associations (Client)

___a. Solicit people who increase client's drug use and problem behavior.
___b. Solicit <u>activities/places</u> that have involved drug use or problem behavior.
___c. Solicit activities/places that have involved drug use or problem behavior from TLDOPB.
   • Record solicited at-risk stimuli in the At-Risk column of the SARAL.
___d. Query if information in at-risk lists should remain confidential, & modify future reviews accordingly.
   • If time permits, solicit things liked and disliked about at-risk items.

Obtaining "At-Risk" Associations (Adult Significant Others)

___a. Solicit people who increase client's drug use and problem behavior.
___b. Solicit <u>activities/places</u> that have involved drug use or problem behavior.
___c. Solicit activities/places that have involved drug use or problem behavior from TLDOPB.
   • Record solicited at-risk stimuli in the At-Risk column of the Safe and At-Risk Associations List.
___d. Query if information in at-risk lists should remain confidential, & modify future reviews accordingly.
   • If time permits, solicit things liked and disliked about at-risk items.

Reviewing Safe and At-Risk Associations List (Client and Adult Significant Others)

___a. Praise client and sig. other in developing lists and being honest.
___b. Review how client & sig. others can each increase client's time & enjoyment w/safe stimuli.
___c. Review how client & sig. others can decrease client's time & risk w/at-risk stimuli.
   • Assist in developing goals to include in Goals Worksheet.
   • Suggest solutions that may help increase time spent in safe situations.
   • Descriptively praise suggestions that assist client in spending more time w/safe stimuli.
   • Descriptively praise suggestions that assist client in spending less time w/at-risk stimuli.

Planning a Family Activity (Client and all Significant Others, Including Children if Available)

___a. Solicit 1 family activity.
___b. Record information about family activity in the FIFF.

Client's Assessment of Helpfulness of the Intervention

___a. After stating client should not feel obligated to provide high scores, as an honest assessment helps better address client needs, solicit how helpful client thought intervention was using 7-point scale:
   7 = extremely helpful, **6** = very helpful, **5** = somewhat helpful, **4** = not sure,
   3 = somewhat unhelpful, **2** = very unhelpful, **1** = extremely unhelpful
   • **Record Client's Rating Here:** _____
___b. Solicit how rating was derived, and methods of improving intervention in future.

Therapist's Rating of Client's Compliance with Intervention

___a. Disclose therapist's rating of client's compliance using 7-point scale:

   7 = extremely compliant, **6** = very compliant, **5** = somewhat compliant, **4** = neutral,
   3 = somewhat noncompliant, **2** = very noncompliant, **1** = extremely noncompliant

   • Factors that contribute to compliance ratings are:
     • Attendance.
     • Participation and conduct in session.
     • Homework completion.

   • **Record Therapist's Rating of Client's Compliance Here:_____**

___ b. Disclose client's compliance rating.

___ c. Explain how rating was derived, and methods of improving performance in future.

End Time:_____

Prompting Checklist 9.2. Environmental Control Therapist Prompting Checklist for Future Sessions.

ENVIRONMENTAL (STIMULUS) CONTROL

THERAPIST PROMPTING CHECKLIST
Future Sessions

Client ID:_____ Clinician:_____ Session #:_____ Session Date:_____

Materials Required

- Safe and At-Risk Associations List
- Family Invitation for Fun Form

Begin Time:_____

Reviewing Safe and At-Risk Associations Recording Sheet (Client and Adult Significant Others)

___a. Provide Safe and At-Risk Associations List.
___b. Instruct client to put checks in boxes for days in which time was spent w/stimuli.
___c. Review Safe & At-Risk list, including:
  ___1. Solicit actions performed w/stimuli to stay clean and free of problems.
  ___2. Encourage/descriptively praise actions consistent w/staying clean & free of problems.
  ___3. Encourage/assist in plans to stay clean & free of problems.
  ___4. Integrate other FBT interventions, including:
    - Determining goals to put in Goals Worksheet (Behavioral Goals and Rewards).
    - Soliciting & performing job interviews (Job-Getting Skills Training).
    - Balancing financial budget (Financial Management).
    - Practicing requests (Positive Request Procedure).
    - Developing impulse control & problem-solving skills (Self-Control).
    - Enhancing overall tone in relationships (I've Got a Great Family).

Reviewing Family Activity (Client and Significant Others, Including Small Children)

___a. Solicit completed copy of Family Invitation for Fun Form.
  - If not complete, instruct to complete in retrospect or discuss what would have been enjoyed if assignment were performed.
___b. Instruct family to discuss what they liked about the activity they performed.
___c. Descriptively praise family for positive experiences, and encourage future family activities.
___d. Provide Family Invitation for Fun Form, & schedule new activity.

Client's Assessment of Helpfulness of the Intervention

___a.   After stating client should not feel obligated to provide high scores, as an honest assessment helps better address client needs, solicit how helpful client thought intervention was using 7-point scale:

> **7** = extremely helpful, **6** = very helpful, **5** = somewhat helpful, **4** = not sure,
> **3** = somewhat unhelpful, **2** = very unhelpful, **1** = extremely unhelpful

- **Record Client's Rating Here:_____**

___b.   Solicit how rating was derived, and methods of improving intervention in future.

Therapist's Rating of Client's Compliance with Intervention

___a.   Disclose therapist's rating of client's compliance using 7-point scale:

> **7** = extremely compliant, **6** = very compliant, **5** = somewhat compliant, **4** = neutral,
> **3** = somewhat noncompliant, **2** = very noncompliant, **1** = extremely noncompliant

- Factors that contribute to compliance ratings are:
  - Attendance.
  - Participation and conduct in session.
  - Homework completion.
- **Record Therapist's Rating of Client's Compliance Here:_____**

___b.   Disclose client's compliance rating.

___c.   Explain how rating was derived, and methods of improving performance in future.

End Time:_____

Worksheet 9.1. Safe and At-Risk Associations List.

SAFE AND AT-RISK ASSOCIATIONS LIST

Client ID: _____   Clinician: _____   Session #: _____   Session Date: _____

Instructions: Please indicate each day you spent time with each item on your safe list and at-risk list over the past week.

Safe List	Mon	Tues	Wed	Thur	Fri	Sat	Sun	At-Risk List	Mon	Tues	Wed	Thur	Fri	Sat	Sun
						X									

Worksheet 9.2. Things to Do and Places I Like to Visit.

THINGS TO DO AND PLACES I LIKE TO VISIT

Client ID:_____ Clinician: _____ Session #: _____ Session Date: _____

Instructions: Put a check mark next to each thing you like to do and place you like to visit that does not involve drug use and/or benefits your family.

Leisure Activities

❐ Attending sporting events, football, baseball, hockey
  • High school sports are an inexpensive way to enjoy a sport
❐ Shopping in malls
❐ Community events
  • Community Centers, Halloween parties
  • City sponsored activities free or low cost
  • Check the paper weekly for activities or community events

School Related Activities

❐ Attending school/vocational events
  • Some activities include free books, crafts, etc.
  • Discount rates at community partners
❐ Participating in choir, a rock band, or band at school, church, or with friends

Religious Activities

❐ Attending Sunday church/temple or attending church outreach events.

Home Activities

❐ Using a computer
❐ Practicing music: guitar, drums, etc.
  • Make homemade instruments
  • Dance to music
  • Play musical pillows (like musical chairs but with pillows)
  • Name that tune
❐ Playing board and card games
  • Make up your own games
  • Play get to know you games

❐ Talking on the phone
❐ Cooking
  • Have a picnic in the living room, backyard
  • Pick favorite meal
❐ Reading
  • Read stories to children
  • Start a book club
❐ Writing
  • Keep a journal and write every week
  • Work on photo album writing stories about the pictures
❐ Playing video games, arcade
❐ Doing repair work (example: carpentry, landscaping, fixing car)
❐ Family gatherings
  • Invite friends over to the house to spend time with family
  • Organize a family reunion

Outdoor Activities

❐ Hiking, picnicking, swimming, camping, skiing

Other Activities

❐ Employment/work
❐ Trips with clean/sober family or friends
❐ County, city or state fairs
❐ Circus or amusement parks
❐ Volunteering
❐ Libraries
  • Reading programs
  • Free arts and crafts
  • Free movies
  • Free family nights
  • Check out books, movies, games

Worksheet 9.3. Things That May Lead to Drug Use and Other Problem Behaviors.

THINGS THAT MAY LEAD TO DRUG USE AND OTHER PROBLEM BEHAVIORS

Client ID:_____ Clinician: _____ Session #: _____ Session Date: _____

Instructions: Please indicate if you have engaged in each of the following items that have been associated with increasing your risk of drug use and problem behaviors.

People

- ❑ Friends
- ❑ Co-Workers
- ❑ Family/friends

Places and Situations

- ❑ Attending parties or get-togethers
- ❑ Smoking cigarettes
- ❑ Drinking alcohol
- ❑ Being angry or sad
- ❑ Stress
- ❑ Being bored
- ❑ Being alone
- ❑ Experiencing tension
- ❑ Having lots of cash available
- ❑ Car
- ❑ Specific times of day
- ❑ Excitement/anxiety
- ❑ Celebrations
- ❑ Being in places where you have used before (e.g., parks, casinos, people's homes)

Worksheet 9.4. Family Invitation for Fun.

Family Invitation for Fun

What?

_____

_____

_____

When?

_____

_____

_____

Who?

_____

_____

_____

Have Fun!

10
Managing Negative Behaviors, Thoughts, and Feelings

Rationale and Overview

Chronic substance use inevitably becomes associated with things that can be sensed in the environment, such as particular places (e.g., back patio, night-club), persons (e.g., friends who use drugs), sounds (e.g., crackling sound of burning "crack" cocaine), smells (e.g., burning pot), or events (e.g., birthday parties, weddings, sporting events). These stimuli often become conditioned to elicit pleasant physiological cravings, images, and thoughts about the rein-forcing aspects of substance use. If these stimuli are permitted to be experi-enced, they may intensify, which in turn increases motivation to use drugs. Therefore, it is important to recognize these triggers when they first occur and are less intense, and consequently engage in thoughts, images, and actions that are incompatible with substance use and other problem behaviors.

Self-Control targets drug use and various impulsive/disruptive behaviors, such as HIV risk behaviors (i.e., sex without condom use), school truancy, symptoms associated with mental health disorders, aggression, arguments, and aversive thoughts associated with traumatic experiences, among others. In the Self-Control intervention, clients are taught to recognize the triggers, or "antecedent" stimuli, to substance use and other problem behaviors early in the response chain, before cravings intensify. After stimulus recognition, they are taught to engage in the following cognitive and behavioral skill sets that are incompatible with drug use and other problem behaviors:

1. Interrupting the association by thinking or shouting, "Stop!"

2. Thinking or stating at least one negative consequence for self and one neg-ative consequence for others that could occur if drug use or other problem behavior is permitted to occur.

3. Relaxing by scanning and relaxing muscles while taking a few deep breaths.

4. Thinking or stating four pro-social alternatives to drug use or other problem behavior for the respective situation.

5. Choosing one or more of the generated alternative behaviors, and imagine out loud engaging in the chosen behaviors.

6. Thinking (or telling) a well-respected friend or loved one how the respective drug or problem behavior was avoided, and imagining the person responding positively.

7. Thinking or stating at least two positive consequences that are likely to result from the avoidance of the respective drug or problem behavior.

The MHP provides descriptive praise and assistance as the client responds correctly throughout practice trials. The number of practice trials in any given session depends on the extent of problem behaviors that were evidenced since last contact in therapy. For instance, if drug use were indicated during the week, four or five Self-Control trials might be performed, whereas no drug use since the last session might require one or two practice trials. Consistent with other FBT interventions, a therapy assignment is prescribed to assist in practicing Self-Control during *real-life* situations that occur between sessions.

Goals for Intervention

➤ Teach clients to recognize antecedent stimuli that act to trigger drug use or other problem behaviors.

➤ Teach clients to interrupt antecedent stimuli with thoughts and behaviors that are incompatible with drug use or problem behavior.

Materials Required

➤ Self-Control Therapist Prompting Checklist for Initial Session (Prompting Checklist 10.1, also located on the CD that accompanies this book)

➤ Self-Control Therapist Prompting Checklist for Future Sessions (Prompting Checklist 10.2, also located on the CD that accompanies this book)

➤ Self-Control Rating Form Worksheet (one copy for client, one copy for Therapist) (Worksheet 10.1, also located on the CD that accompanies this book)

Procedural Steps for Treatment Implementation
Rationale (Client and Adult Significant Others)

The steps for introducing Self-Control are listed in the Self-Control Therapist Prompting Checklist for Initial Session (Prompting Checklist 10.1). The intervention begins with a rationale that is presented to the client and adult significant others. The mental health professional (MHP) explains that Self-Control is a skill set the client can use to assist in decreasing the frequency of drug use and other problem behaviors. MHPs often point out stimuli that have triggered drug use and other problem behaviors for their clients in the past to make the rationale more meaningful. It is explained that Self-Control teaches people to recognize cues or triggers that act to signal drug use and other problem behaviors. It is further explained that Self-Control helps clients to generate actions that are incompatible with drug use or other problem behaviors. While learning Self-Control, these actions are practiced out loud during trials while the MHP provides feedback. MHPs conclude the rationale by explaining how the therapy is expected to help the client from the MHP's perspective, and soliciting from clients how Self-Control will be useful from their perspective. The following sections provide an example of a MHP implementing this rationale.

MHP: Valerie, you're now going to learn a skill that you can use to help decrease drug use and other problem behaviors. First, it might be helpful for you to know that drug use and other problem behaviors are often signaled by things that you associate with drug use from the past, like particular people you used to use drugs with, places where you used to use drugs, and events when drugs were used. These things are called "triggers" and when you come into contact with them, they increase the chances that you will use drugs. For instance, you indicated that seeing roach clips gets you thinking about the good things about drug use, which increases your likelihood of using drugs.

Valerie: That used to happen to me a lot in the past, but now I don't have any positive thoughts or feeling about using drugs. I really don't want to talk about those things, because it will bring up those bad thoughts and feelings again.

MHP: That is a good sign because it means the associations between drug use and various things in your environment are now weak, probably because you have some clean time under your belt. However, you did come up as having used cocaine 3 weeks ago, and it will be important for you to learn how to manage these triggers while not using drugs, in case you see them again and the "perfect storm" occurs. In fact, even though these triggers have weakened over the last 3 weeks, it is still very early in your sobriety, and exposing yourself to these triggers in real life will be too risky. So we will do it only during our sessions in your imagination. We will learn to identify these triggers early, before you experience any positive images or thoughts of drug use. You'll then learn to terminate these positive thoughts or images and refocus on doing behaviors that are inconsistent with drug use. Thus, we will be avoiding the bad thoughts you were probably referring to, but assist you in learning to manage the triggers. Does that sound good to you?

Valerie: I guess so. Let's try it.

MHP: Just like with drug use, there are also cues that may lead to other problem behaviors. For instance, you indicated that kissing may lead to unprotected sex because kissing gets you thinking about the good aspects of sex, while ignoring negative consequences to you that are associated with potential sexual promiscuity with intimate partners who refuse to wear condoms. Self-Control has been very successful in helping my clients recognize triggers to problem behaviors early, so they can instead focus on doing behaviors that will keep them healthy and free of problems. I think this is going to be especially good for you because, although these associations may be weak, you became anxious when I mentioned that I was going to talk about things that have been associated with your drug use in the past, and this intervention has a relaxation component. How do you think this intervention might help you?

Valerie: I think it would help improve my confidence when I have to face drug triggers since I know that will happen.

MHP: Great, do you have any questions?

Identification of At-Risk Situation for Drug Use (Usually Client Alone)

After presenting the rationale with the client alone, the MHP uses brainstorming with the client to identify triggers to drug use to assist the client in becoming keenly aware of their influence. MHPs also explain that it is easier to stop drug urges or desires when these triggers are first recognized, that is, before positive thoughts and images are permitted to intensify. The MHP then instructs the client to disclose a recent situation in which drug use occurred. If the client is unable to think of one, the MHP can choose something from the Environmental Control At-Risk List (see Chapter 9) or provide something that was a trigger for another client. Some clients may feel apprehensive in disclosing such information because they think they are admitting to drug use that could get them into trouble. Such clients are usually early in their recovery or are mandated to treatment by someone from the legal system. In such cases, it is best to simply indicate that the treatment sessions will focus on prevention, and make an attempt to gather scenarios that may have occurred in the distant past, or perhaps ones that are based on hypothetical information. Such scenarios might include being at a party in which marijuana was present, or being offered drugs during a car ride. It is often the case that apprehensive clients will indicate that they are providing a hypothetical situation, but in truth are providing a genuinely experienced scenario. Once a drug use scenario is obtained, the MHP instructs the client to identify the first thought that occurred in the drug use situation. The MHP can use a backward chaining procedure to prompt the very "first" thought of using drugs in this situation, which is illustrated in the following dialogue:

MHP: Tell me about a recent situation in which you used drugs. I'm especially interested in knowing about the first thought or image that you had before you used drugs.

Valerie: The last time I used, which was about 3 weeks ago, I was at my friend's house and saw a guy smoking from a pipe. My first thought was that smoking a rock would be good.

MHP: You did a good job of identifying a thought that eventually led to drug use. However, I want you to think a little harder. I'm sure you had a thought that brought you to the house.

Valerie: I started to think of it while I was driving into the neighborhood and my stomach was turning.

MHP: Good, now go back further—before you were driving into the neighborhood.

Valerie: It was payday, and I was getting off of work. I thought I deserved to do something fun and relaxing after working so hard during the week. And it was then that I started thinking about it, you know, smoking. It was kind of like I just knew. I don't think I really dwelled on it. I just knew what I had to do.

MHP: Any thoughts or images before that?

Valerie: Nope.

MHP *Great, when you had the first thought that you deserved to use, that's the time you would need to do something. By the way, we're going to try to change your thought patterns in the Self-Control. In this scene you thought you knew what you had to do, but smoking a rock sure wasn't it! Right?*

As is evident from this exchange, while Valerie first identified seeing a "guy smoking from a pipe" as the trigger for her drug use, the trigger actually appears to have occurred much earlier, when she received her paycheck from work. The MHP identified the "paycheck" trigger using the backward chaining procedure, which then becomes the focus of the Self-Control practice trial. Once this first thought is identified, it is important for the client to appreciate that thoughts, desires, or physiological responses to environmental triggers generally intensify as the reinforcing aspects of drug use are permitted to occur. To assist in this demonstration, it usually is best to identify the point at which drug use occurred, and query if it would be easier to avoid drug use at this point or the point at which the first thought or image of drug use occurred. Usually, the client will indicate the first drug use thought or image. In this case, Valerie would find it much easier to avoid drug use by addressing the paycheck trigger, rather than the other triggers that occurred when the triggers intensified in their association with drug use, such as seeing the guy smoking crack. Sometimes, clients indicate that the outcome of drug use is not dependent on catching the thought or image early. In these instances, it is possible that the identified thought is, indeed, not the first thought or image of drug use for the respective situation. In such scenarios, MHPs need to reinstate backward chaining for the respective scenario to identify the "true" first thought or image. When clients cannot identify earlier thoughts in response chains, MHPs state that increased awareness will occur with continued practice, as illustrated in the following dialogue:

MHP: Let me ask you this. Would it be easier for you to avoid drug use at the house after you saw and smelled the cocaine or when you were at work?

Valerie: Probably at work, but I knew I was going to use that day, so it didn't really matter.

MHP: That's right. If you're already at the house, it is far more difficult, as you indicated. However, it sounds like we were unable to identify the first thought or image relevant to drug use because even before you got your paycheck, you were already thinking about using. Go back further in the day and tell me if you had any thoughts or images relevant to drug use.

Valerie: I woke up knowing it was payday. You know, I just knew I would use.

MHP: Did you dream about it?

Valerie: Yes. I woke up in the middle of the night sweating about it.

MHP: Now we're getting somewhere. Did you have a thought or image about it during the previous night?

Valerie: No.

MHP: So the dream was the first trigger. It was associated with the first image of you using drugs in this situation, and maybe the first thoughts as well. This would be the point at which you'd have the best shot at doing something incompatible with drug use, and if you didn't do this, it is easy to see how you used later that day.

Valerie: That's right. I just tried to get to sleep, but didn't really know what to do to get to sleep. I kept turning over and over in bed.

MHP: It must have been a terrible experience for you. I'm sorry you had to go through that. The Self-Control intervention would probably be most successful if you used it when you first woke up from the dream. You did a really great job in identifying the "dream" trigger, even though we could not identify it right away and it took some time. The more you practice identifying these triggers, the better you will become at it.

Modeling Self-Control Procedure for Identified Drug Use Situation (Usually Client and Adult Significant Others)

Once the trigger is identified with the client, each of the nine steps in the Self-Control Rating Form (Worksheet 10.1) is modeled in sequence by the MHP for the identified drug use situation. The MHP and client should each have a copy of this rating form. The MHP explains that the steps will be modeled thinking "out loud" while doing the practice trials during sessions so thinking patterns can be better understood. However, in *real-life* situations, the steps are imagined. Adult significant others may be included during this part of the Self-Control instruction if the client desires and the client talks about drug use openly. If not, significant others should be excused. Each step of the Self-Control process is outlined in the following exchanges between client and MHP:

MHP: I am going to teach you the Self-Control Procedure in a series of practice trials here in the office where you will imagine being confronted with triggers for drug use. I'll first model these skills. I'll then have you do them while I help guide you. These trials will permit you to practice getting out of drug use situations and effectively deal with the feeling and thoughts that result when you encounter one of your triggers for drug use. During these trials we will state our thoughts "out loud" so we will each know what the other is thinking, and so I can know how this technique is working for you.

As indicated in the recording form, the first step to model is the termination of the first thought or image associated with drug use in the identified situation, by loudly and forcefully stating, "Stop!" All muscles should be tense during this time (e.g., tight fists).

MHP: The first thing to do when trying to prevent drug use is to firmly yell "Stop!" as soon as you recognize the drug use trigger. During this time, other clients have told me that it helps to tighten their fists, arms, and other muscles, to simulate the tension that they usually experience when they have thoughts about using. I'm going to show you how to do this for the drug use situation you just told me about. I will say two or three things about the situation, and as soon as I recognize a drug thought, I will state, "Stop!" Okay, here I go. I'm at work and I know that I'll be getting done pretty soon. I see that it is 5 o'clock and time to go home. I pick up my paycheck and start to think that it would be good to . . . "Stop!"

For the second and third steps, the client describes at least one negative consequence of drug use for self, and at least one negative consequence for friends or loved ones who are respected. For instance, if the client was upset that children are at risk to develop an addiction to drug use, the client could report how drug use supports the selling of drugs and helps to keep drug pushers in business and ruin the lives of children. During modeling, the MHP should state negative consequences with affect reflecting sadness, anger, disgust, or despair. Muscles should remain tense throughout the trial (e.g., clenched fists). Consequences may be rotated (or added) as trials progress. MHPs should provide details regarding these negative consequences. In the following example, the MHP intentionally elaborates on the details of the negative consequences, to make them more real and to better appreciate their negative ramifications. Clients sometimes gloss over these details, and in these cases, MHPs should assist in developing these details.

MHP: The second and third steps are to describe at least one negative consequence resulting in your drug use for you, and at least one negative consequence for your friends and loved ones, or any other individuals who are affected by your behavior. For example, a negative consequence for me if I were to use drugs is that I could get arrested. That would be terrible because I would lose my freedom and be trapped in a small cell with other people who might want to hurt me or take advantage of me. A negative consequence for others is that it puts stress on my father, and makes it more likely that he will have a heart attack, and my mother would be heartbroken.

The fourth step is to perform deep, rhythmic breathing and conduct a body scan for sensations of tension in major muscle groups to eliminate any tension that is present. Major muscles should be reviewed from head to toe. During this review, if a major muscle is relaxed (e.g., shoulders), the person should state that the muscle is relaxed, calm, and so on. If a muscle is tense, the person should state several relaxing cue words until the muscle is no longer tense; for example, "My arms are getting more and more relaxed. I am imagining a band of relaxation around my arms. They feel relaxed, calm . . . more and more relaxed." Deep, rhythmic breaths should occur throughout the rest of the trial. Statements referring to the relaxed state of the body are acceptable throughout the relaxation period; for example, "I feel so relaxed and comfortable, I feel like I'm floating away." The brief relaxation period should continue until all muscle groups feel relaxed. Although the relaxation period will eventually last 5 to 10 seconds, this phase of the Self-Control intervention may initially last several minutes. Indeed, if stress is present, particularly if there was a delay in recognizing the drug use trigger, the MHP may need to allow more time for the relaxation phase. An example of an MHP doing this step follows:

MHP: The fourth step is to relax your body. Although this relaxation process may last up to a few minutes if I'm stressed or I didn't recognize the trigger, this phase of the trial usually will last only a few seconds. So let me take a few seconds to breathe deeply and focus on my muscles to make sure I'm not tense, upset, or angry. *(While breathing slowly)* I'm letting my shoulders get more and more relaxed. Okay, my shoulders feel loose and relaxed. I'm breathing in relaxation, and exhaling calmness. . . . My legs, toes, and whole body feel completely relaxed now.

The fifth and sixth steps are to review four or more pro-social alternative behaviors that do not involve drugs, including potential pros and cons of each of these alternative behaviors. Trials include stating several alternatives that do not include drug use, briefly checking to make sure the response is unlikely to bring about drug use, and reviewing positive and negative consequences for self and others that are likely to occur. During the client's trial, the MHP may utilize prompts, whenever necessary, including:

1. *Additional alternative behaviors*, for example, "You would probably be hungry in that situation; where could you go?"

2. *How self and others would be positively affected* by alternative behaviors; for example, "What good things would happen in your relationship with your girlfriend and father if you walked away from the party in that situation? How would your girlfriend feel if you walked away?"

3. *What others would do for the client* if alternative behaviors were performed; for example, "What do you think your boyfriend would do for you if he found out that you did that?"

4. *Quickly disclosing negative consequences* when behaviors are stated that lead to drug use; for example, "What negative things might happen if you did that?"

To implement steps 5 and 6, the MHP might say:

MHP: The fifth and sixth steps are to review potential solutions or behaviors that do not involve drugs. For example, some things that I could do to avoid drugs are to go home right after work or I could go to the movies with my friend Angela. I could tell my mom to pick me up at work and plan to take her to the movies or go bowling with my friend Kat. If I go home right after work, I'm getting out of the work situation, but I could get bored and call up my drug buddies. If I call Angela, who doesn't use, I might have a great time and wouldn't use with her. However, my girlfriend may not like this idea! If I went with my girlfriend, she'd probably be able to get me out of risk, and we'd have a great time, especially if we planned something. I can't think of any negative consequences for going out with her, although she may be busy. . . .

Step 7 is to imagine doing one or more of the drug-incompatible behaviors and imagining positive things happening as a result of these behaviors. The behavioral experience should be described in a first-person narrative in the present tense. When the client performs this step, the MHP should provide prompts to elicit detail, including questions as to how the client will successfully resolve difficult situations that are likely to occur; for example, "It really does seem like a great idea to have your coworker over for dinner, but what would you say if he didn't want to leave when it was time for you to go to bed?" It may be necessary to instruct the client to role-play these potentially difficult interpersonal situations that may lead to drug use and subsequently provide feedback regarding correct responding; for example, "Show me how you would tell your coworker that he had to go home. I'll be your coworker." Efforts to engage in the chosen alternative behavior(s) should be presented with positive outcome(s).

> *MHP:*   Step 7 is to imagine doing one or more of the behaviors that were reviewed that are incompatible with drug use. I will tell a story describing myself doing these actions in the first person, and as if it were happening to me right now. Okay, here I go. I think the best thing to do is to call my girlfriend and go home to spend a romantic evening with her. I'm giving her a call, and she answers with a pleasant voice tone. I ask her to spend the night at home watching a movie and eating popcorn. She tells me how proud she is of me and how much she is looking forward to the evening. She tells me she'll be right over to pick me up. I feel fantastic and know I made the right move."

Step 8 is to imagine telling a friend or family member who does not use drugs about having performed the behavior that is incompatible with drug use. Again, the client should use first person and present tense when describing this interaction. The friend or family member should respond in a favorable manner and share positive feelings. The following demonstrates these points:

> *MHP:*   The next step is to imagine telling at least one family member or friend, who does not use drugs, what I did to avoid using drugs. I imagine how I'd feel, and what I'd say. It is important to also imagine the other person responding positively. So, I'm imagining telling my sister that I could have gone to Bob's house and used drugs after work, but instead I went to my girlfriend's house and didn't smoke. I tell her I feel good about myself, and she tells me she's proud of me.

The ninth step is to state several positive consequences that might result due to performance of the drug-free behavior. This step is performed to reinforce the participant for having performed the previous steps. An example follows:

MHP: The final step is to state several positive consequences that might result from my drug-free behavior. For example, I'm really proud of myself for deciding to spend the evening with my girlfriend. That says a lot about the kind of person I am and what a great girlfriend I have. My sister is proud of me, too. Life is positively shining on me!

After the MHP models the steps with ongoing feedback and possible input from the client, it is helpful to model the entire nine steps in sequence, without interruption or feedback as to what is being performed. That is, the MHP performs the steps without stopping to explain what is being performed. In this way, the client is able to appreciate the natural flow of Self-Control through observation. This step may be unnecessary, however, when clients are especially bright and appear to understand the steps or when clients respond well to feedback.

Evaluation of MHP's Performance for First Drug Use Trial (Usually Client and Adult Significant Others)

After modeling, the client and the MHP evaluate the MHP's performance using the Self-Control Rating Form. This evaluation teaches the client how to correctly complete the form, as each of the nine steps is reviewed. In evaluating the MHP's performance, the MHP should ask the client what was generally liked about the modeled performance, and respond with enthusiasm and general agreement, whenever possible.

To complete the Self-Control Rating Form, the date and a cue word describing the modeled situation are recorded in the appropriate places on both the client and MHP copies of the form. The client is instructed to grade each step the MHP performed on her Self-Control Rating Form using a 0% to 100% scale of correctness (0% = forgot to do the step, 100% = did the step perfectly). Clients record their scores on their copy of the rating form, and MHPs also score their performance on their own copy of the rating form. The clients and MHPs then compare their scores. The procedure for this starts with the MHP's asking the client to report the score for the first step. Then, the MHP's score is disclosed. The MHP asks how the client's score was derived and provides descriptive praise. The MHP then states how the scores are consistent and asks what the client might do differently if performing the step. The MHP then points out methods to improve performance in the future. If one of the client's scores is more than 20 percentage points different than the MHP's score, feedback should be given regarding the discrepancy so that the client understands the rationale underlying the rating, and future scores are more accurate. If scores are within 20 percentage points, the MHP praises the client for accurate responses. With practice, the MHP may phase out feedback for each step until feedback is provided only for the step that helped the client the most.

An example dialogue is provided for completion of the first of the nine Self-Control steps.

MHP: What score did you give me for the first step?

Valerie: I gave you a "100."

MHP: Wow, a hundred! That is quite impressive. Did you record that in your rating form?

Valerie: Yes, I recorded all of my ratings here (pointing to the appropriate areas on the form).

MHP: Great. I also gave myself a high score. I gave myself an 85%. How was your score derived? That is, how did you come to give me a 100%?

Valerie: Well, you said "STOP" in a really loud voice, so I thought you should get a "100."

MHP: I also thought our scores were similar, and I thought I was loud and stated it soon after I recognized I was at risk. I think I could have done a little better in stating it sooner because I actually waited until the image of drug use was in my head. Next time, I'll try to knock it off earlier. Would you do anything differently to put this step into your own style?

Valerie: I think I would yell "screw it" instead of "stop" because I think it will work better for me.

MHP: That's great. Anything that will work for you is good.

After reviewing all nine steps in this manner, the MHP then reports a self-rating for his likelihood of using drugs immediately prior to stating "stop," and another self-rating for the likelihood of using drugs after the trial was complete. Ratings are based on a 0 to 100 percentage scale. Zero means the person who conducted the trial is not even thinking or imagining anything associated with drug use, whereas a 100 means the person is using drugs. The MHP provides a rationale to the client after each rating is disclosed, and then describes how the rating was derived. Risk of drug use increases as scores increase. Therefore, the ideal pre-likelihood rating will be less than 10 percentage points. If the prescore is below 10, the post-rating will usually be zero. However, if the pre-likelihood rating is relatively high (e.g., 30 or above), the post-likelihood of drug use score will be hard to bring down to zero. Lower ratings usually result when the drug-associated thought or image is terminated early in the sequence. MHPs provide this information to clients when providing scores in the modeled performance. In this way, clients learn the importance of terminating drug-associated thoughts or images early in the process. These ratings are recorded in the "Pre-Likelihood Rating" and "Post-Likelihood Rating" rows on the Self-Control Rating Form corresponding to the first trial.

MHP: The likelihood of my using drugs just before I yelled "stop" was about a 5 percent on this 0 to 100 percent scale because I yelled "stop" as soon as the thought started to occur. I didn't even let myself finish the sentence; otherwise, I would be increasing my likelihood of drug use. The likelihood of my using drugs after I finished this trial was a zero because I wasn't even thinking of using after I thought about the positive consequences of telling someone I didn't use anymore. Now, if I didn't terminate the drug-associated image early, my pre-likelihood score would have been higher, and it would have been harder to get my post-likelihood score down to zero.

The MHP concludes the critique by disclosing which of the nine steps helped decrease the likelihood of engaging in drug use the most during the trial, including a rationale as to why. The number corresponding to the most helpful step is recorded in the appropriate box of the Self-Control Rating Form.

MHP: I thought the first step was most helpful for me in getting my post-likelihood rating down to zero. I loved how I caught it early, and even though it could be improved, it was still pretty good.

Client's First Self-Control Trial for Drug Use Situation (Usually Client Alone)

After the MHP has modeled the nine Self-Control steps and the performance is critiqued, the client tries to apply the nine steps to a drug use situation. In almost all situations, the client is the only person in the room when conducting initial Self-Control trials. However, in some situations, MHPs may decide it is appropriate for adult significant others to observe. For instance, the adult significant other is a drug user and the client prefers to have the adult significant other in the room. The client should be instructed to perform Self-Control for the drug use situation just modeled by the MHP. The client should be instructed to utilize the Self-Control Rating Form to prompt responding and to "think aloud." MHPs additionally prompt clients to perform components initially; for example, "State one negative consequence for yourself"; "Imagine telling someone who cares about you what you did to avoid drug use." As the client becomes more skilled, MHPs fade out this assistance. For the first step, yelling "stop," it may be necessary to state the situation and prompt the client to yell "stop!"; for example, "You're in the park. Bob unexpectedly comes up to you and asks if you want to smoke reefer. You say . . . go on, yell 'stop!'"). In the latter example, the MHP might use hand signals to prompt the client in yelling "stop!"

Evaluation of Client's First Self-Control Trial for Drug Use Situation (Usually Client Alone)

The MHP initiates a review of the client's Self-Control trial by asking what was generally liked about the client's performance. In this initial session, the client's first trial is recorded under Trial 2 on the Self-Control Rating Form, on both the client and MHP copies. Like the first trial modeled by the MHP, the date and a cue word are recorded to describe the situation (e.g., paycheck) on each of the Self-Control Rating Forms. The client is instructed to grade each of the nine steps using the 0% to 100% scale of correctness (0% = forgot to do the respective step, 100% = did the respective step perfectly). Client scores are recorded on the client's copy of the rating form, and MHP scores on the

MHP's copy of the form. Once completed, the MHP asks the client for her scores, and after each score is reported, the following feedback is provided by the MHP: (1) the MHP's score, (2) how client and MHP scores were consistent, (3) asking how the client might do the step differently if it were performed again, and (4) suggesting methods of improving performance in the future.

The client is queried to provide a rating of the likelihood of using drugs immediately prior to stating "stop!" and a rating for after the trial is completed, as well as rationales as to what influenced derivation of the ratings ("0" = not even thinking of drugs, "100" = using drugs). If the post-rating is above 10%, the MHP should inform client that it is easier to reduce urges when the pre-likelihood rating is low. Therefore, the client will need to catch the drug-associated thought or image earlier in the response chain. The MHP and client then use backward chaining to identify the earliest thought of drug use, and up to three additional trials are performed until the post-likelihood rating is reported to be less than 5%. All likelihood ratings are recorded in the recording form.

MHP: What was the likelihood of your using drugs just before you yelled "stop," and why do you think so?

Valerie: Probably about 25% because I wasn't even thinking about using.

MHP: Remember, 0% is not even thinking about drug use, so 20% would mean you're already thinking about it quite a bit, although you may not have taken any steps to actually get the drug. You know, it's much easier to control these urges when you are about a 5 on the 0% to 100% scale. If you allow the urge to get too high, you're more likely to use. Let's go back and see if there was an even earlier time when you could have stopped yourself from thinking about drugs. Maybe when it is just a brief image. We can do another trial and see if we can get the pre-likelihood rating down to 5% or so.

Additional Trials

Drug use Self-Control trials should be alternated with trials that are focused on other problem behaviors. The trials use essentially the same procedures as drug use trials, and often include adult significant others. Target behaviors often include impulsive problem behaviors (e.g., starting an argument, leaving a child unattended), or problem behaviors associated with distress (i.e.,

lack of energy, crying, nightmares). These problem behaviors are also sometimes antecedents or triggers to drug use. The backward chaining procedure
is used to identify contributing factors that can be addressed in Self-Control
trials. The number of trials should be mutually determined between the MHP
and client. However, it is important to alternate between drug use and other
problem behaviors (see below for application to other problems). The MHP
may also implement Self-Control trials impromptu, while reviewing other
interventions (e.g., Environmental/Stimulus Control, Behavioral Goals and
Rewards), or the trials may be prescribed based on past experiences. The Self-
Control Therapist Prompting Checklist for the Initial Session may be used to
assist in one trial that is focused on drug use and one that is focused on another
problem behavior.

Future Drug Use Trials (Client and Adult Significant Others, if Appropriate)

Future Self-Control trials include the client's modeling the sequence of steps
for drug use or other problem behaviors. This usually includes one trial
for a drug use situation and one trial for another problem behavior. The
number of trials is usually relevant to difficulties clients experience between
therapy sessions. Obviously, drug use or urges since last contact warrant
extended trials for these situations, and difficult life experiences also warrant extended trials. Initial sessions usually involve more practice trials than
subsequent ones due to the accomplishment of therapy goals. In future sessions, the MHP does not typically model trials in their entirety (i.e., all steps
of Self-Control). Indeed, assistance during trials is faded as clients become
more adept at Self-Control. Similarly, the amount of feedback MHPs provide to clients about their performance decreases as clients become more
adept in self-evaluation and enhance their performance. Clients are generally instructed to perform no more than three trials in drug use and three
trials relevant to other problems during each session. The adult significant
others are more involved in these future trials, as they may be encouraged
by the MHP to prompt appropriate responding and descriptively praise the
efforts of clients. The steps for reviewing Self-Control in future sessions are
included in the Self-Control MHP Prompting Checklist for Future Sessions
(Prompting Checklist 10.2).

Concluding Remarks

The Self-Control intervention is extremely robust, as it is capable of managing a wide array of problem behaviors and may be used to assist clients in determining moments when behavioral skills may be optimally implemented. It is also theoretically sound, easy to implement, and comprehensive. Being transportable, it may be used during Environmental Control (Chapter 9) as a skill to assist in refusing drugs, managing urges, and solving problems that may occur when reviewing at-risk stimuli. It may also be used to manage anger prior to conducting the Positive Request Procedure (Chapter 8), assist in identifying optimal times to discipline children, and prevent impulsive undesired behaviors, such as a situation in which vandalism occurred in the near past.

Supporting Materials for Chapter 10: Managing Negative Behaviors, Thoughts, and Feelings

Prompting Checklist 10.1. Self-Control Therapist Prompting Checklist for Initial Session.

SELF-CONTROL

THERAPIST PROMPTING CHECKLIST

Initial Session

Client ID:_____ Clinician:_____ Session #:____ Session Date:_____

Materials Required

• Self-Control Rating Form (SCRF), 1 copy for therapist, 1 copy for client

Note: Although this checklist will be utilized to target drug use primarily, Self-Control (SeC) is robust, and may be utilized to ameliorate various impulsive/disruptive behaviors, such as HIV risk behaviors, school truancy, symptoms associated w/mental health disorders, aggression, arguments, aversive thoughts associated w/traumatic experiences, etc.

Begin Time:_____

Rationale (Client and Adult Significant Others)

• Review the following:
___a. SeC assists in decreasing drug use & other problem behaviors.
___b. SeC improves recognition of cues that signal urges or desires to use drugs or do things that may lead to problems.
___c. SeC assists in learning to generate effective alternatives.
___d. Solicit how SeC will be useful.
___e. Explain how SeC is expected to be useful.
___f. Solicit & answer questions.

Identification of At-Risk Situation for Drug Use (Usually Client Alone)

• Explain each of the following:
___a. Things in environment that lead to drug use called triggers.
___b. Brainstorm drug use triggers for the client.
___c. Easier to stop drug urges or desires when these triggers are 1st recognized, before they intensify.
___d. Practice trials will be performed "thinking out loud" to assist in managing triggers to drug use.
___e. Solicit recent situation in which drug urges or use occurred.
  • If client resistant, choose item from Environmental Control At-Risk list and use hypothetical situation.
___f. Assist client in identifying 1st thought of drug use in solicited situation (use backward chaining).

Modeling SeC Procedure for Identified Drug Use Situation
(Usually Client and Adult Significant Others)

___a. Provide SCRF to client.

___b. Model 9 steps in SeC Rating Form for earliest trigger in solicited situation, including:

    ___1. Stop!

    ___2. State 1 neg. consequence of drug use for self.

    ___3. State 1 neg. consequence for friends/loved ones.

    ___4. 5 to 10 seconds of deep, rhythmic breathing and/or a muscle relaxation.

    ___5. State 4 drug-incompatible behaviors.

    ___6. Briefly evaluate some of the pro's and con's for significant incompatible behaviors.

    ___7. Imagine doing 1 or more of the drug-incompatible behaviors.

    ___8. Imagine telling loved one about drug-incompatible behavior & person responding positively.

    ___9. State several + consequences that might result from drug-incompatible behavior.

Evaluation of Therapist's Performance for 1st Drug Use Trial
(Usually Client and Adult Significant Others)

___a. Record trial 1 and date in client & therapist versions of SCRF.

    ___1. Record word to describe solicited situation in client & therapist versions of SCRF.

       • Client scores therapist's performance on client's copy of this rating form.

___b. Instruct client to grade each step in SCRF using 0 to 100% correctness scale.

___c. After soliciting client scores for each SeC step, do each of the following:

    ___1. Disclose therapist's score.

    ___2. State how client and therapist scores were consistent.

    ___3. Ask what client liked about modeled step.

    ___4. Ask what client would do differently, if anything.

    ___5. Agree w/areas of client's critique, & suggest methods of improving in future.

___d. State likelihood of using drugs immediately prior to stating stop in the trial (0 = not thinking about drugs, 100 = using drug).

    ___1. Show where to record this rating in SCRF.

___e. State likelihood of using drugs immediately after the last step in the trial (0 = not thinking about drugs, 100 = using drugs).

    ___1. Show how to record this rating in SCRF.

___f. Disclose which step helped decrease likelihood of drug use most.

    ___1. Record # of most helpful step in SCRF.

Client's 1st SeC Trial for Drug Use Situation (Usually Client Alone)

___a. For most recent drug use situation, instruct client to do following 9 steps:

    ___1. Stop!

    ___2. State 1 neg. consequence of drug use for self.

    ___3. State 1 neg. consequence for friends/loved ones.

    ___4. 5 to 10 seconds of deep, rhythmic breathing and/or a muscle relaxation.

    ___5. State 4 drug-incompatible behaviors.

    ___6. Briefly evaluate some of the pro's and con's for significant incompatible behaviors.

    ___7. Imagine doing 1 or more of the drug-incompatible behaviors.

    ___8. Imagine telling loved one about drug-incompatible behavior & person responding positively.

___9.   State several + consequences that might result from drug-incompatible behavior.
- Provide the following assistance throughout the trial:
  ___a.   Prompt client in performing steps, fading assistance w/improved performance.
  ___b.   Make suggestions to better performance.

Evaluation of Client's 1st SeC Trial for Drug Use Situation (Usually Client Alone)

___a.   Instruct client to complete SCRF, assisting as necessary.
- Therapist scores client's performance on therapist's copy of this rating form.

___b.   Instruct client to grade each step & record in SCRF using 0 to 100% correct sale.

___c.   Solicit client's scores, and after each score is reported perform the following:
  ___1.   Disclose therapist's score.
  ___2.   State how client and therapist scores were consistent.
  ___3.   Ask what client would do differently in the implementation of the step.
  ___4.   Express areas of agreement w/client's critique, & suggest ways to improve in future.

___d.   Solicit client's rating of likelihood of using drugs immediately prior to stating "stop" in the trial.

___e.   Solicit client's rating of likelihood to using drugs immediately after performing last step in trial.

___f.   Solicit which step helped decrease likelihood to engage in drug use the most.
  ___1.   Encourage client to emphasize this step when practicing SeC.

Identification of At-Risk Situation for Problem Behavior (Usually Client Alone)

- Explain each of the following:
___a.   There are things in environment that lead to problems, called triggers.
___b.   Brainstorm triggers to problems experienced by client.
___c.   Easier to stop problems when triggers are 1st recognized, before they intensify.
___d.   Practice trials will be performed "thinking out loud" to assist in managing triggers to problems.
___e.   Solicit recent situation in which a problem was experienced.
- If client is resistant, choose item from Environmental Control At-Risk list and use hypothetical situation.
___f.   Assist client in identifying 1st thought leading to problem in solicited situation (use backward chaining).

Modeling 1st SeC Trial for Problem Behavior (Usually Client and Adult Significant Other)

___a.   Model 9 steps on SCRF to prevent earliest trigger in solicited situation, including:
  ___1.   Stop!
  ___2.   State 1 neg. consequence of problem behavior for self.
  ___3.   State 1 neg. consequence of problem behavior for friends/loved ones.
  ___4.   5 to 10 seconds of deep, rhythmic breathing and/or a muscle relaxation.
  ___5.   State 4 behaviors that are incompatible w/problem behavior.
  ___6.   Briefly evaluate some of the pros and cons for incompatible behaviors.
  ___7.   Imagine doing one or more of the incompatible behaviors.

___8.   Imagine telling friend/family member about having done the alternative behaviors.

___9.   State several positive consequences that might result from the alternative behaviors.

Evaluation of 1st Trial for Problem Behavior (Usually Client and Adult Significant Other)

___a.   Record trial 3 and date in SCRF for client and therapist.

___b.   Record cue word to describe situation in SCRF.

___c.   Solicit each of the client's scores, and do the following for each step:

    ___1.   Disclose therapist's score.

    ___2.   State how client and therapist scores were consistent.

    ___3.   Ask what client liked about the therapist's performance.

    ___4.   Ask what client would do differently, if anything.

    ___5.   Agree w/areas of client's critique, & suggest methods of improving future performance.

___d.   Solicit client's rating of likelihood of avoiding problem immediately prior to stating "stop" in the trial.

___e.   Solicit client's rating of likelihood of avoiding problem immediately after performing last step in the trial.

___f.   Solicit which step helped decrease likelihood of engaging in problem behavior.

    ___1.   Encourage client to emphasize this step when practicing self-control.

Client's 1st SeC Trial for Problem Situation (Usually Client Alone)

___a.   For most recent problem situation, instruct client to do following 9 steps:

    ___1.   Stop!

    ___2.   State 1 neg. consequence of problem behavior for self.

    ___3.   State 1 neg. consequence of problem behavior for friends/loved ones.

    ___4.   5 to 10 seconds of deep, rhythmic breathing and/or a muscle relaxation.

    ___5.   State 4 behaviors that are incompatible w/problem behavior.

    ___6.   Briefly evaluate some of the pro's and con's for incompatible behaviors.

    ___7.   Imagine doing one or more of the incompatible behaviors.

    ___8.   Imagine telling friend/family member about having done the alternative behaviors.

    ___9.   State several positive consequences that might result from the alternative behaviors.

      • Provide the following assistance throughout the trial:

      ___a.   Prompt client in performing steps, fading assistance w/improved performance.

      ___b.   Make suggestions to better performance.

Evaluation of Client's 1st SeC Trial for Problem Situation (Usually Client Alone)

___a.   Instruct client to complete SCRF, assisting as necessary.

    • Therapist scores client's performance on therapist's copy of this rating form.

___b.   Solicit client's scores, and after each score is reported perform the following:

    ___1.   Disclose therapist's score.

    ___2.   State how client and therapist scores were consistent.

    ___3.   Ask what client liked about the performance.

    ___4.   Ask what client would do differently in the implementation of the step.

    ___5.   Express areas of agreement w/client's critique, & suggest ways of improving.

___c. Solicit client's rating of likelihood of doing problem behavior prior to stating "stop" in the trial.

___d. Solicit client's rating of likelihood of doing problem behavior after last step in the trial.

___e. Solicit which step helped increase likelihood of avoiding problems.

    ___1. Encourage client to emphasize this step when practicing self-control.

- Additional trials are completed at discretion of therapist, but not recorded for adherence.
- Situations for additional trials often come from at-risk list in Environmental Control or Behavioral Goals.
- Can do additional trials w/adolescent or adult significant others at therapist's discretion (usually sig. others are faded into room).

Client's Assessment of Helpfulness of the Intervention

___a. After stating client should not feel obligated to provide high scores, as an honest assessment helps better address client needs, solicit how helpful client thought intervention was using 7-point scale:

    7 = extremely helpful, **6** = very helpful, **5** = somewhat helpful, **4** = not sure,

    3 = somewhat unhelpful, **2** = very unhelpful, **1** = extremely unhelpful

Record Client's Rating Here:_____

___b. Solicit how rating was derived, and methods of improving intervention in future.

Therapist's Rating of Client's Compliance with Intervention

___a. Disclose therapist's rating of client's compliance using 7-point scale:

    7 = extremely compliant, **6** = very compliant, **5** = somewhat compliant, **4** = neutral,

    3 = somewhat noncompliant, **2** = very noncompliant, **1** = extremely noncompliant

- Factors that contribute to compliance ratings are:
  - Attendance
  - Participation and conduct in session
  - Homework completion

Record Therapist's Rating of Client's Compliance Here:_____

___b. Disclose client's compliance rating.

___c. Explain how rating was derived, and methods of improving performance in future.

End Time:_____

Prompting Checklist 10.2. Self-Control Therapist Prompting Checklist for Future Sessions.

SELF-CONTROL
THERAPIST PROMPTING CHECKLIST
Future Sessions

Client ID:_____ Clinician:_____ Session #:_____ Session Date:_____

Materials Required

- Self-Control Rating Form (SCRF)

Note: Although this checklist will be utilized to target drug use primarily, Self-Control (SeC) is robust, and may be utilized to ameliorate various impulsive/disruptive behaviors, such as HIV risk behaviors, school truancy, symptoms associated w/mental health disorders, aggression, arguments, aversive thoughts associated w/traumatic experiences, etc.

Begin Time:_____

Reviewing Drug Use and Problem Behavior Trials (Client and Significant Other, if Appropriate)

___a. Solicit a recent drug use or problem situation.
___b. For most recent drug use or problem situation, instruct client to do following 9 steps:
    ___1. Stop!
    ___2. State 1 neg. consequence of drug use or other problem behavior for self.
    ___3. State 1 neg. consequence of drug use or other problem behavior for friends/loved ones.
    ___4. 5 to 10 seconds of deep, rhythmic breathing and/or a muscle relaxation.
    ___5. State 4 behaviors that are incompatible w/drug use or other problem behavior.
    ___6. Briefly evaluate some of the pro's and con's for incompatible behaviors.
    ___7. Imagine doing one or more of the incompatible behaviors.
    ___8. Imagine telling friend/family member about having done the alternative behaviors.
    ___9. State several positive consequences that might result from the alternative behaviors.
- Provide the following assistance throughout the trial:
___a. Prompt client in performing steps, fading assistance w/ improved performance.
___b. Make suggestions to better performance.
___c. Ask what was generally liked about client's performance.
___d. Instruct client to complete SCRF (therapist completes own copy).
___e. Solicit client's scores, and after each score is reported, perform the following:
    ___1. Disclose therapist's score.
    ___2. State how client and therapist scores were consistent.

___3. Ask what client liked about the performance.

___4. Ask what client would do to enhance scores.

___5. Express areas of agreement w/client's critique, & suggest how to improve performance.

___f. Solicit client's rating of likelihood to perform undesired behavior immediately before stating stop in trial.

___g. Solicit client's rating of likelihood to perform undesired behavior after last step in trial.

___h. Solicit which step decreased likelihood of engaging in undesired behavior the most.

Client's Assessment of Helpfulness of the Intervention

___a. After stating client should not feel obligated to provide high scores, as an honest assessment helps better address client needs, solicit how helpful client thought intervention was using 7-point scale:

> 7 = extremely helpful, 6 = very helpful, 5 = somewhat helpful, 4 = not sure,
> 3 = somewhat unhelpful, 2 = very unhelpful, 1 = extremely unhelpful

Record Client's Rating Here:_____

___b. Solicit how rating was derived, and methods of improving intervention in future.

Therapist's Rating of Client's Compliance with Intervention

___a. Disclose therapist's rating of client's compliance using 7-point scale:

> 7 = extremely compliant, 6 = very compliant, 5 = somewhat compliant, 4 = neutral,
> 3 = somewhat noncompliant, 2 = very noncompliant, 1 = extremely noncompliant

- Factors that contribute to compliance ratings are:
  - Attendance
  - Participation and conduct in session
  - Homework completion

Record Therapist's Rating of Client's Compliance Here:_____

___b. Disclose client's compliance rating.

___c. Explain how rating was derived, and methods of improving performance in future.

End Time:_____

Worksheet 10.1. Self-Control Rating Form Worksheet.

SELF-CONTROL RATING FORM

Client ID:_____ Clinician:_____ Session #:_____ Session Date:_____

Instructions: For each drug use or other problem situation trial, record date and word to describe the situation. Grade steps 1–9 using a 0 to 100% scale of correctness (0% = forgot to do step, 100% = did perfectly) and list solutions and pros/cons. Then record pre- and post-likelihood ratings (0 = not even thinking about drug use or problem, 100 = engaging in drug use or problem behavior). Record which of the 9 steps helped the most in decreasing the likelihood of drug use or problems.

Self-Control Steps	Record details to describe each step	Rate your performance on a scale of 0–100%	Record details to describe each step	Rate your performance on a scale of 0–100%	Record details to describe each step	Rate your performance on a scale of 0–100%
	Trial # 1		**Trial # 2**		**Trial # 3**	
	Date: _____		Date: _____		Date: _____	
	Word to describe situation _____		Word to describe situation _____		Word to describe situation _____	
1) Stop!						
2) One bad thing for self						
3) One bad thing for others						
4) Take a deep breath & relax						
5) State 4 solutions	1. 2. 3. 4.		1. 2. 3. 4.		1. 2. 3. 4.	
6) Briefly evaluate some of the pro's and con's for significant incompatible behaviors.	1. 2. 3. 4.		1. 2. 3. 4.		1. 2. 3. 4.	

7) Imagine doing 1 or more solution(s)					
8) Imagine telling someone about using the solution brainstormed					
9) State positive things that will happen as a result of using the solution					
Pre-likelihood rating					
Post-likelihood rating					
Step that helped the most and why it helped the most					

CHAPTER 11

Gaining Employment

Rationale and Overview

It is often difficult for individuals who have evidenced problems with illicit drugs or other problem behaviors to obtain satisfying jobs that pay well and are consistent with their treatment plan. Some are unable to obtain gainful employment because they have limited education or have not obtained technical or job-specific skills. Others work in bars, nightclubs, or other settings that contribute to their ongoing substance use. Still others are underemployed because they have sporadic work patterns, don't show up for scheduled shifts, don't perform well on the job, or exhibit other behaviors associated with their substance abuse that interfere with stable and rewarding employment. Research indicates that individuals who use cocaine or marijuana more often quit their current jobs than those who do not use these drugs (Hoffman, Dufur, & Huang, 2007). But in addition to these considerations, we have also found that these individuals have poor "job-getting skills." They do not know how to assertively seek employment and often lack the skills or confidence required to perform well during preemployment interviews. Being unemployed or underemployed makes it difficult for the clients to provide themselves and family members with basic necessities, lowers self-esteem, and contributes to stress and boredom, which are highly associated with drug use and other problem behaviors.

Job-Getting Skills Training is an abbreviated application of Job Club, which is one of the most successful job-getting programs developed (Azrin, Philip, Thienes-Hontos, & Besalel, 1981). This intervention is designed to teach clients skills that assist them in effectively requesting interviews from potential employers and prepare them for job interviews. Through modeling and behavior rehearsal, clients learn to be motivated to obtain employment and solicit job interviews. After job-getting skills are performed effectively in simulated scenarios, clients call potential employers and request interviews in the presence of their MHPs. Clients also learn how to present themselves favorably during job interviews.

Goals for Intervention

➤ Motivate clients to pursue employment.

➤ Teach clients to effectively request job interviews from potential employers.

➤ Obtain employment.

Materials Required

➤ Job-Getting Skills Training Therapist Prompting Checklist for Initial Session (Prompting Checklist 11.1, also located on the CD that accompanies this book)

➤ Job-Getting Skills Training Therapist Prompting Checklist for Future Sessions (Prompting Checklist 11.2, also located on the CD that accompanies this book)

➤ Interviewing Skills Worksheet (Worksheet 11.1, also located on the CD that accompanies this book)

Procedural Steps for Implementation

Rationale for Job Interview Solicitation (Client and Adolescent and Adult Significant Others)

The steps for this intervention when it is first implemented are included in the Job-Getting Skills Training MHP Prompting Checklist for Initial Session (Prompting Checklist 11.1). As indicated on the prompting checklist, the client is first provided a rationale for the Job-Getting Skills Training by the MHP. The rationale begins with a very brief assessment to determine if the client is interested in getting a satisfying job. If so, the client is asked to indicate how a satisfying job would be important, and the MHP reinforces statements that suggest a job is important. It is often helpful to solicit components of a "dream job" or career, including the benefits of such a career. It is also helpful to inquire as to how the client can make the dream job or career happen, including generation of solutions to obstacles that might interfere with attainment of the dream job. These queries are designed to instill motivation to pursue employment, which is often lacking in clients who are referred for treatment. Clients are told Job Getting is designed to assist in preparing them for job interviews, including skills that are relevant to obtaining job interviews. It is helpful to remind clients that classified advertisements account for only a small percentage of the jobs that are available and that it is important to practice alternative job-getting strategies, such as telephone networking with potential employers. Clients are told that Job Getting has been successful in achieving employment for others, and they are asked to indicate how Job Getting would be helpful to them. The MHP asks for questions from the client and provides answers, as indicated in the following dialogue.

MHP: Would you be interested in finding a satisfying job?

Chris: I sure would. But there are not a lot of jobs out there right now.

MHP: You are right. We'll talk about some ways to find jobs, but before we do that, tell me why a satisfying job would be important to you.

Chris: If I had a job, I could pay the bills, but I guess these are being paid by welfare and my unemployment benefits right now.

MHP: So it seems like a job might get you a little extra income. How else might it be helpful?

Chris: Well, I guess a job would provide slightly more than I am getting now, and then I might be able to get my cable for TV turned on, and maybe even be able to take a vacation to see my family.

MHP: Fantastic! Additional income is always a big help, and the out-of-state vacations would be great for reestablishing the relationships in your family. Good for you to put an importance on the well-being of your family. What other things would a satisfying job provide you?

Chris: Well, I would feel proud to have a good job—something I could really work at.

MHP: Of course, you have a lot to be proud of presently, like raising a beautiful family. However, I see your point, as you would be independent from the system, and able to model a strong work ethic for your children. What would your dream job or career be like?

Chris: I always wanted to be a chef at a fancy restaurant, like the ones downtown.

MHP: That is wonderful. All the free food you can eat, as well.

Chris: That is true. And the good jobs also have health benefits and you get to work with great people, too.

MHP: Absolutely fabulous. You've got me wanting to switch jobs. What would you need to do to make this a reality?

Chris: I think most people have to go to culinary school for 1 or 2 years. I'd probably have to do that.

MHP: Well, that is certainly achievable.

Chris: I'm not sure about that—I don't have any money, and those places charge a lot for tuition.

MHP: I understand, but perhaps you can begin to build up your resume while saving money for school. Are there any other solutions you can think of to avoid this obstacle or any other obstacles?

Chris: I am not sure, but I really would like to have a good job.

MHP: I love your attitude. The first step in acquiring gainful employment is getting an interview with a potential employer. Many people do this by looking through the paper's classified advertisements. However, this represents only a small percentage of job positions available, as many employers don't advertise their positions in the paper, and many jobs are created only after an outstanding applicant comes to their attention. This Job-Getting Skills Training involves teaching individuals like you to obtain job interviews from potential employers. By getting a job interview you are no longer likely to be treated like just another number. You have an opportunity to show off your skills. Job-Getting Skills Training also helps individuals learn how to best present themselves during interviews. This intervention has been successful with other clients, and I think it will work really well for you because you have a strong work ethic. How do you think this intervention will be able to assist you?

Modeling Job Interview Solicitation (Client and Adolescent and Adult Significant Others)

After discussing the potential benefits of Job Getting to the client and answering any questions, the MHP models how to ask for a job interview with a potential employer. Prior to modeling the solicitation of a job interview, the client should be provided a copy of the Interviewing Skills Worksheet (Worksheet 11.1) to prompt correct responding during Job Getting role-plays. The Interviewing Skills Worksheet contains simple, step-by-step prompts that help clients prepare to ask for a job interview, and also assists them as they make the actual phone calls to request an interview. The MHP then models how to ask for a job interview, instructing the client to pretend to be an office manager or secretary answering the telephone for a potential employer. The potential employer may be an ex-employer of the client or a business for which the client is interested in working. This permits the MHP an opportunity to manage potential problems that are enacted by the client. MHPs are usually able to manage such resistance with experience, practice, and preparation, which further assists in motivating clients to feel confident in Job Getting.

First, the MHP calls the potential employer (i.e., client in role-play) and provides basic salutary remarks. After an introduction, the MHP solicits the name of the manager or supervisor. Once this is accomplished, the MHP asks to speak with this person. The client is told that if the person who answers the phone asks why the manager is desired, the response should be, "It's personal." Clients should not disclose that they are calling for a job interview to a secretary or other employee who first answers the phone because they may state that there are no jobs available, and the client will not have an opportunity to talk directly with the supervisor or manager. Speaking directly with a supervisor or manager is critical because they are in a better position to know of potential job opportunities at their companies or to know of other, similar jobs that might be available at other companies. Sometimes it helps to explain to the client how getting a job is "personal," as clients sometimes feel insecure in not disclosing that they are looking for jobs. If the manager is unavailable, the client should request a good time to call back, but not leave a message for the manager because these messages are often not returned.

MHP:	Hello, my name is Jennifer Ramirez. Who is the manager on shift today?
Receptionist:	The manager on shift today is Paula.
MHP:	And what is Paula's last name?
Receptionist:	Her last name is Jones, Paula Jones.
MHP:	Great, may I speak with her, please?
Receptionist:	What is the reason for your call?
MHP:	It's personal.
Receptionist:	She is not in right now. Can I take a message?
MHP:	No, that's fine. Is there a good time that I can call back and speak with her?

If the manager is able to come to the phone, the MHP provides an introduction and thanks the manager for accepting the call. The interviewer (MHP) then lists a few personal strengths and/or qualifications and requests an in-person interview to further discuss personal qualifications and strengths. Strengths that are often reported include something about having a strong work ethic, being trustworthy, being passionate about work, or being positively assertive. Two or three qualifications are usually drafted prior to the call and are specific to the job position or workplace. These might include outstanding math skills, ability to type quickly, physical strength, ability to operate basic landscaping equipment, and so on. Thus, if done smoothly, a job interview is never requested. That is, the only thing that is requested is to meet in person to discuss the candidate's strengths and qualifications. Of course, most employers are able to recognize that the interviewee is attempting to gain employment, but in a sophisticated and unique manner. If the manager is not able to meet due to a lack of job opportunities, the interviewee attempts to schedule the meeting anyway in case a job opportunity should become available in the future. If the manager still cannot arrange an interview, the interviewee solicits potential employers who may be hiring. If the manager is aware of potential employers, he or she is asked if it would be fine to indicate that the manager referred the interviewee to this employer (or business). The client would later call the referral and indicate that the manager referred the client to call the referral.

MHP: Hello, Mrs. Jones. My name is Jennifer Ramirez. Thank you for taking the time to speak with me. I'm a very motivated, loyal, and extremely hardworking person with a lot of experience cooking in outstanding restaurants such as yours. I would enjoy meeting with you at your earliest convenience to discuss my qualifications further. I think you'd really be impressed with me.

Manager: You said your name was Jennifer, is that right? I am sorry to say that we are not hiring anybody right now. We're in a hiring freeze.

MHP: I understand. Perhaps I could meet with you anyway, just in case something should open up later? I really think you'd find that I have a lot to offer.

Manager: Right now is not a good time for me. I just don't have time to meet with you.

MHP: Okay, I understand. May I ask, do you know of any other employers who may be interested in someone with my qualifications?

Manager: Hmmm . . . I did hear that Alan's Steak House is looking for a new cook. You know, the place over on State Street?

MHP: Yes, I do. Thank you. Is it all right if I tell the manager at Alan's that you referred me?

Manager: Sure, that would be fine.

Client Role-Play of Job Interview Solicitation (Client and Adolescent and Adult Significant Others)

After the MHP models how to request a job interview, the client is instructed to attempt to ask for a job interview, with the MHP playing an accommodating and compliant potential employer. It is important for the MHP to be compliant during the role-play to build the client's self-efficacy in requesting job opportunities. To assist in this endeavor, the client should be instructed to utilize the Interviewing Skills Worksheet to prompt correct responding. It may be necessary to instruct the client to make several attempts until the steps are executed with ease. The MHP may also conduct further modeling throughout the process whenever indicated. Of course, the MHP will gradually phase out assistance as the client's performance improves. It is also very appropriate to instruct adolescent and adult significant others to role-play the job interview solicitation.

MHP: I would now like you to go through the steps I just modeled in requesting a job interview. We'll pretend I'm a secretary answering the phone, and later I'll pretend to be a potential employer. What restaurant do you want me to be?

Chris: Why don't we do Alan's Steakhouse?

MHP: Sounds like a great restaurant to work at. Remember to refer to your Interviewing Skills Worksheet to help you go through the steps, and take your time, as you're not expected to memorize them. Even later, you'll always be able to use the worksheet you have in your hand, as the people on the other end of the telephone line won't know you have it there. You're going to be on the phone, so feel free to read it as you go. Let's write a couple of strengths and qualifications in the spaces by the fourth step so you're prepared to smoothly list them off when you get there in the phone interview.

Chris: I've always been hardworking and loyal to my employer. And I have worked in the restaurant business for many years.

MHP: That's fantastic. So, ring, ring. Hi, this is Joe from Alan's Steakhouse.

Chris: Hello, this is Chris Alvarez. Who is the manager working today?

MHP: Great stuff, Chris. You were polite and right to the point. Go ahead and ask if you can speak with the manager. . . .

The role-play would continue in this manner, with the MHP praising the client for each step that is performed correctly, and offering suggestions about how to improve performance as needed, until all of the steps were completed. It is important to consider potential nervousness of clients, as similar efforts may have resulted in rejection. Thus, the MHP should avoid commentary about signs of nervousness and provide ample encouragement and praise throughout the role-play. Significant others are often instructed to praise efforts of clients and potentially attempt job-getting role-plays themselves, whenever appropriate.

Client Job Interview Solicitation With Potential Employer (Client and Adolescent and Adult Significant Others)

Once the client and, potentially, the significant others have successfully solicited job interviews during two or three role-plays, it is important to instruct them to attempt interviews with potential employers during the session utilizing the Interviewing Skills Worksheet (Worksheet 11.1). Common interview questions are listed at the bottom of the worksheet, as well as space for clients to write their responses. Common questions include, for example: Tell me about yourself. Why do you want to work here? What are some of your strengths and weaknesses? Why did you leave your last job? Why should I hire you? The MHP provides verbal prompts throughout the interview, and may also point to specific instructions in the Interviewing Skills Worksheet if the client gets lost during the telephone interview. Clients should identify potential employers in telephone books or based on personal knowledge of businesses in their area that might be appropriate. It is best to start with employers who are geographically far away from the client's residence to assist in gaining practice with less desirable jobs. Jobs that are particularly desired should be the last ones called. The client will need to have a pen or pencil to record potential leads. Clients are often very nervous in making these calls; thus, it is particularly important to keep critique of these interviews positive, avoiding suggestions unless specifically requested. If the client hangs up due to nervousness or embarrassment during an interview, immediately reinforce positive actions and tell the client the interview was good practice.

Preparation for Job Interview (Client and Adolescent and Adult Significant Others)

It is important to prepare clients for job interviews. Along these lines, the MHP first queries the client's understanding of how to properly dress for a job interview. This provides an assessment of the client's insights into dress codes, as well as the client's receptivity to dressing formally (suit and/or tie for men, suit or dress for women), which is highly encouraged. They are encouraged to conservatively hide tattoos and take off nose rings, hats, and ill-fitting, baggy, or worn clothing. Conservative colors are also recommended, such as gray, black, and blue tones. They are also encouraged to avoid gaudy jewelry.

It is important to assess the client's understanding of what to say during the interview. Generally, clients are encouraged to keep conversation focused on client's strengths, being honest, expressing passion about various opportunities, and stating positive qualities about past employers and the potential employer. Clients are also advised to avoid derogatory aspersions about others. General interviewing strategies should be extensively and spontaneously role-played to assist the client in being comfortable during the interviewing process. Responses to a prescribed list of common interview questions listed in the Prepare for Common Interview Questions section of the Interviewing Skills Worksheet are also role-played. Appropriate responses to interview questions should be reviewed prior to role-playing.

MHPs should assign clients to practice job-interviewing skills with family members and seek job interviews until a job is obtained. They should be forewarned that the strategy of soliciting job interviews is likely to be successful only when a high number of calls are attempted.

Future Sessions

Future sessions that review this intervention follow the steps outlined in the Job-Getting Skills Training Therapist Prompting Checklist for Future Sessions (Prompting Checklist 11.2). Job Getting may be utilized in future sessions to assess skills during calls to employers and improve skills through practice. It is also important to continuously review in-person job interviewing skills, as well as things to avoid during job interviews.

Concluding Remarks

Job-Getting Skills Training is a skill-based intervention with demonstrated effectiveness in helping clients successfully obtain employment by providing them with strategies to assist in obtaining job interviews and performing well once interviews are obtained. Clients value these basic skills. Indeed, many gain a sense of self-confidence as they apply these skills to interviews. It is important, however, that clients practice making telephone calls to potential employers during their intervention sessions so MHPs will have opportunities to descriptively praise them and support them through the process, as many will be nervous and give up quite easily without such encouragement. After the first call is made to a potential employer, it will be very important to avoid critique. That is, no suggestions should be offered regarding changes in behavior to raise self-efficacy to attempt more telephone calls, which is the key to eventual employment.

Supporting Materials for Chapter 11: Gaining Employment

Prompting Checklist 11.1. Job-Getting Skills Training Therapist Prompting Checklist for Initial Session.

JOB-GETTING SKILLS TRAINING

THERAPIST PROMPTING CHECKLIST
Initial Session

Client ID: _____   Clinician: _____   Session #:_____   Session Date:_____

Materials Required

• Interviewing Skills Worksheet (ISW)

Begin Time:_____

Rationale for Job Interview Solicitation (Client and Adolescent and Adult Significant Others)

___a.   Ensure client is interested in obtaining a satisfying job.
___b.   Query why a satisfying job would be important.
___c.   Solicit components of a dream job or career.
___d.   Solicit benefits of a dream job or career.
___e.   Solicit methods of making the dream job or career happen.
___f.   Determine solutions to obstacles involved in obtaining a "dream job" or career.
    • Problem-solve if necessary.

___g.   State JG is designed to obtain job interviews.
___h.   State JG helps individuals learn how to present themselves well during interviews.
___i.   State JG has been successful w/others.
___j.   State why JG is expected to be particularly effective w/client.
___k.   Solicit questions and provide answers as indicated.

Modeling Solicitation of Job Interview (Client and Adolescent and Adult Significant Others)

• Provide client a copy of ISW.
• Model the following telephone interviewing components:
___a.   Introduce self.
___b.   Solicit name of manager on shift.
___c.   Ask to speak w/manager.
    ___1.   If asked what it is regarding, state it is "personal."
    ___2.   If unavailable, disclose that you will call back (do not leave a message to call back).

___d.   When manager answers do the following:
     ___1.   Introduce self.
     ___2.   Thank manager for taking call.
     ___3.   List a few qualifications or personal strengths.
     ___4.   Solicit an in-person interview to discuss qualifications.
          ___a.   If scheduled, state you're looking forward to the interview.
          ___b.   If manager can't arrange interview, attempt to schedule later time.
          ___c.   If not scheduled, solicit referral to other employers & verify it's okay to reference manager.

Client Role-Play of Job Interview Solicitation (Client and Adolescent and Adult Significant Others)

___a.   Instruct client to solicit interview w/MHP pretending to be potential employer via phone using ISW.
___b.   Prompt or descriptively praise client for performing each of the following:
     ___1.   Introduce self.
     ___2.   Solicit manager on shift.
     ___3.   Ask to speak w/manager.
          ___a.   If asked what it is regarding, state it is "personal."
          ___b.   If unavailable, disclose that you will call back.
     ___4.   When manager answers do the following:
          ___a.   Introduce self.
          ___b.   Thank manager for taking call.
          ___c.   List a few qualifications or personal strengths.
          ___d.   Solicit an in-person interview.
               ___i.   If scheduled, state you're looking forward to the interview.
              ___ii.   If manager can't arrange interview, attempt to schedule later time.
              ___iii. If not scheduled, solicit referral to other similar employers.

Client Job Interview Solicitation w/Potential Employer (Client and Adolescent and Adult Significant Others)

___a.   Instruct client to solicit interview w/potential employer via phone using ISW.
___b.   Prompt client in performing each of the following steps, if not initiated by client:
     ___1.   Introduce self.
     ___2.   Solicit manager on shift.
     ___3.   Ask to speak w/the manager.
          ___a.   If asked what it is regarding, state it is "personal."
          ___b.   If unavailable, disclose that you will call back.
     ___4.   When manager answers do the following:
          ___a.   Introduce self.
          ___b.   Thank manager for taking call.
          ___c.   List a few qualifications or personal strengths.
          ___d.   Solicit an in-person interview.
               ___i.   If scheduled, state you're looking forward to the interview.
              ___ii.   If manager can't arrange interview, attempt to schedule later time.
              ___iii. If not scheduled, solicit referral to other similar employers.
___c.   Descriptively praise client after call is completed.

Preparation for Job Interview (Client and Adolescent and Adult Significant Others)

___a. Solicit client's understanding of how to dress for job interview, & assist when appropriate.

___b. Indicate usually important to dress formally/conservatively (suit and/or tie for men, suit or dress for women).

___c. Indicate to hide tattoos; don't wear nose rings, hats, torn, ill-fitting, baggy, or worn clothing, or gaudy jewelry.

___d. Solicit client's understanding of what to say during interview, and assist when appropriate.

- Generally keep conversation focused on client's strengths, being honest, being passionate about opportunities, stating positive qualities of employer and agency.
- Don't speak derogatorily about other employers or other people.

___e. Review the following list of common interview questions w/client, including potential solutions.

   ___1. Tell me about yourself.
   ___2. Why do you want to work here?
   ___3. What are some of your strengths and weaknesses?
   ___4. Why did you leave your last job?
   ___5. Why should we hire you?

- State if offer is made client should indicate happiness w/offer, but that hoping for more given personal strengths and qualifications.

Client's Assessment of Helpfulness of the Intervention

___a. After stating client should not feel obligated to provide high scores, as an honest assessment helps better address client needs, solicit how helpful client thought intervention was using 7-point scale:

   7 = extremely helpful, 6 = very helpful, 5 = somewhat helpful, 4 = not sure,
   3 = somewhat unhelpful, 2 = very unhelpful, 1 = extremely unhelpful

- **Record Client's Rating Here:_____**

___b. Solicit how rating was derived, and methods of improving intervention in future.

Therapist's Rating of Client's Compliance with Intervention

___a. Disclose therapist's rating of client's compliance using 7-point scale:

   7 = extremely compliant, 6 = very compliant, 5 = somewhat compliant, 4 = neutral,
   3 = somewhat noncompliant, 2 = very noncompliant, 1 = extremely noncompliant

- Factors that contribute to compliance ratings are:
  - Attendance
  - Participation and conduct in session
  - Homework completion
- **Record Therapist's Rating of Client's Compliance Here:_____**

___b. Disclose client's compliance rating.

___c. Explain how rating was derived, and methods of improving performance in future.

End Time:_____

Prompting Checklist 11.2. Job-Getting Skills Training Therapist Prompting Checklist for Future Sessions.

JOB-GETTING SKILLS TRAINING

THERAPIST PROMPTING CHECKLIST
Future Sessions

Client ID: _____ Clinician: _____   Session #:_____ Session Date:_____

Materials Required

• Interviewing Skills Worksheet (ISW)

Begin Time:_____

Client Solicits Interview with Therapist's Assistance (Client and Adolescent and Adult Significant Others)

___a. Instruct client to solicit an interview w/a potential employer over the telephone utilizing the ISW as a guide.

___b. Assist client in performing each of the following:

    ___1. Introduce self.

    ___2. Solicit manager on shift

    ___3. Ask to speak w/manager.

        ___a. If asked what it is regarding, state it is "personal."

        ___b. If unavailable, disclose that you will call back.

    ___4. When manager answers do the following:

        ___a. Introduce self.

        ___b. Thank manager for taking call.

        ___c. List a few qualifications or personal strengths.

        ___d. Solicit an in-person interview to further discuss qualifications.

___i.   If scheduled, state you're looking forward to the interview.

___ii. If manager can't arrange interview, attempt to schedule later time.

___iii. If not scheduled, solicit referral to other similar employer & verify it's okay to reference the manager.

___c. Descriptively praise client for performance once call is completed.

___d. Review things to focus on during job interviews, as well as things to avoid during job interviews.

Client's Assessment of Helpfulness of the Intervention

___a. After stating client should not feel obligated to provide high scores, as an honest assessment helps better address client needs, solicit how helpful client thought intervention was using 7-point scale:

    7 = extremely helpful, **6** = very helpful, **5** = somewhat helpful, **4** = not sure,

    3 = somewhat unhelpful, **2** = very unhelpful, **1** = extremely unhelpful

- **Record Client's Rating Here:_____**

___b. Solicit how rating was derived, and methods of improving intervention in future.

Therapist's Rating of Client's Compliance with Intervention

___a. Disclose therapist's rating of client's compliance using 7-point scale:

7 = extremely compliant, **6** = very compliant, **5** = somewhat compliant, **4** = neutral,

3 = somewhat noncompliant, **2** = very noncompliant, **1** = extremely noncompliant

- Factors that contribute to compliance ratings are:
  - Attendance
  - Participation and conduct in session
  - Homework completion

- **Record Therapist's Rating of Client's Compliance Here:_____**

___b. Disclose client's compliance rating.

___c. Explain how rating was derived, and methods of improving performance in future.

End Time:_____

Worksheet 11.1. Interviewing Skills Worksheet.

INTERVIEWING SKILLS WORKSHEET

THERAPIST PROMPTING CHECKLIST
Future Sessions

Instructions: Follow these steps when attempting to set up an interview with an employer over the phone.

1.	Introduce yourself.
2.	Ask the name of the manager on shift.
3.	Ask to speak with the manager. • If asked why or what it is regarding, answer that it's personal. • If manager is unavailable, state that you will call back.

4.	**When manager answers do the following:**
	• Introduce self.
	• Thank manager for taking call (& indicate if someone referred you).
	• State a few qualifications or personal strengths:
	    a. _____
	    b. _____
	    c. _____
	• Ask to schedule an in-person interview to further discuss qualifications.
	    a. If scheduled: state you're looking forward to the interview.
	    b. If manager can't arrange interview: attempt to schedule a later time.
	    c. If manager can't schedule later time: ask for referral.

Prepare for Common Interview Questions
1. Tell me about yourself.
2. Why do you want to work here?
3. What are some of your strengths and weaknesses?
4. Why did you leave your last job?
5. Why should we hire you?

12

Managing Finances

Rationale and Overview

Maintaining financial well-being is extremely important to clients who have a history of drug abuse and other problem behaviors, as they are often unemployed, spend excessive amounts of money on illicit drugs or things that are immediately gratifying but do not contribute to their future welfare, and lack basic vocational and financial management skills. Therefore, this intervention is focused on assisting clients in balancing their budget, including any money that they receive, and other resources, such as food stamps. Learning to identify precursors to financial deficits, prioritize spending, and obtain and manage additional income permits these clients to better allocate money to appropriate sources, and avoid financial crises that may habitually increase motivation to use drugs to reduce stress or engage in other problem behaviors (e.g., stealing).

Financial Management Skills Training involves listing monthly expenses, listing types and amounts of monthly income, determining financial deficit or surplus, and learning to obtain and manage additional income. When deficits are determined, clients are taught to prioritize expenses and eliminate or reduce low-priority expenses. In cases where eliminating or reducing low-priority expenses is infeasible or undesirable, MHPs assist clients in brainstorming methods of increasing income.

Goals for Intervention

➣ Accomplish a financial budget.

➣ Prioritize expenditures and eliminate unnecessary expenses.

➣ Generate methods of increasing income and decreasing financial deficits.

Materials Required

➤ Financial Management Therapist Prompting Checklist for Initial Session (Prompting Checklist 12.1, also located on the CD that accompanies this book)

➤ Financial Management Therapist Prompting Checklist for Future Sessions (Prompting Checklist 12.2, also located on the CD that accompanies this book)

➤ Financial Management Worksheet (Worksheet 12.1, also located on the CD that accompanies this book)

Procedural Steps for Treatment Implementation

Presenting Rationale for Financial Management (Client and Significant Others)

Using the Financial Management Therapist Prompting Checklist for Initial Session (Prompting Checklist 12.1), mental health providers (MHPs) initiate this intervention by reporting that financial stress often acts as a trigger to drug use and other problem behaviors. They are told that many clients have indicated it is difficult to balance a budget (i.e., amount of income from employment or other resources is equal to the amount of expenses going out of the home). MHPs attempt to gain a commitment from clients that they will find it helpful to increase income and lower expenses. If interested, they are told that Financial Management Skills Training involves generating a list of both income and expenses so that financial needs and surpluses can be determined. Most importantly, they are told that Financial Management Skills Training involves prioritizing expenses, determining how best to cut expenses, brainstorming methods of saving and obtaining greater income, and then implementing these methods of saving or obtaining greater income. Consistent with FBT rationales, clients are asked to provide reasons the intervention is expected to be beneficial. However, when clients evidence difficulties coming up with viable benefits, MHPs are encouraged to offer benefits that have been indicated by others, such as paying bills, rent, or mortgage on time; purchasing desired items when desired; and decreased stress. When clients are involved in the judicial system, they can be reminded that caseworkers and probation and parole officers usually provide more freedom to clients who are financially secure. An example of an MHP presenting this rationale to a client and significant others is presented in the following sections.

MHP: As you've indicated, financial stress often acts to trigger drug use and insomnia, which are two problems that you've recently experienced. Others have indicated that it is very hard to balance financial budgets, particularly in tough economic times. So Financial Management was developed to help our clients effectively balance a budget so the money coming in is more than what's going out! Isn't that wonderful?

Chris: That does sound great. I think my family could really use something like that since we always seem to be short on money.

MHP: Fantastic! First, we're going to generate a list of money coming in and money going out so your financial needs, or extra money, can be determined exactly. The second step will be to prioritize your expenses and figure out how best to cut your expenses, if at all. The third step will involve putting our heads together and thinking of a bunch of things we can do to save money and achieve greater income. The last step involves setting up a plan and actually doing the plan. I think this is going to be great for you because it will take away the stressor that seems to be weighing heavily on your mind. You don't deserve that! Why do you think this will be good?

Chris: It would help get my credit score up again, and then I wouldn't have to be afraid answering my phone because there is a bill collector on the other end.

MHP: That's exactly right. And good credit in a bad economy is very important. Would it be good to not have to worry about paying your bills and having those bill collectors calling?

Chris: Yeah, that would be a big relief.

MHP: Good for you to recognize this. You could also be able to buy healthy snacks for your kids and not have to feel bad about spending the money. How would that be?

Chris: That would be good, too.

MHP: Great! What would your probation officer say if he knew you were able to balance a budget for your family?

Chris: I think she would probably respect me and my ideas more.

MHP: Yes, and respect is everything when you're trying to get full custody of your kids back from the state.

Determining Financial Need or Surplus (Client and Significant Others)

The MHP may provide each family member a copy of the Financial Management Worksheet to review (Expenses section, and Income and Total Budget sections; Worksheet 12.1). However, recordings occur only in the client's copy. The client is instructed to first review the expense items, and indicates personal expenses for the average month in the "amount" column. The client is then instructed to review the income items, and report income gained in the average month in the "amount" column. The total monthly expenses are then quickly subtracted from the total monthly income and recorded in the bottom left column of the Income and Total Budget section of the Financial Management Worksheet. This amount may indicate a deficit or surplus. The MHP discloses the monthly balance, and asks the client how it would help to enhance surplus to help motivate the client to increase income. Of course, all responses that suggest more money would be helpful are descriptively praised with enthusiasm.

MHP: Here's a copy of the Financial Management Worksheet. On the first page are expenses some families experience. I'd like you to indicate how much you usually spend in each of these areas during each month on average, and record your answers in the amount column, as appropriate.

Client completes the assignment.

MHP: Outstanding, you should have been an accountant! The next page identifies sources of income some families experience. I'd like you to indicate how much income you obtain each month in each of these areas, and record your answers in the amount column, as appropriate.

Client completes the assignment.

MHP: Great job getting your monthly expenses and incomes recorded. Now, I'd like you to subtract your total monthly income from your total monthly expenses and record them at the bottom of this worksheet.

This will tell us if you have extra money at the end of the month or owe money.

Client completes the assignment.

MHP: Great work, your balance seems to be $10, indicating that at the end of each month you probably have about $10 cash. How would it help to enhance your surplus of cash each month?

The client and MHP conclude by discussing methods of increasing income.

Brainstorming Methods of Decreasing Expenses (Client and Significant Others)

The MHP refers the client and participating family members to the Expenses section of the worksheet and helps the client brainstorm ways of decreasing expenses. This is usually a wonderful opportunity for the family to work together on a common and very important goal. All methods of decreasing expenses are recorded in the Ways to Decrease Expenses column, in the rows corresponding to their respective expenses. After all potential expenses are reviewed, the total amount of estimated savings is computed at the bottom of the "projected savings" column, and this amount is subsequently recorded in the box to the right of the projected savings column at the bottom of the Income and Total Budget sections of the worksheet, as illustrated in the following exchange:

MHP: Okay, let's look at the Expenses section of the worksheet and think of ways of decreasing these expenses. The first one listed is the rent. You're paying $800 a month. How can we lower that?

Chris: I don't think there is anything we can really do about that. This is about the cheapest place we can find that is big enough for our family.

MHP: At first it may seem like that, but we could do a number of things.

Fabiola: You know, Chris, we could ask the landlord to lower our rent.

MHP: That's a great idea.

Chris: I guess we could try that positive request thing we went over a couple of sessions ago.

MHP: Now you're thinking. You have nothing to lose, and you have a lot you can put into that request. Heck, you've been here forever paying the rent on time, right? *(Client laughs)* Super, so make sure the landlord knows that. How much do you think you can get the landlord to go down?

Fabiola: I was talking with that lady that just moved in downstairs, and she said she is paying $750.

MHP: Great, so you can at least ask for that. I'll put $50 in the decreasing expenses column. You can also make sure you let the landlord know there are other options for you, but first you may want to explore your options. There are a lot of places in the neighborhood you could move to so you could keep your kids in the same school district. Even if you didn't move, you could at least know that was an option when you talk with the landlord. *(The MHP, client, and his wife review all remaining expenses in a similar manner.)* That was amazing! Let's add these all up and discover your savings. . . ."

Brainstorming Methods of Achieving Greater Income (Client and Significant Others)

The next step is to assist the client in brainstorming ways of increasing income. Each method is recorded in the Ways to Increase Income column, and later totaled in the Total Projected Gains column. The total amount is also recorded in the box to the right of the Projected Gains box.

MHP: Now for the fun! We get to review the Income column and try to think of ways of increasing income. I like this one because it will give us a chance to be creative, and keep you too busy to experience any problems! *(Family laughs.)* So, what can we do to increase income from your main job?

Fabiola: I could ask my boss for a raise.

MHP: Outstanding! How would you ask for a raise, and how much would you ask for?

Fabiola: I wasn't really thinking about asking for a specific amount. I figured I could leave it up to my boss—if he said yes.

MHP: Well, that is one strategy, but, really, you have all the control because you can determine when you ask and how you ask. For instance, you can bring him his favorite dessert to soften him up, tell him how long you have worked together, give him a well-thought-out Positive Request, and so on.

Chris: Yeah, you could remind him that you never charge him for gas during business trips, and the price of gas has gone up.

MHP: Excellent idea! You could also ask for a small amount, say 25 cents an hour. That's only $2 a day extra, but it comes out to $40 a month!

Fabiola: Wow, I never thought about it like that.

MHP: Yeah, $480.00 a year, but we're getting ahead of ourselves. Things are going great already. Let's do the rest and add up our projected gains. . . ."

Determining Projected Financial Need or Surplus (Client and Significant Others)

The last step in the initial session is to add the total projected savings to total projected gains to get projected extra income. The MHP congratulates the client for developing plans to earn extra money. The MHP then works with the family to further develop implementation plans, role-play implementation skills, and transfer plans to the Behavioral Goals and Rewards and Environmental Control Worksheets, as indicated in the following narrative:

MHP: We're almost done. Let's add the total projected savings to the total projected gains and see what we get. Wow, if you're able to carry out the plan, you would have $275 extra per month. Let's get some of these things into action. One of the things I wanted to put on your Behavioral Goals and Rewards Worksheet (see Chapter 5) is the goal of setting up a savings account for you in which your wife has to cosign in order for you to withdraw money, and getting your paychecks automatically deposited into this bank account. You said you'd be willing to do this for a month and see how it goes, so you can make this a focus goal for next week.

Chris: We could try that for a couple of months to see how it goes.

MHP: Great. We have some more time left in the session, so let's keep working on some of these other plans until we run out of time.

Future Sessions

Implementing Methods of Saving or Achieving Greater Income (Client and Significant Others) Future Financial Management Skills Training sessions are conducted according to the Financial Management Therapist Prompting Checklist for Future Sessions (Prompting Checklist 12.2). These sessions are focused on distributing the completed Financial Management Worksheets, and assisting clients in (1) decreasing existing expenses, (2) increasing income, and (3) establishing plans to implement brainstormed methods for saving or achieving greater income and decreasing expenses.

Concluding Remarks

Financial Management Skills Training is a great complement to Job Getting and is very valuable for clients who have secure jobs as well. For instance, some clients are quite capable of achieving high-paying jobs but, due to their fast-paced lifestyle or lack of responsibility, experience difficulties maintaining a financial surplus. It is also important to point out that financial management is a skill that is often taken for granted. Of course, some are quite thrifty but do not have the insights to realize how they may be able to actively reduce debts and expenses. In any event, however, Financial Management Skills Training may be used as a quick assessment to determine if these problems do exist, and clients frequently appreciate this intervention.

Supporting Materials for Chapter 12: Managing Finances

Prompting Checklist 12.1. Financial Management Therapist Prompting Checklist for Initial Session.

FINANCIAL MANAGEMENT

THERAPIST PROMPTING CHECKLIST
Initial Session

Client ID:_____ Clinician: _____ Session #: _____ Session Date: _____

Materials Required

• Financial Management Worksheet (FMW)

Begin Time:_____

Presenting Rationale for Financial Management (Client and Significant Others)

___a.   State financial difficulties often trigger drug use & other problem behaviors.
___b.   State many people have difficulties balancing a financial budget.
___c.   Determine if client is interested in learning Financial Management (FM) skills.
___d.   State FM involves:

    ___1.   Developing a list for both income and expenses to determine financial need or surplus.
    ___2.   Prioritizing expenses, and determining how best to cut expenses.
    ___3.   Brainstorming methods of saving or achieving greater income.
    ___4.   Making specific plans to implement methods of saving or achieving greater income & cutting expenses.

___e.   Solicit reasons FM skills are beneficial.

    • For each of following if not mentioned, query if client believes reason is important:
    ___1.   Ability to pay utility bills and rent on time.
    ___2.   Ability to purchase desired healthy foods.
    ___3.   Less stress.
    ___4.   Purchase things that are desired.
    ___5.   People usually give more freedom to clients who are financially secure.

Determining Financial Need or Surplus (Client and Significant Others)

___a.   Provide copy of FMW.
___b.   Instruct to review expense prompts, & report monthly expenses in amount column of Expense Section of FMW.
___c.   Instruct to review income prompts, & report monthly income in amount column of Income & Total Budget Sections of FMW.
___d.   Assist in subtracting total income from total expenses, and record in appropriate boxes at the bottom of the Income & Total Budget Sections of FMW.
___e.   Disclose the extent client is in a surplus or deficit.

Brainstorming Methods of Decreasing Expenses (Client and Significant Others)

___a.   Identify methods of decreasing expenses, and record in "ways to decrease expenses" column of the Expenses Section of FMW.
  • Estimate amount of money that would be saved by managing costs in each area.
___b.   Indicate total estimated amount of money saved.
  • Record estimated amount of money in appropriate sections of Expense section of FMW.

Brainstorming Methods of Achieving Greater Income (Client and Significant Others)

___a.   Identify methods of achieving extra income, and record in "ways to increase income" column of Income & Total Budget sections of FMW.
___b.   Indicate total amount of money that would be gained by incorporating these new sources of income.
  • Record total estimated amount gained in Income and Total Budget Sections of FMW.

Determining Projected Financial Need or Surplus (Client and Significant Others)

___a.   Add total projected savings to total projected gains to get projected extra income.
___b.   Assist client in developing plans relevant to implementing methods of saving or achieving more income & decreasing expenses.
___c.   Add developed plans to Behavioral Goals & Rewards and Environmental Control Worksheets.

Client's Assessment of Helpfulness of the Intervention

___a.   After stating client should not feel obligated to provide high scores, as an honest assessment helps better address client needs, solicit how helpful client thought intervention was using 7-point scale:
    7 = extremely helpful, 6 = very helpful, 5 = somewhat helpful, 4 = not sure,
    3 = somewhat unhelpful, 2 = very unhelpful, 1 = extremely unhelpful
  • **Record Client's Rating Here:**_____
___b.   Solicit how rating was derived, and methods of improving intervention in future.

Therapist's Rating of Client's Compliance with Intervention

___a.   Disclose therapist's rating of client's compliance using 7-point scale:
    7 = extremely compliant, 6 = very compliant, 5 = somewhat compliant, 4 = neutral,
    3 = somewhat noncompliant, 2 = very noncompliant, 1 = extremely noncompliant
  • Factors that contribute to compliance ratings are:
    • Attendance
    • Participation and conduct in session
    • Homework completion
  • **Record Therapist's Rating of Client's Compliance Here:**_____
___b.   Disclose client's compliance rating.
___c.   Explain how rating was derived, and methods of improving performance in future.

End Time:_____

Prompting Checklist 12.2. Financial Management Therapist Prompting Checklist for Future Sessions.

FINANCIAL MANAGEMENT

THERAPIST PROMPTING CHECKLIST
Future Sessions

Client ID:_____ Clinician:_____ Session #:_____ Session Date:_____

Materials Required

- Financial Management Worksheet (FMW)

Begin Time:_____

Implementing Methods of Saving or Achieving Greater Income (Client and Significant Others)

___a. Utilize and/or modify the FMW to assist client in saving or achieving greater income, & reducing expenses.

Client's Assessment of Helpfulness of the Intervention

___a. After stating client should not feel obligated to provide high scores, as an honest assessment helps better address client needs, solicit how helpful client thought intervention was using 7-point scale:
    7 = extremely helpful, **6** = very helpful, **5** = somewhat helpful, **4** = not sure,
    3 = somewhat unhelpful, **2** = very unhelpful, **1** = extremely unhelpful
- **Record Client's Rating Here:_____**

___b. Solicit how rating was derived, and methods of improving intervention in future.

Therapist's Rating of Client's Compliance with Intervention

___a. Disclose therapist's rating of client's compliance using 7-point scale:
    7 = extremely compliant, **6** = very compliant, **5** = somewhat compliant, **4** = neutral,
    3 = somewhat noncompliant, **2** = very noncompliant, **1** = extremely noncompliant
- Factors that contribute to compliance ratings are:
    - Attendance
    - Participation and conduct in session
    - Homework completion
- **Record Therapist's Rating of Client's Compliance Here:_____**

___b. Disclose client's compliance rating.

___c. Explain how rating was derived, and methods of improving performance in future.

End Time:_____

Worksheet 12.1. Financial Management Worksheet.

FINANCIAL MANAGEMENT WORKSHEET

Expenses Section

Monthly Expenses	Amount	Ways to Decrease Expenses	Projected Savings
Rent/Mortgage	$		$
Average spent on food per week $_____._____ × 4 =	$		$
Electric Bill	$		$
Gas Bill	$		$
Water Bill	$		$
House Phone	$		$
Car Payment	$		$
Car Insurance	$		$
Car Repair Bills	$		$
Cell Phone	$		$
Cable	$		$
Credit Cards	$		$
Medical	$		$
Home Products and Furniture	$		$
Fun Things: Movies, Bowling, Restaurants, Gym Memberships, etc.	$		$
Bad Habits: Alcohol, Drugs, Gambling, Cigarettes, etc.	$		$
Other:	$		$
Total Monthly Expenses =	$	Total Projected Savings =	$

FINANCIAL MANAGEMENT WORKSHEET

INCOME & TOTAL BUDGET SECTIONS

Monthly Income	Amount	Ways to Increase Income	Projected Gains
Main Job	$		$
Part time job(s)	$		$
Child Support	$		$
Legal Settlement Awards	$		$
State & Federal Assistance	$		$
Private or Church-Based Assistance	$		$
Inheritance &/or Investment Income (e.g., Stocks, Bonds, Real Estate Sales)	$		$
Assistance from Family/Friends	$		$
Other	$		$
Total Monthly income:	$	Total Projected Gains:	$

Total Monthly Income:	$	Projected Savings:	$
Total Monthly Expenses:	$	Projected Gains:	$
Remaining Balance: (income – expenses)	$	Projected Extra Income: (savings + gains)	$

13

Concluding Treatment and Planning for Success

Rationale and Overview

FBT usually occurs for about 6 months, and its timing of termination is mutually determined between clients and their treatment providers. Treatment termination is ideally based on the clients' demonstration of positive results from various therapeutic progress indicators, such as negative urinalysis testing, decreased symptoms based on validated questionnaires, demonstrated skills during role-plays, and collateral reports of behavioral goal accomplishment.

In the last session, the MHP queries family members to indicate how their personal strengths, particularly those addressed during therapy, may be utilized to maintain accomplishment of goals that were a focus in therapy. Thus, clients and their families are assisted in reviewing how treatment effects will be generalized to future endeavors. The session concludes with all family members communicating things they love, admire, and respect about each other. The emphasis on acquired skills is important because it substantiates self-efficacy in clients.

Goals for Intervention

➤ Identification of family strengths that may be used to assist in generalizing treatment effects to future endeavors.

Materials Required

➤ Last Session: Concluding Treatment and Planning for Success Therapist Prompting Checklist (Prompting Checklist 13.1, also located on the CD that accompanies this book)

Procedural Steps for Treatment Implementation
Reviewing Strengths (Client and Adult Significant Others)

The first half of the last session involves the client and adult significant others. As indicated in the Last Session: Concluding Treatment and Planning for Success Therapist Prompting Checklist (Prompting Checklist 13.1), mental health providers (MHPs) initiate the session by instructing clients and their adult significant others to report how they will utilize their strengths and skills to assist in avoiding drug and alcohol use, maintaining cohesive and functional family relationships, and personal achievement (e.g., employment, school graduation). For instance, clients may be asked, "What personal strengths and abilities will you use to help Kendra keep living a clean and healthy life?" Thus, adult significant others are free to contemporaneously choose specific topics within the umbrella of these nonspecific goals. Of course, MHPs provide enthusiastic and descriptive praise for all positive responses and disallow statements that are consistent with self-deprecation. MHPs may also implement FBT interventions and solicit discussion about methods of accomplishing future aspirations whenever appropriate throughout the last session.

MHP: I'm so excited for you both and can't wait to do this last session exercise because I'm so very proud of each of you. First, I'd like each of you to answer a few questions I've prepared to assist in identifying the strengths and abilities in your family that are going to be used to maintain the goals we've set in therapy. The first one I have concerns how both of you are going to use your strengths and abilities to keep Kendra living a clean and healthy life. *(Kendra and her husband, Howard, indicate a number of things each of them will be able to do.)* I absolutely love what I'm hearing. It is music to my ears to hear that you will all be walking around the neighborhood together to lose weight and build your relationships back to how good they used to be. I also think it might give you opportunities to meet some of your neighbors to establish a new, healthy social network. How could you increase the likelihood of establishing new friends from these walks?

Howard: I could invite them over for a barbecue if we liked them.

MHP: That's great how you're using your cooking skills.

Kendra: He's also using his assertiveness skills!

After reviewing the remaining goals, children would be invited to enter the room.

Family Exchange of Positive Remarks (All Family Members)

When all goals are addressed, usually after about 20 to 35 minutes, children are invited into the room to participate. Without recording forms for the family, MHPs instruct all family members to exchange things they love, admire, and respect about each other. Of course, this procedure is consistent with the guidelines established earlier when utilizing the I've Got a Great Family intervention. However, the exercise is less formal, and the MHP is involved in the role of an additional "family member." That is, family members are provided an opportunity to tell the MHP things they love, admire, and respect about the MHP, and the MHP reciprocates these comments. The session usually ends with a group hug or other signs of affection.

MHP: This is the last time you'll all be able to share things you love, admire, and respect about yourselves with me in the room so I thought I'd like to join you all this time if that's okay.

Vincent: I have something for you. I respect how you helped my mom and dad listen to what I had to say during therapy.

MHP: Thank you, Vincent. I really appreciate your saying that. It's those kinds of comments that motivate me to never forget how important it is to listen. I also respect you for asking your parents to trust you with more freedom using PR. I know that was hard for you at the time to do, but it comes naturally now. Do you have something to say to Vincent, parents? . . .

Concluding Remarks

The last session encourages family members to experience pride in their performance during the past few months, and assists them in looking to the future with optimism. Although the session solicits positive affect, it is also very skill oriented. That is, when reviewing strengths and skills in family members, MHPs provide descriptive praise and query how family members will be able to overcome obstacles. Of course, the reviewed obstacles are typically identified during the previous treatment sessions, so family members are usually quite adept at generating viable solutions. It is also important to emphasize the importance of having the MHP listed in the positive remarks, as family members usually experience great joy in using this exercise to show their appreciation of the MHP.

Supporting Materials for Chapter 13: Concluding Treatment and Planning for Success

Prompting Checklist 13.1. Last Session: Concluding Treatment and Planning for Success Prompting Checklist.

LAST SESSION: CONCLUDING TREATMENT AND PLANNING FOR SUCCESS

THERAPIST PROMPTING CHECKLIST

Client ID:_____ Clinician: _____ Session #: _____ Session Date: _____

Materials Required

• NA

Begin Time:_____

Reviewing Strengths (Client and Adult Significant Others)

___a. Solicit/Provide strengths of family to assist client in having great family relationships.
___b. Solicit/Provide strengths of family to assist client in living a healthy/clean life.
___c. Solicit/Provide strengths of family to assist client in personal achievement.
___d. Solicit/Provide strengths of family to assist client in other treatment goals.
   • Role-play FBT modules as needed if obstacles are reported.

Family Exchange of Positive Remarks (All Family Members)

___a. Instruct family in <u>exchanging what is loved, admired, or respected</u> about each other, including therapist.
   • Therapists exchange positive remarks w/family, as well.

Client's Assessment of Helpfulness of the Intervention

___a. After stating client should not feel obligated to provide high scores, as an honest assessment helps better address client needs, solicit how helpful client thought intervention was using 7-point scale:
   7 = extremely helpful, **6** = very helpful, **5** = somewhat helpful, **4** = not sure,
   3 = somewhat unhelpful, **2** = very unhelpful, **1** = extremely unhelpful

   • **Record Client's Rating Here:_____**
___b. Solicit how rating was derived, and methods of improving intervention in future.

Therapist's Rating of Client's Compliance with Intervention

___a.   Disclose therapist's rating of client's compliance using 7-point scale:

   7 = extremely compliant, **6** = very compliant, **5** = somewhat compliant, **4** = neutral,
   3 = somewhat noncompliant, **2** = very noncompliant, **1** = extremely noncompliant
   • Factors that contribute to compliance ratings are:
     • Attendance
     • Participation and conduct in session
     • Homework completion

   • **Record Therapist's Rating of Client's Compliance Here:_____**

___b.   Disclose client's compliance rating.
___c.   Explain how rating was derived, and methods of improving performance in future.

End Time:_____

References

Allen, D. N., Donohue, B., Sutton, G., Haderlie, M., & LaPota, H. (2009). Application of a standardized assessment methodology within the context of an evidence-based treatment for substance abuse and its associated problems. *Behavior Modification, 33*(5), 618–654.

Azrin, N. H., Acierno, R., Kogan, E. S., Donohue, B., Besalel, V., & McMahon, P. T. (1996). Follow-up results of supportive versus behavioral therapy for illicit drug use. *Behaviour Research and Therapy, 34*, 41–46.

Azrin, N. H., Donohue, B., Besalel, V. A., Kogan, E. S., & Acierno, R. (1994). Youth drug abuse treatment: A controlled outcome study. *Journal of Child & Adolescent Substance Abuse, 3*(3), 1–15.

Azrin, N. H., Donohue, B., Teichner, G., Crum, T., Howell, J., & DeCato, L. (2001). A controlled evaluation and description of individual-cognitive problem solving and family-behavioral therapies in conduct-disordered and substance dependent youth. *Journal of Child and Adolescent Substance Abuse, 11*, 1–43.

Azrin, N. H., McMahon, P. T., Donohue, B., Besalel, V. A., Lapinski, K. J., Kogan, E. S., Acierno, R. E., & Galloway, E. (1994). Behavior therapy for drug use: A controlled treatment outcome study. *Behavior Research and Therapy, 32*(8), 856–866.

Azrin, N. H., Philip, R. A., Thienes-Hontos, P., & Besalel, V. A. (1981). *Journal of Vocational Behavior, 18*(3), 253–254.

Azrin, N. H., Sisson, R. W., Meyers, R. J., & Godley, M. D. (1982). Alcoholism treatment by disulfiram and community reinforcement therapy. *Journal of Behavior Therapy and Experimental Psychiatry, 3*, 105–112.

Bartholomew, N. G., Joe, G. W., Rowan-Szal, G. A, & Simpson, D. D. (2007). Counselors assessments of training and adoption barriers. *Journal of Substance Abuse Treatment, 33,* 193–199.

Bender, K., Springer, D. W., & Kim, J. S. (2006). Treatment effectiveness with dually diagnosed adolescents: A systematic review. *Brief Treatment and Crisis Intervention, 6*(3), 177–205.

Burgard, J., Donohue, B., Azrin, N. H., & Teichner, G. (2000). Prevalence and treatment of substance abuse in the mentally retarded population: An empirical review. *Journal of Psychoactive Drugs, 32,* 293–298.

Carroll, K. M., & Onken, L. S. (2005). Behavioral therapies for drug abuse. *American Journal of Psychiatry, 162,* 1452–1460.

Carruth, A. K., Tate, U. S., Moffett, B. S., & Hill, K. (1997). Reciprocity, emotional well-being, and family functioning as determinants of family satisfaction in caregivers of elderly parents. *Nursing Research, 46,* 93–100.

Del Boca, F. K., & Darkes, J. (2007). Enhancing the validity and utility of randomized clinical trials in addictions treatment research: I. Treatment implementation and research design. *Addiction, 102,* 1047–1056.

Donohue, B., Allen, D. N., Romero, V., Hill, H. H., Vasaeli, K., LaPota, H., et al. (2009). Description of a standardized treatment center that utilizes evidence-based clinic operations to facilitate implementation of an evidence-based treatment. *Behavior Modification, 33,* 411–436.

Donohue, B., Azrin, N. H., Lawson, H., Friedlander, J., Teichner, G., & Rindsberg, J. (1998). Improving initial session attendance of substance abuse and conduct disordered adolescents: A controlled study. *Journal of Child and Adolescent Substance Abuse, 8,* 1–13.

Donohue, B., Romero, V., Herdzik, K., LaPota, H., Abdel Al, R., Allen, D. N., et al. (2010). Concurrent treatment of substance abuse, child neglect, bipolar disorder, post-traumatic stress disorder, and domestic violence: A case examination involving family behavior therapy. *Clinical Case Studies, 9,* 106–124.

Donohue, B., & Van Hasselt, V. B. (1999). Development of an ecobehavioral treatment program for child maltreatment. *Behavioral Interventions, 14,* 55–82.

Dutra, L., Stathopoulou, G., Basden, S. L., Leyro, T. M., Powers, M. B., & Otto, M. W. (2008). A meta-analytic review of psychosocial interventions for substance use disorders. *American Journal of Psychiatry, 165,* 179–187.

Hoffman, J. P., Dufur, M., & Huang, L. (2007). Drug use and job quits: A longitudinal analysis. *Journal of Drug Issues, 37,* 569–596.

Hunt, G. M., & Azrin, N. H. (1973). A community reinforcement approach to alcoholism. *Behavior Research and Therapy, 13,* 1115–1123.

Madson, M. B., Campbell, T. C., Barrett, D. E., Brondino, M. J., & Melchert, T. P. (2005). Development of the Motivational Interviewing Supervision and Training Scale. *Psychology of Addictive Behaviors, 19,* 303–310.

Morgan, M. M., & Sprenkle, D. H. (2007). Toward a common-factors approach to supervision. *Journal of Marital and Family Therapy, 33*(1), 1–17.

Moyer, A., Finney, J. W., & Swearingen, C. E. (2002). Methodological characteristics of quality of alcohol treatment outcome studies, 1970–98: An expanded evaluation. *Addiction, 97,* 253–263.

National Institute on Drug Abuse, National Institutes of Health. (1998, April). *Principles of drug addiction treatment: A research based guide* (Publication No. 99-4180). Retrieved August 25, 2008, from NIDA NIH Reports Online via: www.nida.nih.gov/PDF/PODAT/PODAT.pdf

National Institutes of Alcoholism and Alcohol Abuse. (2005). Adolescents and treatment of Alcohol Use Disorders. In *NIAAA: Social work education for the prevention and treatment of alcohol use disorders* (Module 10A). Retrieved December 27, 2008, from http://pubs.niaaa.nih.gov/publications/Social/Module10AAdolescents/Module10A.html

National Registry of Evidence-Based Programs and Practices (2008, June). *Anonymous reviews.* Retrieved July 14, 2008, from www.nrepp.samhsa.gov/

Power, T. J., Blom-Hoffman, J., Clarke, A. T., Riley-Tillman, T. C., Kelleher, C., & Manz, P. H. (2005). Reconceptualizing intervention integrity: A partnership-based framework for linking research with practice. *Psychology in the Schools, 42*(5), 495–507.

Romero, V., Donohue, B., & Allen, D. N., (2010). Treatment of concurrent substance dependence, child neglect and domestic violence: A single case examination involving family behavior therapy. *Journal of Family Violence, 25*(3), 287–295.

Romero, V., Donohue, B., Hill, H. H., Gorney, S., Van Hasselt, V., & Allen, D. N. (2010). Family Behavior therapy for use in child welfare: Results of a case study involving an abused woman formally diagnosed with alcohol dependence, bipolar disorder, and several anxiety disorders. *Clinical Case Studies, 9,* 353–368.

Rowan-Szal, G. A., Greener, J. M., Joe, G. W., & Simpson, D. D. (2007). Assessing program needs and planning change. *Journal of Substance Abuse Treatment, 33,* 121–129.

Sheidow, A. J., Donohue, B., Hill, H. H., Henggeler, S. W., & Ford, J. D. (2008). Development of an audio-tape review system for supporting adherence to an evidence-based practice. *Professional Psychology Research & Practice, 39,* 553–560.

Sisson, R. W., & Azrin, N. H. (1989). The community reinforcement approach. In R. K. Reid & W. R. Miller (Eds.), *Handbook of alcoholism treatment approaches: Effective alternatives* (pp. 242–258). Elmsford, NY: Pergamon Press.

Author Index

Subject Index

About the Authors

Brad Donohue is a licensed clinical psychologist and professor in the Department of Psychology at the University of Nevada, Las Vegas, where he is Director of the Achievement Center. The Achievement Center is focused on the development of evidence-based protocols for use in disadvantaged populations. He is editor of the *Journal of Child & Adolescent Substance Abuse*, and editorial board member for seven other scientific journals. He has directed projects funded by the National Institute on Drug Abuse, Substance Abuse and Mental Health Services Administration, and National Institute of Mental Health. He has published more than 100 manuscripts, including 60 peer-reviewed journal articles and 30 book chapters. He is one of the developers of FBT and other evidence-based protocols, and he has received awards for his research, including the Outstanding Research Award from the Western Psychological Association and the Outstanding Faculty Member and Barrick Scholar Awards.

Daniel N. Allen is a licensed clinical psychologist and professor in the Department of Psychology at the University of Nevada, Las Vegas. He has published 115 scientific manuscripts. His research focuses on the neuropsychological correlates of mental illness, including substance use disorders, and FBT applications for treatment of substance use disorders in those with serious mental illnesses. He has been honored twice by the National Academy of Neuropsychology with the Nelson Butters Award and Early Career Award, and he has been elected a Fellow of the American Psychological Association, National Academy of Neuropsychology, and Western Psychological Association.

STUDY PACKAGE
CONTINUING EDUCATION
CREDIT INFORMATION
Treating Adult Substance Abuse Using Family Behavior Therapy

Our goal is to provide you with current, accurate and practical information from the most experienced and knowledgeable speakers and authors.

Listed below are the continuing education credit(s) currently available for this self-study package. *Please note: Your state licensing board dictates whether self study is an acceptable form of continuing education. Please refer to your state rules and regulations.*

COUNSELORS: PESI, LLC is recognized by the National Board for Certified Counselors to offer continuing education for National Certified Counselors. Provider #: 5896. We adhere to NBCC Continuing Education Guidelines. This self-study package qualifies for **3.75** contact hours.

SOCIAL WORKERS: PESI, LLC, 1030, is approved as a provider for continuing education by the Association of Social Work Boards, 400 South Ridge Parkway, Suite B, Culpeper, VA 22701. www.aswb.org. Social workers should contact their regulatory board to determine course approval. Course Level: All Levels. Social Workers will receive **3.75** (Clinical) continuing education clock hours for completing this self-study package.

PSYCHOLOGISTS: PESI, LLC is approved by the American Psychological Association to sponsor continuing education for psychologists. PESI, LLC maintains responsibility for these materials and their content. PESI is offering these self- study materials for **3.5** hours of continuing education credit.

ADDICTION COUNSELORS: PESI, LLC is a Provider approved by NAADAC Approved Education Provider Program. Provider #: 366. This self-study package qualifies for **4.5** contact hours.

Procedures:

1. Review the material and read the book.

2. If seeking credit, complete the posttest/evaluation form:

   -Complete posttest/evaluation in entirety; including your email address to receive your certificate much faster versus by mail.

   -Upon completion, mail to the address listed on the form along with the CE fee stated on the test. Tests will not be processed without the CE fee included.

   -Completed posttests must be received 6 months from the date printed on the packing slip.

Your completed posttest/evaluation will be graded. If you receive a passing score (70% and above), you will be emailed/faxed/mailed a certificate of successful completion with earned continuing education credits. (Please write your email address on the posttest/evaluation form for fastest response) If you do not pass the posttest, you will be sent a letter indicating areas of deficiency, and another posttest to complete. The posttest must be resubmitted and receive a passing grade before credit can be awarded. We will allow you to re-take as many times as necessary to receive a certificate.

If you have any questions, please feel free to contact our customer service department at 1.800.844.8260.

PESI LLC
PO BOX 1000
Eau Claire, WI 54702-1000

PESI

Treating Adult Substance Abuse Using Family Behavior Therapy

PO BOX 1000
Eau Claire, WI 54702
800-844-8260

Any persons interested in receiving credit may photocopy this form, complete and return with a payment of $15.00 per person CE fee. A certificate of successful completion will be sent to you. To receive your certificate sooner than two weeks, rush processing is available for a fee of $10. Please attach check or include credit card information below.

Mail to: PESI, PO Box 1000, Eau Claire, WI 54702 or fax to PESI (800) 554-9775 (both sides)

CE Fee: $15: (Rush processing fee: $10)   **Total to be charged** _____

Credit Card #: _____ **Exp Date:** _____ **V-Code*:** _____
(*MC/VISA/Discover: last 3-digit # on signature panel on back of card.) (*American Express: 4-digit # above account # on face of card.)

	LAST	FIRST	M.I.

Name (please print): _____ _____ _____

Address: _____ Daytime Phone: _____

City: _____ State: _____ Zip Code: _____

Signature: _____ Email: _____

Date Completed: _____ Actual time (# of hours) taken to complete this offering: _____ hours

Program Objectives After completing this publication, I have been able to achieve these objectives:

1. Identify etiological factors influencing the development and maintenance of substance abuse.   1. Yes   No

2. Determine the style and process of implementing FBT, including methods of effectively engaging clients and their family members in evidence-supported therapies that are fun and exciting.   2. Yes   No

3. Recognize how to use written prompts to guide evidence-supported therapies while being flexible to proactively address day-to-day problems of clients that often interfere with treatment integrity.   3. Yes   No

4. Understand family supported contingencies for sobriety that are likely to endure long after therapy is withdrawn.   4. Yes   No

5. Demonstrate to clients how to manage drug use situations, including generation of negative consequences for substance use, relaxation, problem-solving, and imagery.   5. Yes   No

6. Apply standardized record keeping procedures and quality assurance methods that complement FBT and prevent liability.   6. Yes   No

7. Implement techniques that have demonstrated success in managing difficult clients.   7. Yes   No

PESI LLC
PO BOX 1000
Eau Claire, WI 54702-1000

ZNT043220   CE Release Date: 12/16/10

Participant Profile:
1. Job Title: _____ Employment setting: _____

1. When conducting Environmental Control, the primary task for therapists is to assist clients in
a. managing consequences to problem behavior
b. managing antecedents to problem behavior
c. maintaining exposure to stimuli that have become conditioned to problem behavior
d. none of the above

2. After reviewing the pros and cons of generated solutions during Self Control trials clients should:
a. engage in thought stopping
b. engage in relaxation
c. imagine themselves performing an optimum solution aloud
d. imagine themselves experiencing positive reinforcement

3. When attempting to solicit a job interview over the telephone, if the person answering the telephone asks what the nature of the call concerns, the best response is to:
a. indicate it's none of the person's business
b. state a call will be attempted later
c. request a job interview
d. state it's personal

4. Financial Management doesn't involve which of the following:
a. identification of current income
b. identification of current expenses
c. identification of current methods of decreasing expenses
d. none of the above

5. In Behavioral Goals and Rewards, who provides rewards to the client?
a. the client's children
b. the therapist
c. the client's adult significant others
d. the client

6. Treatment session agendas are:
a. determined by the client during the respective treatment session
b. determined by the therapist during the respective treatment session
c. determined by both the client and therapist during the respective treatment session
d. determined by the therapist immediately prior to the treatment session

7. The following should be avoided by therapists during the implementation of FBT:
a. confrontation
b. praise
c. descriptive praise
d. role-playing

8. The last treatment session is primarily designed to do which of the following:
a. review potential obstacles to future goal accomplishment
b. review personal strengths that may be used to maintain goal accomplishment
c. review methods of improving relative weaknesses
d. the final Self Control trial

9. Self Control should be initiated:
a. when the trigger or antecedent to problem behavior is first experienced
b. immediately after the problem behavior has occurred
c. immediately after the desired behavior has occurred
d. as soon as the optimum solution is chosen

10. When conflicts occur during FBT sessions between clients and their significant others, which of the following interventions should be implemented:
a. I've Got a Great Family
b. Environmental Control (Stimulus Control)
c. Positive Request
d. Behavioral Goals and Rewards

PESI LLC
PO BOX 1000
Eau Claire, WI 54702-1000

About the CD-ROM

Introduction

This appendix provides you with information on the contents of the CD that accompanies this book. For the latest information, please refer to the ReadMe file located at the root of the CD.

System Requirements

> A computer with a processor running at 120 MHz or faster

> At least 32 MB of total RAM installed on your computer; for best performance, we recommend at least 64 MB

> A CD-ROM drive

Using the CD with Windows

To install the items from the CD to your hard drive, follow these steps:

1. Insert the CD into your computer's CD-ROM drive. The license agreement appears (for Windows 7, select Start.exe from the AutoPlay window or follow the same steps for Windows Vista).

    The interface won't launch if you have autorun disabled. In that case, click Start➤Run (for Windows Vista and Windows 7, click Start➤All Programs ➤Accessories➤Run). In the dialog box that appears, type D:\Start. exe. (Replace D with the proper letter if your CD drive uses a different letter. If you don't know the letter of your CD drive, see how it is listed under My Computer.) Click OK.

2. Read through the license agreement, and then click the Accept button if you want to use the CD.

3. The CD interface displays. Select the lesson video you want to view.

Using the CD with Macintosh

To install the items from the CD to your hard drive, follow these steps:

1. Insert the CD into your computer's CD-ROM drive.

2. The CD icon will appear on your desktop; double-click to open.

3. Double-click the Start button.

4. Read the license agreement and click the Accept button to use the CD.

5. The CD interface will appear. Here you can install the programs and run the demos.

What's on the CD

The following sections provide a summary of the software and other materials you'll find on the CD.

Content

Any material from the book, including forms, slides, and lesson plans, if available, are in the folder named "Content."

This companion CD-ROM contains worksheets, handouts, and checklists intended to provide resources for practitioners and clients within therapy sessions. These practical materials will help practitioners throughout the therapeutic process: from organizing a client's file to treatment checklists, implementing strategies, and client assignments. Included on the CD-ROM in an easy-to-use and reproducible format, these worksheets are organized to correspond to the book's chapters and follow the evolution of the FBT treatment process. Some of the forms are intended to assist in the maintenance of client record-keeping procedures. Therefore, it is recommended that appropriate administrative staff review and potentially customize these forms to be consistent with the agency's culture and relevant state and federal laws, if applicable.

Applications

The following applications are on the CD:

OpenOffice.org   OpenOffice.org is a free multi-platform office productivity suite. It is similar to Microsoft Office or Lotus SmartSuite, but OpenOffice.org is absolutely free. It includes word processing, spreadsheet, presentation, and drawing applications that enable you to create professional documents, newsletters, reports, and presentations. It supports most file formats of other office software. You should be able to edit and view any files created with other office solutions.

Notes

Shareware programs are fully functional, trial versions of copyrighted programs. If you like particular programs, register with their authors for a nominal fee and receive licenses, enhanced versions, and technical support.

Freeware programs are copyrighted games, applications, and utilities that are free for personal use. Unlike shareware, these programs do not require a fee or provide technical support.

GNU software is governed by its own license, which is included inside the folder of the GNU product. See the GNU license for more details.

Trial, demo, or evaluation versions are usually limited either by time or functionality (such as being unable to save projects). Some trial versions are very sensitive to system date changes. If you alter your computer's date, the programs will "time out" and no longer be functional.

Customer Care

If you have trouble with the CD–ROM, please call the Wiley Product Technical Support phone number at (800) 762-2974. Outside the United States, call 1(317) 572-3994. You can also contact Wiley Product Technical Support at http:// support.wiley.com. John Wiley & Sons will provide technical support only for installation and other general quality control items. For technical support on the applications themselves, consult the program's vendor or author.

To place additional orders or to request information about other Wiley products, please call (877) 762-2974.